JANE AUSTEN & GEORGE ELIOT

JANE AUSTEN & GEORGE ELIOT

THE LADY & THE RADICAL

EDWARD WHITLEY

Biteback Publishing

First published in Great Britain in 2025 by
Biteback Publishing Ltd, London
Copyright © Edward Whitley 2025

Edward Whitley has asserted his right under the Copyright, Designs and Patents Act 1988 to be identified as the author of this work.

All rights reserved. No part of this publication may be reproduced, stored in a retrieval system or transmitted, in any form or by any means, without the publisher's prior permission in writing.

This book is sold subject to the condition that it shall not, by way of trade or otherwise, be lent, resold, hired out or otherwise circulated without the publisher's prior consent in any form of binding or cover other than that in which it is published and without a similar condition, including this condition, being imposed on the subsequent purchaser.

Every reasonable effort has been made to trace copyright holders of material reproduced in this book, but if any have been inadvertently overlooked the publisher would be glad to hear from them.

ISBN 978-1-78590-954-2

10 9 8 7 6 5 4 3 2 1

A CIP catalogue record for this book is available from the British Library.

Set in Adobe Caslon Pro

Printed and bound in Great Britain by
CPI Group (UK) Ltd, Croydon CR0 4YY

*With love to
Ella, Honor, Josie and Ned*

CONTENTS

Acknowledgements   ix

Prologue   Bluestocking Passion   xiii
Chapter 1   From Regency to Radical   1
Chapter 2   The Lady Novelists   35
Chapter 3   Love and Marriage   65
Chapter 4   Fortunes and Finance   99
Chapter 5   Gentlemen and Trade   135
Chapter 6   The Heroine's Journey   171
Chapter 7   Villains and Victims   203
Chapter 8   Endings and Echoes   229

Epilogue   A Meeting of Minds   261
Index   269

ACKNOWLEDGEMENTS

My overwhelming thanks are, of course, to Jane Austen and George Eliot, whose novels and letters provide us all with such extraordinary worlds to explore. They are authors of genius and their books have provided the world with endless pleasure.

This book was inadvertently started when my client and friend Ellyn Daniels gave me a handsome, green leather-bound notebook with the provocative caption embossed on the front cover:

'*Brilliant ideas, profound inspirations and a list of my favourite clients.*'

Ellyn invariably tops one of these lists, but she might be surprised to hear where the other lists took me – *brilliant ideas* led me to re-read the brilliant novels of my favourite authors, Jane Austen and George Eliot, and finally to take up the challenge of reading *Romola*. The green notebook filled up as I began to write my reactions to these two magnificent authors and added my reading of the Brontë sisters.

The *profound inspiration* came when I was exploring Charlotte Brontë's letters and came across the pivotal moment when the literary critic George Lewes was given a copy of a first-time novel to review. The novel was *Jane Eyre*. Lewes wrote to the author, who apparently enjoyed the original name of Currer Bell, and proffered some helpful if patronising advice to him; namely, that he should endeavour to write more like Jane Austen. Currer Bell was eventually unmasked as Charlotte Brontë, and her powerful and indignant responses to this advice ran to several letters, all of which were kept by Lewes. I believe that Brontë's letters, which contain not only a scathing riposte to his advice but also her poignant account of the challenges facing a lady novelist at the time, profoundly influenced the novels of Lewes's partner, Mary Ann Evans, when she started to write her novels under the name George Eliot. Lewes acted as a lightning conductor, and the connection through him between Jane Austen, Charlotte Brontë and George Eliot was the inspiration for me to write this book.

I wrote *Jane Austen and George Eliot: The Lady and the Radical* to pass on my love and admiration for these two authors (three, including Charlotte Brontë) to our children, Ella, Honor, Josie and Ned, whom I thank for having been my first readers and always providing unconditional and dynamic support. I would also like to thank Victoria Gray and Sigrid Rausing, who were early readers and who kindly gave me unflinching encouragement.

After twenty years since my last book, a financial thriller, my literary agent Mark Lucas was only momentarily blindsided by this account of Jane Austen and George Eliot. With his deft touch of ingenuity, Mark introduced me to Alan Samson, who helped me turn it from a collection of miscellaneous essays into a coherent manuscript. With similar literary alchemy, Laura Palmer then helped transform the book into the state where it became publishable. Olivia Beattie emerged as the publisher who I had always hoped and dreamed might be out there. She and her team at Biteback

ACKNOWLEDGEMENTS

Publishing shared my vision of combining these two authors and looking at each of them through the lens of the other, learning so much more about them both in the process.

There are many extraordinary Austen and Eliot scholars who have paved the way. The extensive work of Deirdre Le Faye, including her collection and editing of *Jane Austen's Letters*, and the works of Claire Tomalin, John Mullan, Kathryn Sutherland, Emma Clery, Jenny Uglow, Lucy Worsley and Clare Carlisle are exemplary blends of scholarship and pragmatism.

I would like to pay tribute to and celebrate Dorothy Bednarowska ('Mrs Bed'), my late English tutor at St Anne's College, Oxford. She was so inspiring, and together with Ann Pasternak Slater she opened my eyes to a detailed and rigorous reading of Austen and Eliot. (She also taught Jenny Uglow.) Dorothy Bednarowska died in 2003, but, Ann, I hope that this book goes a little way to thank you for your patience, your kindness and your tenacity in continuing your tutorials with me. You stirred up something that has taken forty years to emerge in this form. As you used to greet my inventive excuses for a late essay: 'Well, let's hope that it's worth the wait!'

Finally and above all, I would like to thank my wife, Araminta, who is my bedrock of support. We met when we were both studying English at Oxford and over the subsequent years I have now understood that, with her lightning quick observation and profound wisdom, Araminta combines all the best qualities of Jane Austen the lady and George Eliot the radical.

PROLOGUE: BLUESTOCKING PASSION

It was 6 October 1851. In London's Hyde Park, the Great Exhibition of the Works of Industry of All Nations was about to enter its final week. Already over 6 million visitors, twice the size of the population of London, had made the pilgrimage to the Crystal Palace to see what became known simply as the Great Exhibition, a spectacular series of towering glass pavilions in which Prince Albert had arranged for the wonders of Victorian invention, technology and industry to be showcased to the world.

But among the tourists teeming along Piccadilly that October afternoon, two Londoners had a different destination in mind. Unknown to each other and coming from different directions, they were both heading to William Jeff's bookshop in the Burlington Arcade.

Like much of Victorian London, the Burlington Arcade operated on two different levels. Along the ground floor were a variety of jewellers, gold and silversmiths and luxury boutiques selling gloves, silks, watches, perfume and handbags to the swelling ranks of London's wealthy shoppers, much as they do today. William Jeff's bookshop was halfway along at No. 15. Meanwhile, running along the first-floor gallery above the shops were a series of brothels that advertised their presence by hanging black stockings out of their windows. The boutiques on the ground floor made good sales from eager customers impulsively buying presents on their way upstairs.

Coming from her lodgings in The Strand and passing by Nelson's Column, the startling latest addition to the city skyline, Mary Ann Evans had recently arrived in London. At thirty, the same age as Queen Victoria, Mary Ann already had a formidable record of scholarly achievement. The major literary endeavour of her twenties had been the painstaking translation of a lengthy German academic treatise *Das Leben Jesu* by the philosopher David Strauss, in the course of which she had taught herself German, Greek, Latin and Hebrew. Determined to avoid being stuck in the Midlands, after her father died Mary Ann had packed her carpet-bag and left Coventry and her brother behind her in order to live an independent literary life in London. In the words of Henry James, Mary Ann was a 'bluestocking' – a female scholar, fierce and intelligent, who would soon be known as the best-read woman in London.

Coming across from his bohemian household in Bayswater was George Lewes, a freelance journalist who was always on the lookout for the next story. The illegitimate son of an obscure and itinerant poet and brought up partially in France, Lewes had gravitated to London, where he had tried his hand at various things – he had worked in a Russian trading house, he had toured with a troupe of actors when he had acted with Charles Dickens and played Shylock in *The Merchant of Venice*, he had written book reviews and miscellaneous articles for magazines and he had even published a novel. Lewes had been the first reviewer to spot the talent of a first-time author with the unusual name of Currer Bell, who had written a novel called *Jane Eyre*. Lewes had engaged in a long correspondence with Bell in which he advised him to improve his writing style by reading a slightly forgotten Regency author called Jane Austen, who had died some thirty-five years previously. Notoriously, Lewes was living in a commune with Thornton Hunt, his best friend and co-editor of *The Leader*, a periodical magazine. Hunt, who would go on to become the first editor of the *Daily Telegraph* and *The Spectator*, had already fathered one son with Lewes's wife Agnes. Lewes had happily adopted the baby along with his own sons, which would later have significant repercussions for any possible divorce proceedings. Short, heavily bearded with whiskers, long straggling hair and so invariably described as 'simian', Lewes was mercurial, extroverted, a dazzling raconteur and he loved a party. He was, wrote Jane Carlyle in 1849, 'the most amusing little fellow in the whole world – if you only overlook his unparalleled impudence, which is not impudence at all but man-of-genius bonhomie'.

Mary Ann Evans's powerful intellect coexisted with a rebellious and passionate streak. When she had first arrived in London and taken lodgings with John Chapman, the publisher of her translation *The Life of Jesus*, they had also become lovers. In a dramatic intervention, Chapman's wife Susanna and his existing mistress Elisabeth had joined forces to demand that he put an end to his affair with Mary Ann. Reluctantly he had done so, but she remained a lodger at his house at 142 The Strand and Chapman had just appointed her as deputy editor of the *Westminster Review*. It was Chapman who had walked with Mary Ann to the Burlington Arcade that October day, where he promptly recognised Lewes and made the introduction.

As between any freelance journalist and magazine editor, there would have been a frisson of interest. With his antennae finely tuned to detect whatever the next best article might be, Lewes would have been keen to bag a lucrative commission. Equally, Mary Ann would have been keen to impress on John Chapman that she could go toe to toe with a bright writer, no matter how brilliant or impudent his conversation.

While less immediately blatant than what was going on above them in the brothels upstairs, this meeting in William Jeff's bookshop between the 'bluestocking' and 'the most amusing little fellow in the whole world' clearly also had a powerful charge of physical attraction. Later that week, Mary Ann let slip to Charles Bray this brief and beguiling mention: 'I was introduced to Lewes the other day in Jeff's shop – a sort of miniature Mirabeau in appearance.'

The Comte de Mirabeau was a flamboyant figure from the French Revolution. Looking at Mirabeau's portrait today, it is difficult to fathom his appeal, yet he was infamous for his many scandalous love affairs. Despite Lewes's simian looks and straggly hair, Mary Ann Evans had identified in him the pull of a magnetic charisma and in herself, perhaps, the beginning of an attraction.

Lewes, for his part, had no doubt heard the gossip about John Chapman's and Mary Ann Evans's affair. Did he know enough to see this young, erudite editor in a different light? Did she suspect that he suspected? Would this meeting rip off the sticking plaster from her scholarly exterior, revealing the passionate radical beneath? Mary Ann's subsequent letters are coy about when she and Lewes started their affair, but since he was impulsive and she was a radical thinker who was prepared to blow away all social conventions, I do not think that they waited very long. At any rate, their lives were soon entangled. At first, it was a secret affair, conducted through the editing of articles and visits to the theatre and opera. While mentioning Thomas Carlyle and Robert Browning as possible contributors to the *Westminster Review* in her letter to Charles Bray of November 1851, Mary Ann includes the aside: 'Lewes says his article on Julia von Krudener will be glorious. He sat in the same box as us at *The Merry Wives of Windsor* and helped to carry off the dolorousness of the play.'

By 1854, the scholar from the Midlands threw caution to the winds. In a scene as exciting and passionate as any of the romantic novels which she would later satirise, Mary Ann and Lewes caught a cross-Channel steamer and fled to the Continent. Her journal takes up the story:

'I said a last farewell to Cambridge Street on 20th July 1854 and found myself on board the *Ravensbourne*, bound for Antwerp.'

Mary Ann was now committed. Living out the reality of the biggest gamble of her life, she arrived at St Katharine Docks before Lewes. Understandably she was anxious – might he have had second thoughts? Had he been able to say goodbye to his wife and children?

'I had 20 minutes of terrible fear least something should have delayed G. Before long I saw his welcome face looking for me over the porter's shoulder and all was well.'

All really was well. Clearly immune to the night chill, they sat out on the deck – presumably in each other's arms – and watched the dawn break over the Antwerp skyline. They were heading into uncharted territory and Mary Ann knew that their trip abroad would irrevocably change her life. Her journal entry catches the sublime excitement of the moment:

The day was glorious and our passage perfect. The sunset was lovely, but still lovelier the dawn as we were passing up the River Scheldt between two and three in the morning. The crescent moon, the stars, the first faint blush of the dawn reflected in the glassy river, the dark mass of clouds on the horizon which sent forth flashes of lightning.

Until this point Mary Ann's letters to her three Coventry friends, Sara Hennell, her sister Cara and Cara's husband Charles Bray, were generally long, wordy and discursive. Keen to impress upon them how important she was becoming in London literary life, Mary Ann often listed various great men of letters who were in and out of her office and while apparently self-deprecating, she liked to imply how reliant they were upon her judgement. The trio in Coventry would have been thunder-struck to receive these terse three lines scribbled to them as she dashed to catch the steamer:

'Dear Friends, I have only time to say good-bye and God bless you. *Poste Restante* Weimar for the next six weeks and afterwards Berlin.'

Mary Ann's excitement and rush of adrenaline is palpable. By the time the letter arrived, she had left with Lewes. Their affair was out in the open and there was no way back. Determined to start a new life, Mary Ann threw herself out of Victorian society. Her poetic journal entry could stand as the mantra to this new life: '*Still lovelier the dawn.*'

* * *

That chance meeting at William Jeff's bookshop changed the lives of Mary Ann Evans and George Lewes. With Lewes's help, Mary Ann not only reinvented herself, but as a writer she reinvented English literature and the art of the novel. And if Lewes was looking for the next story, in Mary Ann the bluestocking he found the story of the rest of his life. She would become his lover and lifelong partner and he would help shape her writing career as she became the most important literary figure of her generation and a bestselling author to rival Charles Dickens.

In fact, I believe that the momentous meeting in William Jeff's bookshop on that October day in 1851 was the occasion of not just one highly charged encounter but two. The second encounter was less vivid, but it was no less consequential. For in that bookshop, I think that Mary Ann Evans most likely had her first introduction to the work of the novelist Jane Austen, who had died two years before Mary Ann had been born.

Lewes was one of Austen's most committed fans. He invariably invoked Austen as his first line of reference in any literary context and had recently provoked the author Currer Bell into violent indignation by telling him that he should endeavour to write more like her. Given his evangelical love of Austen, I like to imagine Lewes pointing her out on the bookshelves, skipping over and leaping up onto a chair to pull out one of her novels and brandish it under Mary Ann's nose, probably declaiming his favourite expression of praise: 'This is capital!'

Certainly at that time Mary Ann Evans, a high-brow scholar of the classics and a specialist in German philosophy, would not have read Austen. Indeed, for Lewes to admire Austen and to pick her out was surprising. By the 1850s, novels were written in a very different literary style from Jane Austen. This style was exemplified by the bestselling works of Charles Dickens, then at the towering height of his powers, whose vast novels with huge casts, implausible plots and indignant social commentary were serialised on a monthly basis to a mass market. Described by Henry James as 'large loose baggy monsters with their queer elements of the accidental and the arbitrary', these sprawling Victorian novels had eclipsed the neatly structured romantic comedies of Austen and the Regency period she portrayed. This was 1851, after all, and as the Great Exhibition so magnificently displayed, bonnets, barouches and calling cards left on silver trays had given way to railways, steamships and telegraph wires. The manners and values of the Regency era had been overtaken and outpaced by the extraordinary progress of the Victorian industrial revolution. Before reading Austen, Mary Ann might easily have confused her with the throngs of female authors who she would later poke fun at in her essay 'Silly Novels by Lady Novelists'.

Whether as the first upshot of the William Jeff's bookshop meeting or not, Lewes was indeed duly commissioned by the new young assistant editor to write an article for the *Westminster Review*. Austen was the trigger. Lewes wrote an article that reviewed Austen's novels in depth alongside other female novelists such as the Brontë sisters (now revealed as the women behind their male pseudonyms of Currer, Ellis and Acton Bell) and George Sand. In his article 'The Lady Novelists', Lewes laments how little Austen was then recognised and champions her as 'the greatest artist that has ever written, using the term to signify the most perfect mastery over the means to her end'. He goes on to praise her novels as demonstrating 'the special quality of womanliness in tone and point of view. They are novels written by a woman, an Englishwoman, a gentlewoman.'

If Mary Ann was attracted to Lewes – as she was – she could now also readily see that in turn he found Jane Austen highly attractive. Lewes also fell for the convenient male fantasy (which still prevails today) that Jane Austen herself was most like her beguiling heroine Elizabeth Bennet, writing in a later review: 'We may picture her as something like her own sprightly, natural but by no means perfect Elizabeth Bennet in *Pride and Prejudice*, one of the few heroines one would seriously like to marry.'

As well as providing some insight into the character of Austen, this declaration of love for her would have given Mary Ann greater insight into Lewes himself. As we shall see, there is a great deal to unpack between Jane Austen and Mary Ann Evans. In a mirror image of the role he played when he had his extensive dialogue with Currer Bell (who was of course revealed as Charlotte Brontë), Lewes would stand as a lightning conductor between Mary Ann Evans, by then his lover, and Jane Austen, his great literary love.

* * *

That meeting in William Jeff's bookshop shaped their destiny. If Lewes did talk about Austen he laid the groundwork not just for his next commissioned article but also for the time when Mary Ann Evans would stop writing literary articles and take up the challenge of writing novels. Five years later in 1856, both Lewes and Austen provided the key influences to Mary Ann when she began to write her first fiction.

As well as reinventing the English novel, Mary Ann Evans also reinvented herself. Most obviously she reinvented her own name. Today we do not recognise and know her as Mary Ann Evans in the way we recognise and know Charles Dickens or Jane Austen, we know her and discuss her as *George Eliot*, which was the name that she used to conceal her female identity when she started to write fiction.

The choice of the name George Eliot is itself significant. Many years later after Lewes had died, Mary Ann explained how she had chosen it to her financial advisor John Cross, whom she married in the last year of her life. In his edited edition of her letters, Cross recalled: 'My wife told me the reason she fixed on this name was that *George* was Mr Lewes's Christian name, and *Eliot* was a good mouth-filling, easily pronounced word.'

The 'George' is clear enough, but I have a slightly different view of the 'Eliot'. During the summer of 1856, when she was planning her first fiction, Lewes had encouraged Mary Ann to read Jane Austen's novels. Among Austen's heroines, one in particular is likely to have caught her attention: Anne Elliot, the heroine of *Persuasion*. The personal similarities between Anne Elliot and Mary Ann Evans are striking. With her mother long dead and her remote father failing to understand her, Anne Elliot is trapped by her family; furthermore, aged twenty-seven Anne has lost the bloom of her youth and is universally considered too plain to attract a partner. If Henry James had met Anne Elliot, he might have also described her as a 'bluestocking'. However, thrillingly, Austen turns the tables and by the end of *Persuasion* Anne casts off this haggard appearance, regains the light in her eyes and is passionately pursued and embraced by Captain Wentworth. Lewes might not have been Captain Wentworth, and he was certainly no Darcy, but he was mesmerising, provocative and sexually attractive to Mary Ann. Equally, while Mary Ann might have appeared ostensibly more Mary Bennet than Elizabeth Bennet (Mary Ann's clothes were notoriously dowdy), she was a radical who was clearly highly attractive to him.

From the first spark in William Jeff's bookshop, theirs was a bluestocking love affair that grew to sustain them for the rest of their lives. Their passion was invariably heightened when Mary Ann was in the creative process of writing. They established a pattern whereby every evening she would read aloud to him the prose that she had written that day and if he liked it, he would exclaim 'That's capital!' and jump up from his chair and come over to kiss her. Writing as George Eliot, Mary Ann wrote seven lengthy novels full of magnificent prose. There would have been a great many kisses.

* * *

Conscious or not, the choice of 'Eliot' as a pseudonym has a strong flavour of *Persuasion* and Lewes clearly approved. Nevertheless, on the face of it Jane Austen and George Eliot have little in common. Austen was genteel and ironical. Staying single all her life, she remained under the wing of her family and rarely strayed from her native Hampshire. As Virginia Woolf commented: 'Of all great writers, she is the most difficult to catch in the act of greatness.' The title pages of Austen's original editions bore a simple if enigmatic byline: 'By a Lady.'

Eliot, on the other hand, was no lady. Her pseudonym was deliberately masculine. Unlike Austen, she had several affairs with married men before she met her partner Lewes and they lived together in an atmosphere of radicalism, sexual liberty and scandal. Most of all, if Austen was hard to catch in the act of greatness, Eliot was immediately recognised and celebrated for achieving greatness. Her first novel *Adam Bede* was a runaway bestseller and reprinted seven times in its first year of publication. Writing in her journal after the first print run had sold out, Eliot noted with some surprise: 'John Blackwood writes to say, I am a popular author as well as a great author.' The reaction of the poet Emily Dickinson to Eliot's *Middlemarch* captures the spirit of the ecstatic contemporary critical responses. 'What do I think of *Middlemarch*? What do I think of glory?' Sight unseen, Eliot's fourth novel *Romola* attracted the highest advance any publisher had then ever paid for a novel. Henry James considered *Romola* to be her masterpiece and like all her other books it was a bestseller and made Eliot very wealthy.

It would have surprised Victorian critics to know that today it is Jane Austen rather than George Eliot who is the household name. Despite the focus of her work upon a privileged sector of Regency society, on the face of it not an area where we share much common ground with her, Austen is widely loved. Her books have been turned into a sequence of popular films and banner television series. As one of our most cherished British authors, her iconic image adorns the back of £10 notes and we all have our own view of what 'Jane Austen's world' looks like, which might include horse-drawn carriages pulling up with a crunch of the gravel outside country vicarages (ideally enhanced by the strobe effect of the wheel spokes spinning backwards), ladies spilling out in a flurry of white muslin dresses and bonnets, gentlemen tall, straight and attentive in dress coats and top hats with quick-witted repartee fizzing between them.

I was first introduced to the works of Jane Austen and George Eliot as a student. Reading and examining Austen alongside Eliot illuminates many aspects of their respective works and writing techniques. Understanding Austen's greatness requires close attention to detail. The perceptive and detailed views of Charlotte Brontë, which wash through Lewes and are evident in the later work of Eliot, both challenge and illuminate her genius. Likewise, looking at Eliot with the lens provided by Austen gives insight into the areas which Eliot addresses. Eliot is a profoundly radical writer who takes the literary world established by Austen as her starting point and breaks it apart. She then picks her way through and explores the extensive wreckage and difficult psychological territory that lies beyond.

Both authors were impacted by their fathers' early deaths and decided to try to support themselves by their writing. With widely differing levels of family support, they each followed this tenuous and daunting literary path. While the lives of Austen and Eliot were utterly unrecognisable from each other, using the contemporary material they witnessed they each managed to produce works of profound genius. They also achieved something virtually no other women of their generations managed: they each earned their own income and – to the extent they wished – their independence.

Written between 1795 and the year of Austen's death in 1817, Austen's novels have one foot in the eighteenth century. Eliot lived until 1880 and the themes and characters in her books anticipate the concerns of twentieth-century fiction. Among the many classic novels of the nineteenth century, the six by Jane Austen and seven by George Eliot act as bookends to the beginning and the end of the nineteenth century. A close reading of these two sets of magnificent novels casts a revealing light on each other and on the different themes that preoccupied the authors and the different techniques they used to explore them. Their novels and their slightly overlooked letters also reveal their personalities and the lives they led and illustrate the shifting worlds that they lived in at either end of the nineteenth century.

I hope this book will inspire readers who love and know Jane Austen's work but who are less familiar with George Eliot to take a chance and reach along the bookshelf for her novels and read them with admiration and enjoyment. And if any reader reaches right along the shelf and picks out two of George Eliot's least read novels, *Romola* and *Daniel Deronda* (pausing with respect mingled with apprehension as you weigh them in your hand), I will have exceeded all my hopes – and you will be in for two of the greatest literary treats of your lifetime.

CHAPTER 1

FROM REGENCY TO RADICAL

Jane Austen started writing extensively in the 1790s, and just after the turn of the new century in 1800 she had completed three draft manuscripts that she would repeatedly revise, initially with the working titles of *Elinor & Marianne*, *First Impressions* and *Susan*. In 1803, six years after her father unsuccessfully tried to sell *First Impressions*, her brother Henry managed to sell *Susan* for £10 to the London publisher Crosby & Co. of Stationer's Court. This £10 was the first money Austen received for her writing and should have marked the start of her writing career. However, inexplicably Richard Crosby failed to publish the novel. Perhaps Crosby was concerned that *Susan*, which was a mocking parody of the sort of Regency gothic thrillers that he was successfully publishing, might dent their credibility and damage their overall sales.

By 1809, frustratingly Austen was still an unpublished author. *First Impressions*, telling the story of the romance between Elizabeth Bennet and the curiously named Mr Darcy, had been gathering dust for twelve years, and her hopes for *Susan* and her adventures in the gothic Northanger Abbey had been thwarted. Breaking the convention that men managed business affairs, Austen decided to take action herself. Signing herself off as MAD, Mrs Ashton Dennis, to emphasise her mounting frustration, on 5 April 1809 she wrote to Richard Crosby to point out that six years had passed since he had purchased the copyright of *Susan* and to ask whether he intended to publish it. Provocatively suggesting that the only reason for the 'extraordinary circumstances' of his failure to publish must be that 'by some carelessness' the manuscript had been lost, she gave Crosby an ultimatum: if he did not publish *Susan*, she would feel at liberty to secure its publication by applying elsewhere.

The letter itself is revealing – when studied under ultraviolet light, it is possible to detect the first draft of the letter which she wrote in pencil. In this pencil draft, Austen signed the letter using her own name. However, when she rubbed out the pencil draft and wrote the fair copy in ink, she changed her signature to Mrs Ashton Dennis, which both made the pun of MAD and protected her identity. In due course, this concealment of her identity would prove significant. Jane Austen vigilantes have also pointed out that when read backwards, 'Ashton Dennis' is revealed as 'has not sinned'. Prompt in his reply, writing on Saturday 8 April 1809 to Mrs Dennis addressed to her at the Post Office at Southampton, Richard Crosby archly pointed out that having bought the copyright there was 'not any time stipulated for its publication, neither are we bound to it'. Mrs Ashton Dennis may not have sinned, but Crosby was not going to forgive her for the threat to seek to publish *Susan* elsewhere. While threatening to take legal action himself 'should you or anyone else [publish it], we shall take proceedings to stop the sale', he offered to sell it back to her for the original £10. Austen baulked at this. Leaving *Susan* gathering dust with Crosby, her careful pious anagram ignored and her sarcasm repudiated, she turned her attention to her other manuscripts and reworked the structure of *Elinor and Marianne* from a sequence of letters between the two Dashwood sisters to a more dramatic narrative.

Two years later, Austen finally became a published author. In 1811, her brother Henry, who since leaving the Oxfordshire Militia in 1801 had established himself as a successful private banker in London, managed to arrange for the private publication of the manuscript by Thomas Egerton, who was a publisher of miscellaneous military works and dictionaries based in Whitehall. The printing costs for 750 copies have been estimated at £180, well beyond Austen's budget. It has been suggested that her brothers Henry and Edward (who was adopted by the wealthy Knight family in Kent and was the richest) paid Thomas Egerton. Austen had changed the title so that rather than *Elinor & Marianne*, the novel that appeared as a private, anonymous publication 'Printed for the Author' enjoyed the witty alliterative title *Sense and Sensibility*. At last, Jane Austen's writing career was launched.

Happily, *Sense and Sensibility* was well received and sold sufficient copies to allow Austen to repay whichever brother had paid for the printing costs and to move from having to pay to publish her second book to negotiating the sale of its copyright. In November 1812, Jane and Henry agreed a price of £110 for the copyright and she altered the title from *First Impressions* to a more catchy, thought-provoking one that echoed the lively alliteration of *Sense and Sensibility* and neatly encapsulated the attributes of the leading couple. And so it was that *Pride and Prejudice* was published and the iconic Regency romantic couple of Elizabeth Bennet and Mr Darcy were introduced to the world. While it now seems impossible to imagine English literature without them, the first print run was perhaps only 1,500 copies. By October 1813, this pair of novels were reprinted and there were profits to be distributed. Reporting news of the second edition to her brother Francis, now an officer rising up through the ranks in the Royal Navy, Austen writes with pride and pleasure: 'I have now therefore written myself into £250, which only makes me long for more – I have something in hand.'

Jane Austen was certainly attracted to earning money. The 'something in hand' that might provide the further money she 'longed for' was *Mansfield Park*, which was published by Egerton in 1814 with a first edition print-run of 1,250 copies. Although this edition sold well and would eventually sell out, Jane and her brother Henry appear to have decided that Egerton, which specialised in military books, was not really an appropriate publisher of her novels. The print-run was perhaps rather low (John Murray noted his 'astonishment that so small an edition of such a work should have been sent into the world' – although that is an easy and cheap criticism for a rival publisher to make) and there was a disappointing lack of advertising and general reviews.

Writing to her niece Fanny Knight, the daughter of the richest Austen brother Edward, on 20 November 1814 after the first edition of *Mansfield Park* sold out, Austen remarks:

'You will be glad to hear that the first edition of *MP* is all sold. Your Uncle Henry is rather wanting me to come to Town to settle about a second edition.'

She adds rather archly almost in the vein of what Mrs Norris, a notorious miser and the Austen family's favourite character of *Mansfield Park*, might have written to her own niece in the novel, also called Fanny:

'I am very greedy and want to make the most of it, but as you are much above caring about money, I shall not plague you with any particulars.'

Expressing a sentiment of which Mrs Norris would have approved, Austen concludes:

'People are more ready to borrow and praise than to buy, but though I like praise as well as anybody, I like what Edward calls *"pewter"* too.'

In order to satisfy her longing for more *pewter* (money), and with her brother Henry now acting as her literary agent, Austen decided to sell her next novel *Emma* to a more recognised literary publisher. Their choice was John Murray, who had recently moved his office to 50 Albemarle Street in Mayfair and was the celebrated publisher of the sensationally successful Romantic poet Lord Byron. With queues forming along the length of Albemarle Street and jostling outside his office to buy copies of Lord Byron's work, John Murray was certainly providing his authors with plenty of eye-catching publicity and *pewter*. Unashamedly, Austen wanted both.

As the negotiations over the publication of *Emma* took place, three surviving letters provide insight into the various tactics and reactions surrounding the deal. William Gifford, John Murray's reader, was an early fan of Austen's three published novels. John Murray gave him the manuscript of *Emma* to read, and he came back with the following advice:

'Five hundred pounds seems a good deal for a novel ... cannot you get the third novel thrown in, *Pride and Prejudice*? I have lately read it again – 'tis very good.'

Meanwhile, Austen had come to stay with Henry in London to be on hand for the negotiations, and on 17 October she provided an update to her sister Cassandra:

'Mr Murray's letter is come. He is a rogue of course, but a civil one. He offers £450 – but wants to have the copyright of *MP* and *S & S* included. It will end in my publishing for myself, I daresay.'

John Murray had clearly taken Gifford's advice and reduced his offer by £50, although he does not appear to have asked for the copyright of *Pride and Prejudice* to be 'thrown in'.

As the negotiations continued, Henry pushed back to John Murray in a magnificently self-assured response of 21 October, which still speaks for all aggrieved writers and their indignant literary agents who have ever felt that their work has been inexplicably undervalued by publishers:

'The terms you offer are so very inferior to what we had expected that I am apprehensive of having made some great error in my arithmetical calculations.'

I like to imagine Jane and Henry drafting this letter together from his house in Hans Place, chortling and congratulating each other as they put the final flourishes to their chosen adjectives. '*Apprehensive* – that's a good one!'

As Austen anticipated, the deal they eventually agreed with John Murray was a commission agreement, rather than the sale of the copyright. They now had the money to underwrite the printing costs. In a rather eye-catching manner, Austen dedicated *Emma* to the Prince Regent himself, who – bombastic, decadent and repulsive to Austen as he was – was above all the figure who defined the Regency period.

The dedication was arranged by Reverend James Clarke, the Prince Regent's librarian, whom Austen had met through Henry (they shared the same London doctor). Given their mutually exclusive sense of morality, Austen presumably swallowed a good deal of her pride to make this dedication, but she was also sufficiently commercial to realise that having the Prince Regent headline the publication might help attract publicity for *Emma* – and the more publicity, the more *pewter*.

Austen might well have expected to make some compromises in the course of promoting her work, but what she might not have expected was that James Clarke would pursue her, inviting her to come and stay with him at his house in Golden Square 'when you come to Town'. Such a brazen invitation (when Clarke knew that she stayed with her brother Henry) is an indication of the sort of London life that a celebrated single female author could have been drawn into. Life in Regency London was racy and Clarke was blatantly offering Austen something very different from the time she spent in her muddy Chawton parish in Hampshire.

Undeterred by her initial rejection, after the publication of *Emma* James Clarke also made extensive suggestions about the next novel she should write, which he recommended should involve 'an English Clergyman ... fond of and entirely engaged in Literature. Carry your Clergyman to sea as the Friend of some distinguished Naval Character about a Court.' Seeing through this semi-disguised, blatantly self-serving plotline, Austen demurred. Even more ludicrously, James Clarke tried to sway her towards another idea where he could offer her the patronage of Prince Leopold of Saxe-Coburg, who was about to marry Princess Charlotte, the Prince Regent's daughter and only heir. Clarke suggested: 'Perhaps when you again appear in print you may choose to dedicate your Volumes to Prince Leopold: any Historical Romance illustrative of the History of the august House of Saxe-Coburg would just now be very interesting.'

While this suggestion strikes us now as wholly absurd, it nevertheless reveals the insidious pressure put upon an artist to bend their art to patronage. Just imagine – if Austen had yielded to this pressure (and there were the implications that there might be more money provided along this route), *Persuasion* would have been based in some world involving 'the august House of Saxe-Coburg'.

As a German naval officer, Kapitan Wentworth might have turned out very differently.

Austen was having none of it. Her letter of 1 April 1816 robustly rejects James Clarke and illuminates her effervescent, decisive personality. She insists that she must do things her own way:

> You are very, very kind in your hints as to the sort of Composition which might recommend me at present, and I am fully sensible that an Historical Romance, founded on the House of Saxe-Coburg might be much more to the purpose of Profit or Popularity than such pictures of domestic Life in Country Villages as I deal in – but I could no more write a Romance than an Epic Poem – I could not sit seriously down to write a serious Romance under any other motive than to save my Life, and if it were indispensable for me to keep it up & never relax into laughing at myself or other people, I am sure I should be hung before I had finished the first Chapter. No – I must keep to my own style and go on in my own Way; and though I may never succeed again in that, I am convinced that I should totally fail in any other.

Austen echoes the words that Mr Bennet uses in *Pride and Prejudice* when he asks Elizabeth: 'For what do we live, but to make sport for our neighbours, and laugh at them in our turn.'

Vivacious and independent, her comments go to the heart of her writing. Above all else, Austen determinedly defines herself as a comic writer. Dancing away from the ponderous interference of James Clarke, she merrily and caustically follows her own path. We see in her the same spirit that she gave to Elizabeth Bennet in *Pride and Prejudice* when Miss Bingley tries to muscle her out of a walk in the garden:

The path just admitted three. Mr Darcy felt their rudeness and immediately said: 'This walk is not wide enough for our party. We had better go into the avenue.' But Elizabeth, who had not the least inclination to remain with them, answered laughingly: 'No; no; stay where you are – you are charmingly group'd and appear to uncommon advantage. The picturesque would be spoilt by admitting a fourth. Good-bye.' She then ran gaily off, rejoicing as she rambled about.

Emma was published on 23 December 1815 'by the Author of *Pride and Prejudice*'. Austen's future looked bright and assured – she was now an established author with four successful novels. After a long wait of almost twenty years since her father had so proudly yet ineffectually tried to sell *First Impressions*, the ultimate Regency love story between Mr Darcy and Elizabeth Bennet, Austen was now at last earning 'praise and money'. The much-prized *pewter* was coming in, and John Murray, the top London publisher, was looking forward to her next manuscript. As well as working on a story to which she gave the provisional title *The Elliots*, Austen was also finally able to afford the £10 to buy back the copyright of *Susan* from Crosby & Co., who had still not published it. In the intervening years, another novel called *Susan* had been published and so before submitting it to John Murray, Austen changed the heroine's name from Susan to Catherine – Catherine Morland. Among other edits, she also took the liberty of making a snide reference to Richard Crosby in the opening paragraph, a private joke between her and her brother Henry. Describing the apparently unprepossessing qualities of her heroine Catherine, Austen writes: 'Her situation in life, the character of her father and mother, her own person and disposition were all equally against her. Her father was a clergyman, without being neglected or poor, and a very respectable man.' So far, so gently amusing, and this feels as if it was the original text. Then Austen adds bitingly: 'Though his name was Richard and he had never been handsome.' Given that Catherine's father makes no further appearance in the book, this was an easy manual edit to make and it feels like a fresh sharp stab at Richard Crosby.

Austen's fiction was contemporary. The year 1815 had seen not only the publication of *Emma* but also the final defeat of Napoleon at the Battle of Waterloo. There was something almost Austen-like about the last movement of the Napoleonic Wars. When Napoleon made his final unexpected advance in the evening before the battle, the Duke of Wellington and his officers were enjoying a sumptuous if rather makeshift ball hosted by the Duchess of Richmond in Brussels. From the fictional army officers scattered across Austen's novels, we can imagine the cast of Regency characters who were dancing the quadrilles and waltzes at the ball – unscrupulous villains like George Wickham from *Pride and Prejudice* taking their turn alongside decent younger sons of earls like Colonel Fitzwilliam; Captain Denny bowing deferentially to his senior officer Colonel Brandon from *Sense and Sensibility*. The officers finished their dancing before leaving to take up their positions at Waterloo. Some officers danced all night and with no time to change fought the battle in their evening dress.

In the long term, the victory over Napoleon at Waterloo left Regency Britain in a dominant position on the world stage, which the next generation, the Victorians, would enjoy and systematically exploit. Unfortunately for the Regency generation, the immediate consequence of the end of the lengthy Napoleonic Wars was a severe recession caused by the disbanded soldiers returning back home. This recession was compounded by a freak climate that washed out two successive harvests, and it also destroyed a number of banks and struck the Austen family very close to home. In 1816, Henry Austen's London bank, Austen & Maunde, went bust, and Henry was himself declared personally bankrupt. In Regency times, banks were unregulated and customers had no protection for their cash deposits. Along with other customers of the bank who had placed their cash deposits at Austen & Maunde, the Austen family lost a significant amount of their savings.

Jane Austen never dwelt for long on bad news. Her attitude was that she would 'let other people's pens dwell on anything odious'. After briefly lamenting the bankruptcy, she bounced back to encourage her brother Henry in his new incarnation as a curate, the lowest rung of the clergy in the Church of England. She also immediately introduced new themes of bankruptcy into her next book, still provisionally called *The Elliots*. The story opens with the Elliot family, who are teetering on the edge of financial ruin. Austen follows their moves to avoid catastrophe and intertwines their story with that of a young naval officer, Captain Wentworth, who has won a spectacular fortune for himself by capturing French ships. In a new departure for Austen, family fortunes are now prone to wild swings. In parallel with the financial success of Captain Wentworth, Austen creates her oldest heroine, Anne Elliot, who defies her age and wins back her former lover. Written in the bruising aftermath of Henry's personal bankruptcy when all his possessions were publicly auctioned to pay his creditors and the family had to come to terms with the fact that there was no chance of them recouping any of the money that they had entrusted to him, it is an inspiring story of encouragement to both Henry and to herself. No matter how bad life is, Austen was determined to demonstrate that it is always possible to turn the tables and win back both money and love.

With both the newly rewritten manuscripts of *Susan* and *The Elliots* almost ready to send to John Murray, Austen even started a new novel. This one promised to be a story of financial speculation around a fast-changing Regency seaside resort called Sanditon. As 1816 progressed after the bankruptcy, on the surface Austen was as busily creative and engaged as she had always been. Later in the year, she received her first royalty cheque from the 'civil rogue' John Murray. Dated 21 October 1816 and addressed to 'Jane Austin' (spelling was more variable then, and in any event it represented *pewter*, so nobody was going to return it) the cheque was for £38 18s 1d.

Jane Austen did not submit any more manuscripts to John Murray. She did not live to see any more of her novels published or to celebrate the receipt of any more royalty cheques they earned. By the spring of 1817, after sketching out only the opening twelve chapters, Austen was too ill to continue writing the manuscript that she had provisionally called *The Brothers*. The exact nature of her illness is unclear, but Addison's disease, Hodgkin's and lupus have each been cited. Austen was an unflinchingly brave patient, but her symptoms were ominous.

Writing on 25 March 1817, she admits: 'I have had a good deal of fever at times and indifferent nights, but am considerably better now and recovering my looks a little, which have been bad enough, black and white and every wrong colour. I must not depend upon being ever very blooming again'. She adds, with black humour which still makes us catch our breath and read it again to admire her self-deprecating courage: 'Sickness is a dangerous indulgence at my time of life.'

Her illness was sufficiently threatening that on 24 May, her sister Cassandra arranged for her to move to Winchester, to be closer to medical care. Her last known letter, dated 29 May 1817, describes her rapidly fading world: 'I live chiefly on the sofa, but am allowed to walk from one room to the other. I have been out once in a sedan-chair and am to repeat it, and be promoted to a wheel-chair as the weather serves.'

Describing the man who will deliver this letter, she signs off: 'You will find Captain [Clement] a very respectable, well-meaning man, without much manner, his wife and sister all good humour and obligingness and I hope (since the fashion allows it) with rather longer petticoats than last year.'

It is both poignant and uplifting that even as her life was closing down around her, Austen's last known written letter contains one of her classic gently barbed jokes.

Six weeks later, on 18 July 1817, aged just forty-one, Austen died. She left a surprise for Henry – her last two completed manuscripts were found in her desk. One of them was the reworked manuscript of *Susan*, which for all those years had been sitting moribund on Richard Crosby's shelves. Now it was rewritten with a new heroine's name, Catherine Morland, and an energetic hero, pointedly called Henry. Henry would also have read the manuscript of *The Elliots* and recognised the themes of financial turmoil and an ageing sister fighting to regain her bloom.

After arranging for her burial in Winchester Cathedral, Henry discussed the publication of Austen's last two novels with John Murray. While *Susan* had been written some twenty years earlier as her first novel when she was as young, dynamic and headstrong as the naive heroine herself, and *The Elliots* was her last novel written with the private knowledge that she was suffering from a fatal illness, the two books were jointly published by John Murray. Henry chose the titles. He chose well: *Susan* was changed to the more evocative and gothic *Northanger Abbey*, which chimed with the Regency craze for gothic novels. Echoing the key event of Anne Elliot's past when she was persuaded to turn down the young naval officer's ambitious proposal of marriage, he decided to change the title of *The Elliots* and called her final novel *Persuasion*.

* * *

Two years after Jane Austen's death, in November 1819, Mary Ann Evans was born in a different part of the country and with a very different family background. Almost immediately, the Regency period itself officially ended when the old, tragically 'mad' King George III finally died in January 1820 and the Prince Regent became King George IV. Bloated and unhealthy, George IV only reigned for ten years and his brother William IV for a further seven. With the rest of the Hanoverians failing to produce any heirs, in 1837 the crown went to their eighteen-year-old niece Victoria, who had been born in the same year as Mary Ann Evans. While still in her teenage years, the Regency period of Mary Ann's birth had turned into the Victorian age.

From the beginning of Jane Austen's life in 1775 to the end of George Eliot's life in 1880 is a span of just over 100 years. During these years, the industrial revolution transformed the world and the role of Britain as an industrial superpower. The span of their lives and their novels tell the story of the nineteenth century.

In the Regency time of Austen, the Royal Navy was a fleet of sailing ships that were hand-built from oak. Their masts carried billowing canvas sails that were unfurled by men climbing up and down the rigging while the officers with brass telescopes and sextants directed operations from the poop decks, where they gathered behind elaborately decorated balustrades. Two of Austen's brothers, Francis and Charles, served in the Royal Navy and helped her with the naval vocabulary in *Mansfield Park*, where the description of the fleet anchored at Portsmouth rings true with its vigour and national pride:

> 'By God, you lost a fine sight by not being here in the morning to see the *Thrush* go out of harbour. I would not have been out of the way for a thousand pounds. Old Scholey ran in at breakfast time to say she had slipped her moorings and was coming out. I jumped up and made but two steps to the platform. If ever there was a perfect beauty afloat, she is the one. And there she lays at Spithead and anybody in England would take her for an eight-and-twenty. She lays close to *Endymion*, between her and the *Cleopatra*, just to the eastward of the sheer hulk.'
>
> 'Ha!' cried William. 'That's just where I should have put her myself. It's the best berth at Spithead.'

HMS *Thrush*, *Endymion* and *Cleopatra* were real warships of the Royal Navy. Charles Austen started his naval career as a midshipman on HMS *Endymion*, built in 1795 as a forty-gun frigate with a crew of 300 sailors. *Endymion* was celebrated in her day as the fastest-sailing ship in the Royal Navy, and she captured a string of French and Spanish ships. As Admiral Nelson's fleet was trying to close in on the French and Spanish Navies in 1805, *Endymion* was dispatched to collect supplies from Gibraltar, so Charles Austen missed the Battle of Trafalgar. In 1810, Charles was promoted to captain of HMS *Cleopatra* and ended his career as a Vice Admiral. Elsewhere in *Mansfield Park*, Austen also mentions HMS *Elephant*, a 74-gun ship of the line that was Nelson's flagship in the Battle of Copenhagen in 1801 (when he put his telescope to his blind eye and so truthfully claimed that he could not see Admiral Parker's signal ordering him to withdraw), which her other brother Francis later captained. This mentioning of real ships was a delicate matter, and Jane had asked Francis for his permission in advance:

'And by the bye, shall you object to my mentioning *Elephant* and two or three other of your old ships? I have done it, but it shall not stay to make you angry – they are only just mentioned.'

By the time George Eliot was at the height of her writing career, all these magnificent timber warships with their painted bowsprits and balustrades were redundant and dismantled. Naval records confirm that HMS *Elephant* was broken up in 1830 and Charles Austen's first ship HMS *Endymion* was broken up in Plymouth in June 1868.

This change in technology moved across the industrialised world. In 1862, Count Otto von Bismarck concluded a speech to the Prussian National Association with the now notorious observation: 'It is not by speeches and majority resolutions that the great questions of the time are decided – that was the big mistake of 1848 and 1849 – but by iron and blood.'

The American Civil War of 1861–65 was indeed defined by iron and blood. The army fought with early versions of repeating 'machine' guns and the navy was a fleet of iron-clad, steam-powered gunboats. The killing power of this new machinery, which would later dominate the conflicts of the twentieth century, meant that military deaths soared to industrial levels.

In 1870, the Franco-Prussian War broke out. In both France and Germany, all the railways that had been recently laid and were operated by private regional companies were nationalised by their respective governments and passed to military control. Immediately after the declaration of war in 1870, there is an account of 1,000

French trains leaving Paris within three weeks to transport 300,000 soldiers and 65,000 horses to meet the Prussian Army. Yet even these troop movements were too slow, because the Germans moved their troops faster and were more organised in the first example of what was later called 'Blitzkrieg'.

While in Austen's Regency time, Napoleon's troops with muskets on their shoulders and swords on their belts marched on foot across Europe covering ten miles a day into – and then so painfully back out of – Russia, by Eliot's Victorian adulthood the Prussian military machinery and troops moved with devastating speed along railways from Denmark to Austria and then doubled back to demolish France and invade Paris. There is even an account of the steam from the trains' boilers being used to brew coffee for the troops, an early and remarkably inventive and industrial-scale espresso coffee machine. It's no wonder that Jane Austen's novels had one foot stuck in the eighteenth century, while George Eliot was striding towards the twentieth.

George Eliot lived twenty years longer than Jane Austen. Throughout her adult life, she travelled widely and the broader scope of her experience is reflected in the settings of her novels. Austen wrote only about the upper-class Regency society with which she was familiar. While some of the male characters occasionally gallop off to conduct business further afield, the action of the novels rarely goes beyond an English village, echoing the advice Austen once gave to her niece Anna, who in 1814 was writing a novel:

'You are now collecting your people delightfully, getting them exactly into such a spot as is the delight of my life – 3 or 4 families in a country village is the very thing to work on.'

The single momentous visit to Derbyshire in *Pride and Prejudice* forms the northern boundary of Austen's settings. Socially too, the range is narrow. Wherever they find themselves, her characters use the same language and respect the same niceties of social etiquette. With no tradesmen or servants speaking more than the shortest line, there is no dialect.

George Eliot's novels span a much broader world socially, geographically and even historically. *Romola* is an exception as it is set in Renaissance Florence and the other novels take place between ten and sixty years before they were written: *Adam Bede* is set in 1799, which overlaps Austen's era and provides extensive local dialect of the sort that Austen would have heard spoken around her. Both *Felix Holt* and *Middlemarch* are set around the 1832 Reform Act. *Daniel Deronda* is her most contemporary setting where a joke about Lord John Russell, then Prime Minister, dropping in for tea gives us a date of 1865.

The locations are as varied as the periods and reflect Mary Ann and Lewes's extensive travels on the Continent. *Romola* is set in Florence, where the city map is so painstakingly recreated that we sense Mary Ann pacing out the streets and moving her characters around the city in her footsteps. She chooses Rome for part of *Middlemarch*; Leubronn, a fictional German spa town, and Genoa in Italy provide settings for *Daniel Deronda*. While horsepower predominates in her earlier novels, by the time of *Daniel Deronda* the characters travel by train to London and around Europe. Unlike Jane Austen, so rooted in her time and place, George Eliot roams freely between centuries, continents and class.

* * *

Unlike Jane Austen, who was the daughter of a well-to-do, well-connected vicar with a well-stocked library in bosky Hampshire, Mary

Ann Evans was the daughter of an estate manager in a newly developed coalmining area near Coventry, in the Midlands. The world of Mary Ann Evans's childhood was very different from the genteel tranquillity of the Austen rectory – there is no character in any Austen book who resembles Mary Ann or her family.

Mary Ann's father was Robert Evans, the manager of the Arbury Hall estate, just outside Coventry. Robert Evans had to be much more pragmatic and commercially minded than the Reverend George Austen. His job involved assessing the value of coal, crops, livestock and timber and negotiating the costs of repairs and improvements across the estate. Robert Evans, who inspired the character of Caleb Garth in *Middlemarch*, worked across society, managing both the expectations of his employer Lord Newdigate, who lived at Arbury Hall, and the various tradesmen and tenants who lived or worked on the estate.

In 1836, Mary Ann's mother died. Mary Ann was sixteen and she left school in order to look after her father and brother Isaac. The following year, her older sister Chrissey married and left home, leaving Mary Ann to run the household. Mary Ann continued her education by herself. Lady Newdigate had given her permission to use the library at Arbury Hall and Mary Ann, a voracious reader, would make the two mile walk from Griff House. It is still an impressive sight. From Griff House, Mary Ann would have walked between the tall ornate gates at the start of the driveway into the estate. As the drive bends around a wood, suddenly Arbury Hall, celebrated as the finest of all Gothic Revival houses in England, is revealed standing tall over a lake resplendent with swans. Inside, the library is unchanged from Mary Ann's day. It is unsurprising that Arbury Hall features in Mary Ann's first work of fiction and that the tall, serene library with shelves reaching high and filled with rich leather-bound volumes is recreated in *Romola*. Mary Ann had just five years to read as much as she could of this fully stocked collection of all the classics before her father retired in 1841 and handed Griff House and the management of Arbury Estate to her brother, Isaac. Robert Evans moved to Foleshill on the outskirts of Coventry and Mary Ann went to live with him.

Coventry, one of the great old towns of medieval England, was changing fast. The opening of the Coventry Canal in 1769 had connected Coventry to the growing markets of London and beyond. The ribbon-weaving and clock-making industries now employed thousands of skilled workers in the town. The surrounding countryside was also changing. In 1829, the launch of George Stephenson's famous 'Rocket' locomotive had triggered a railway-building frenzy. Journeys that would have taken days for Austen to complete in a horse-drawn carriage would soon be conducted in hours by train. The development of the next generation of steam engines provided power, which allowed miners to dig into the deep seams of coal that ran through the Midlands. The fields and farms of Mary Ann's childhood were being transformed into an industrial landscape that people in nearby Birmingham were already calling the Black Country.

While in Austen's time, a village common might have appeared as a pastoral oasis as painted by John Constable (a year younger than her), by Mary Ann's time the country landscape had been overtaken by the industrial revolution. A description in *Scenes of Clerical Life* encapsulates her impression of the change:

'Paddiford Common … was hardly recognisable as a common at all, but was a dismal district where you heard the rattle of the handloom and breathed the smoke of coalpits.'

This was the new Britain of the Victorian age. Like many Victorians, Robert Evans may have appreciated the technological and commercial progress that was being made, but in other areas of life he was a traditionalist. When he and Mary Ann moved to Coventry, she promptly met a radical group of free thinkers who challenged some of the traditional ideas. The scene was set for Mary Ann's radical education to begin, which would cause an increasing series of ructions between her and her family and friends.

In November 1841, Mary Ann met Charles Bray, a wealthy ribbon manufacturer who hosted regular gatherings of radicals and free-thinking philosophers at his house in Rosehill. Sitting out on bearskin rugs under the acacia tree in his garden, members of the 'Rosehill circle' discussed religion and religious dogma. Some rejected organised religion; others denied the divinity of Christ altogether. Questions were freely asked and debated that would have been unthinkable in the traditional schools of Mary Ann's childhood and certainly would never have crossed the mind of her father. Charles Bray's wife Cara and her sister Sara were at the centre of this group and became close friends of Mary Ann.

In January 1842, Mary Ann dropped her first family bombshell. She announced to her father that she had lost religious faith and to his mortification refused to attend church. With characteristic honesty and directness, Mary Ann wrote him a letter to explain her radical decision: 'While I admire and cherish much of what I believe to have been the moral teaching of Jesus himself,' she declared, 'the system of doctrines built on his life was most dishonourable to God and most pernicious in its influence on individual and social happiness.' Her father was distraught and for two years she was ostracised by her family and became something of an outcast, a role that she was later to experience again. Eventually, Mary Ann softened her uncompromising radical line and agreed to come to church with her father, not to worship but for the sake of his feelings.

Yet Mary Ann never changed her mind on the underlying principles. Remaining agnostic, her research increasingly centred upon trying to disentangle the elements of myth from the proven facts of Christianity. This resulted in her first literary task of translating *Das Leben Jesu* by the influential German theologian David Friedrich Strauss. When published in Germany, it had caused a scandal because its central argument was that the miracles of the New Testament were fictionalised additions to the biographical account of the real historical Jesus. Joseph Parkes, the radical MP for Birmingham, paid the commission that Mary Ann took two years to complete. In this intense, ambitious and rather unappreciated labour, we can glimpse the origins of Dorothea Brooke and her subservient desire to help Casaubon's monumental (if deluded) work, or Romola's selfless decision to help her father in the library. *The Life of Jesus* with the new, loaded subtitle '*Critically Examined*' was published in 1845 by London publisher John Chapman. It was considered highly radical. One reviewer called it 'the most pestilential book ever vomited out of the jaws of hell'. Mary Ann received £20 for her work and while her name does not appear as a by-line in the publication, it set in motion many of the key parts of her future life.

When her father died in 1849, Mary Ann travelled with Charles and Cara Bray to Lake Geneva. There, far from the coal fields and factories of the Midlands, she considered her future. She was at a turning point. There are very few portraits of Mary Ann, either of her in her youth or in later life as George Eliot. One portrait that does survive and is now in the National Portrait Gallery was painted while she was on this trip in Switzerland. After Charles and Cara Bray left, Mary Ann stayed on for a few weeks. She found a guest house in Geneva run by Monsieur and Madame D'Albert Durade, with whom she quickly felt at home and formed a deeply affectionate friendship. As a boy, François D'Albert had suffered an accident which had left him almost doubled over with a bent spine. He was a keen painter and would later provide the inspiration for Philip Wakem in *The Mill on the Floss*. To her evident surprise, Monsieur D'Albert asked her if he could paint her portrait. Mary Ann was self-deprecating about her appearance and wrote to the Brays:

> You will be amused to hear that I am sitting for my portrait – at M. D'Albert's request – not mine. If it turns out well, I shall long to steal it to give to you; but M. D'Albert talks of painting a second and in that case I shall certainly beg one. The idea of making a study of my visage is droll enough.

The portrait of Mary Ann is gentle but intense. It shows a young woman on the cusp of making a crucial life decision. With no father, no mother, a distant married sister and a coldly remote brother who could not tolerate her radicalism, she is making up her mind what to do. Her gaze is calm and steady and with her head slightly on one side and leaning towards us, she appears gentle and understanding. But the portrait is a very subtle one and shows her gaze just fractionally not meeting our eye. This creates the sense of her looking so preoccupied and introspective.

Mary Ann was under no illusions as to how difficult it would be to earn her own money and be a professional writer – £20 for two years' work was not a viable income. Far too well read and intellectually ambitious to settle into domestic life in the Midlands, she saw a narrow path open to her. Rather than living off her family and being overwhelmed with domestic chores at Griff House, Mary Ann realised she could earn her own living as a professional writer. To have any chance of success, she would have to move to London.

When she returned home, Mary Ann cast the dice. She wrote to ask Sara Hennell:

'Will you also send me an account of Mr Chapman's prices for lodgers in London? Will you tell me what you can? I am not asking you merely for the sake of giving you trouble, I am really anxious to know.'

Fresh back from Switzerland, she was committed to changing her life. Upon returning home after a long stay abroad, it is almost a universal human reaction to feel disappointment that everything is still all the same – the same old people living the same old lives, especially if the same old bad weather is thrown in for good measure:

'Oh the dismal weather, and the dismal country and the dismal people,' Mary Ann lamented. 'It was some envious demon that drove me across the Jura. However I am determined to sell everything I possess except a portmanteau and carpet-bag and the necessary contents, and be a stranger and a foreigner on the earth for evermore.'

But unlike so many people who idly dream of escaping from their normal life, Mary Ann actually did pack her portmanteau and her carpet-bag. In 1851, she kicked over the traces of her tedious domestic life in the Midlands and escaped. She became a Londoner.

* * *

As we have seen, 1851 was a heady year for London. When the city hosted the Great Exhibition, it must have been an exhilarating time. Intoxicated by the opening ceremony, the young Queen Victoria's diary entry that evening had summed up the mood of the nation as she acknowledged the historic occasion:

'This day is one of the greatest and most glorious days of our lives.'

Mary Ann Evans slipped into London with less fanfare. To commemorate her new life, she changed her name from Mary Ann to Marian (though to avoid confusion I have called her Mary Ann until she wrote her first fiction and morphed into George Eliot). Her first destination was board and lodgings with the publisher John Chapman. The Chapman setup was rambling, disorganised and louche. His house was at 142 The Strand, from where he also operated his publishing company and had rooms available over five or six floors, which he rented out to a ragbag variety of young freelance journalists who were all vying for roles in the literary mainstream of London. In short, all people very like Mary Ann Evans.

John Chapman's wife, Susanna, had brought money to their marriage, but aged forty to his twenty-eight she was fading. On 10 August 1851, Chapman despondently noted in his diary: 'Susanna's incapability of walking far or fast and general debility presses upon me how much she has aged latterly and makes the future look sad.'

Susanna was nevertheless sufficiently tolerant, or perhaps just sufficiently downtrodden, to accept an unusual marriage. Chapman had a mistress, Elisabeth, who was ostensibly the governess and lived with them at 142. As soon as Mary Ann arrived in January 1851, she too started an affair with Chapman. This was a catastrophic misjudgement. Within weeks, Susanna and Elisabeth closed ranks and insisted to John Chapman that Mary Ann leave her lodgings. In March, humiliatingly, Mary Ann returned home. She had literally been 'sent to Coventry'. Her dream of making a new life in London appeared to be in tatters.

Happily, it was not long before she was summoned back. The hopelessly disorganised John Chapman was given the opportunity to purchase and relaunch the quarterly magazine the *Westminster Review*, and he needed someone who was well-read, well-organised and – crucially – cheap to help him edit the magazine. In August 1851, Chapman visited Mary Ann in Coventry and invited her back to London. She needed little persuasion. Within days, she had repacked her carpet-bag and returned to London. She resumed her residency on the top floor at 142 The Strand, this time on an exclusively professional basis, and set about her new career of commissioning articles, selecting books to review and editing the relaunched *Westminster Review*. Unsurprisingly she turned out to be an outstanding editor.

This episode of Mary Ann's early life in London would later be rather glossed over by John Cross when he published the first collection of Eliot's letters and journals. Exercising the discretion of a high Victorian widower, John Cross's publication appears to imply that the young Mary Ann Evans arrived in London and worked as a selfless and chaste academic until she met Lewes in October 1851, and even then little happened until that dramatic night in July 1854 when they left for the Continent. John Chapman is barely mentioned in her letters. John Cross had merely noted:

> Miss Evans seems to have been in London from the beginning of January till the end of March 1851; and Mr Chapman made another fortnight's visit to Rosehill at the end of May and beginning of June. It was during this period that, with Miss Evans's assistance, the prospectus of the new series of *The Westminster Review* was determined and put into shape.

John Cross's version of Mary Ann's first years in London was given fresh light in 1913, when Chapman's diary was discovered in a bookshop in Nottingham. John Cross would have been mortified because Chapman used a very simple code to denote when he had made love with each of the three women in his household and how they had conspired and railed against him.

Whatever the truth of her early relationship with John Chapman, as the effective editor of the *Westminster Review* Mary Ann seemed completely at home. She showed shrewd and patient judgement between the various contributors pushing their different articles. Mary Ann steered a course between these jostling, ambitious and opinionated men (and they were all men), admittedly rather favouring George Lewes and keeping John Chapman himself largely out of the magazine. Along with her work, she was happily engaged attending the opera at Covent Garden and various literary gatherings, where she was often the only professional woman. The 1850s were a time of radical reform and invention, and Mary Ann was happy to work long hours for little money, taking great pride at being in the mainstream of the literary discussions about philosophy, social and political reform, evolution and even phrenology. The first phase of her London life came to a crescendo on that July night in 1854.

* * *

After their dramatic departure to Antwerp that summer night, Mary Ann Evans and George Lewes spent eight months in Germany. Lewes was researching and writing his autobiography of Johann Wolfgang von Goethe, enjoying how his widespread and various interests mirrored his own. Mary Ann stayed in touch with John Chapman and managed to write a few articles. She was effectively a freelance journalist. No longer sitting in the editors' office at The Strand commissioning and editing what was published, she was now very much at the fringes of the magazine and at the back of the queue of those journalists jostling for commissions.

Mary Ann tried to stay in touch with her Coventry friends, and it is painful to read this poignant and tentative letter of 23 October 1854 to Charles Bray:

> I am ignorant how far Cara and Sara may be acquainted with the state of things, and how they may feel towards me. I am quite prepared to accept the consequences of a step which I have deliberately taken and accept them without irritation or bitterness. The most painful consequence will, I know, be the loss of friends. If I do not write, therefore, understand that it is because I desire not to obtrude myself.

In their correspondence, Sara and Cara often maintained that they were as close to Mary Ann as they had always been, but their friendship never fully recovered. Sara wrote to her in November: 'I have a strange sort of feeling that I am writing to someone in a book and not the Mary Ann that we have known and loved so many years.'

During their eight months in Germany, Mary Ann and Lewes lived as man and wife. Both of them were fluent in German and they were welcomed into society. In Weimar, they became friends with the composer Franz Liszt and they joined in literary and musical gatherings. They might not have known, or might not have cared, that their affair was being gossiped about in literary London as the leading scandal of the day.

When Mary Ann and Lewes returned from Germany, they both knew that Mary Ann would be ostracised by society. Lewes himself would be able to carry on attending society events, but not Mary Ann. They knew that they could not appear as man and wife; indeed, they would even be unable to check into a guest house together. It must have been a daunting prospect. As if reflecting their changed future, the ferry crossing back to Dover was stormy and made them both sick. This time there was no sitting up on deck to celebrate and admire the rising sun of their new life together, no more euphoric journal entries of 'still lovelier the dawn'. When they landed, they parted company. Mary Ann stayed discreetly behind in a guest house in Dover while Lewes went ahead to find lodgings for them in London. It was not the homecoming welcome that a radical returning heroine might have dreamed of, but this was the new reality.

The most galling aspect of their rejection by their friends must have been the hypocrisy, especially of those people who Mary Ann had counted as being as radical as herself. Charles Bray himself was not only known to have various affairs with other women, but he also had a separate family with a long-term mistress. Mary Ann would not have seen this letter, which Bray had written to George Combe, a typical Victorian amateur scientist who published papers on the popular quasi-science of phrenology:

'My wife and Miss Hennell are sadly troubled by all this and wish me to say that Miss E's going had not their sanction because they knew nothing about it.'

Combe replied to Bray in a letter that sums up the general society's verdict. Mary Ann would not have seen this letter either, but it speaks for what everyone was saying about her behind her back:

> If you receive her into your family circle, while present appearances are unexplained, pray consider whether you will do justice to your own female domestic circle, and how other ladies may feel about going into a circle which makes no distinction between those who act thus and those who preserve their honour unspotted.

Conflating two streams of radical philosophy, the freedom to love and the freedom to worship, Combe illogically argued: 'T Hunt, Lewes and Miss Evans have in my opinion by their practical conduct inflicted a great injury on the cause of religious freedom.'

Even Mary Ann's original sponsor, Joseph Parkes, who still invariably attracts the moniker 'the radical MP' and who was famous for proposing the radical social reform that led to the Reform Act of 1832, was apparently outraged by their affair. He reacted 'in a white rage as if on the verge of a paralytic stroke'. Like Charles Bray and like many other Victorian husbands, Parkes had conveniently overlooked the mistress whom he kept alongside his wife, or perhaps like so many others he simply thought that different rules applied to a radical man compared to a radical woman. Society closed rank and radicals were not so radical after all.

Worst of all, closer to home Mary Ann's brother Isaac was still implacably opposed to any reconciliation. Unless she renounced her agnostic beliefs, they would not see each other again. Upon her return to London, Mary Ann had hoped that her sister Chrissey might be more understanding, but here too she was disappointed. Isaac insisted that Chrissey and their half-sisters not only never visited her, but also stopped any correspondence. Eventually in 1859, Chrissey broke the embargo, but tragically, the reconciliation took place too late. Suffering from consumption, Chrissey wrote to Mary Ann from her deathbed. Mary Ann immediately replied, but she was unable to see her before she died. Taciturn and utterly unyielding in his logic, at least Isaac was not a hypocrite. Without a hint of irony and certainly not a jot of apology, a lifetime later in 1878, when Lewes died and Mary Ann confounded everyone by marrying her young financial advisor John Cross, Isaac would be the first to write to her to congratulate her upon her marriage. Dutifully, soon afterwards Isaac would come to his sister's funeral when, reinstated as her brother, he would be one of the leading mourners.

Mary Ann was paying a high price for her radical approach to life. Just like the hustling Burlington Arcade, Victorian society really did operate on two levels, and rather than being welcomed in the open social mix downstairs, free to meet anyone in a bookshop, Mary Ann was now cast away in the same invisible category as the prostitutes upstairs whose availability was only indicated by their black stockings hanging out of the windows.

Unable to attend social gatherings, it was not worth their while living in the centre of London. Nobody would visit them or invite them as a couple. Lewes therefore found a series of houses where they could live in the London suburbs ranging from East Sheen to Hampstead. Lewes was also paying a price for his earlier radical life. When he had adopted his wife Agnes's baby, fathered by Thornton Hunt, Lewes had effectively condoned their adultery. There was obviously plenty of proof of Hunt's adultery (he had actually gone on to father four children with Agnes), but Lewes could not cite adultery as a cause for any divorce proceedings. Since Lewes was unable to divorce Agnes, he was unable to marry Mary Ann.

In the absence of strong relationships and by necessity living in isolation, Mary Ann turned exclusively for support to Lewes. Initially they muddled by with little money. Lewes's miscellaneous journalism brought in some cash and there were royalties from his biography of Goethe. Mary Ann also managed to win some commissions from John Chapman. They did not seem to worry very much about money. Unlike so many other radicals who proved flawed, they were two true radicals together. The most luminous entries in Mary Ann's journal describe time together that no amount of money could buy. There is a simplicity of this account of a day in the park with George in Munich which glows with her love for him:

'We walked in the Englische Garten and heard the band and saw the Germans drinking their beer. The park was lovely.'

Or this account of their Christmas Day together in Richmond, which shows them equally content in isolation from the world and with each other:

'Christmas Day 1857: George and I spent this lovely day together – lovely as a clear spring day. We could see Hampstead from the Park so distinctly that it seemed to have suddenly come near to us. We ate our turkey together in a happy solitude *a deux*.'

Despite society speculating that he would soon tire of her, Lewes remained faithful and loving to Mary Ann throughout the rest of his life. There are no surviving letters between them because Mary Ann asked for all their correspondence to be buried in her coffin with her. However, I do not think that there would have been many letters in the first place, if only because they spent virtually all their time together. Lewes seems to have lost none of his boundless enthusiasm, and he continued to be described in slightly derogatory terms by his visitors. Writing later in 1869 during a visit to London, the Harvard University professor Charles Eliot Norton noted that Lewes was still the life force of any party:

> Lewes received us at the door with characteristic animation; he looks and moves like an old-fashioned French barber or dancing master, very ugly, very vivacious, very entertaining. You expect him to take up his fiddle and begin to play ... all the action of his mind is rapid and it is so full that it seems to be running over.

But none of this implies faithlessness. Time and again in her journal Mary Ann writes of her gratitude to George and appreciates his wise advice, and time and again he does not disappoint her.

So it was that these two radical thinkers who had so much to offer society were marginalised. Writing is a solitary activity, and while Mary Ann was content in her own company, she clearly lit up in George's company. However, she was finding it increasingly difficult to win commissions to write journalism. From her position in Richmond (to where they had moved), she was rather remote, but equally she might have tired of journalism as being too humdrum and superficial for her. As she had seen from her role as editor, being a successful journalist involved constantly keeping in the editor's face, being able to drop by their office or see them at the opera or the next literary event. It was becoming impossible for Mary Ann to succeed at this. So as her life of isolation continued and she saw how she could not contribute to any radical writing through journalism, her mind turned to writing novels.

In 1856, Mary Ann's journal noted this shift for the first time. A new identity was about to be born – a change that would not have happened without George Lewes.

At the time, there was a prevailing craze for collecting coral, rock pools and fossils. It was not long before Charles Darwin, an avid fossil collector, would publish *On the Origin of Species*. All along any rocky stretch of British coastline, the only sound all day was of Victorian amateur naturalists hammering away to unearth fossils and remove interesting rock formations to bring home and display in little grottos. As they did so, they irreparably destroyed the rock pools around the coastline. Taking advantage of this fashion, Lewes had the idea to write a book called *Seaside Studies*. In June, he took Mary Ann on a seaside trip to Ilfracombe on the Devon coast and then to Tenby in south Wales, where he set about collecting various sea creatures from the rock pools. Armed with a shrimping net and a bag of tools, Mary Ann was his eager assistant. While in Tenby, she noted in her journal:

'St Catherine's Rock with its caverns is our paradise. We go there with baskets, hammers and chisels, and jars and phials and come home laden with spoils.'

Lewes would complete his research for *Seaside Studies*, which would add to his miscellaneous collection of publications and bring in a tiny royalty to keep them going. Far more significant than *Seaside Studies*, however, is this short sentence in Mary Ann's journal of 20 July 1856: 'Mr Chapman invites me to contribute to the *Westminster* for this quarter. I am anxious to begin my fiction writing and so am not inclined to undertake an article that will give me much trouble.'

In fact, Mary Ann did take the time and trouble to write the article that John Chapman wanted. It turned out to be very prescient. The title itself was provocative: 'Silly Novels by Lady Novelists.' Just as she planned her first fiction, it stands as her writing manifesto. By the time she wrote the article, Mary Ann had decided to become a novelist. She would not write silly novels, however; she was going to write novels that were radical for their realism and psychological insight into their characters. Moreover, she would not be a 'lady novelist' – she had already been judged for her actions as a woman, so she was going to write as a man. Mary Ann Evans was about to take her most radical step of all – she was going to become George Eliot.

* * *

CHAPTER 2

THE LADY NOVELISTS

Placed exactly between Jane Austen and George Eliot, Charlotte Brontë proved to be a vital hinge in their work. In an extraordinary turn of events, these three lady novelists were each connected through George Lewes. Austen's novels profoundly influenced Lewes, and he in turn insisted that both Brontë and Eliot read and learned from her. The arguments over Austen can be seen in the passionate, indignant and insightful letters from Brontë to Lewes; the consequences of these arguments can be seen in the novels of Eliot.

Between November 1847 and January 1850, Brontë wrote seven letters to Lewes, which he carefully kept and which have been preserved. Although none of his letters to her survive, it is possible to deduce some of what he wrote because as she subjects his 'sermonising' to detailed analysis, interrogation and rebuttal in her letters, Brontë helpfully quotes verbatim some of the key sentences that Lewes wrote. As a result, Brontë's letters offer unique insight into a critical turning point in literary history.

On the face of it, Brontë and Lewes were unlikely correspondents. She lived in Haworth, a remote Yorkshire village high up beside the moor. A vicar's daughter, Brontë was unmarried and lived with her puritanical father along with her sisters, Emily and Anne. She was an outsider to London literary circles and her first manuscript, *The Professor*, had been rejected by six publishers.

George Lewes, then aged thirty (a year younger than Brontë), was anything but puritanical. It would be another four years before he met Mary Ann Evans in William Jeff's bookshop, and during this time he was living with his wife in a commune in Bayswater. Their artistic commune was known as a 'phalanstery', and within their group marriages were not considered exclusive. As well as sharing their love life, they also shared their literary ideas and it was through this phalanstery that Lewes and Charlotte Brontë came together. *Jane Eyre* was published in 1847 by Smith, Elder & Co. The publisher William Smith Williams was also a member of the phalanstery. Williams gave Lewes an early copy of *Jane Eyre* for him to review. Lewes was deeply impressed, so much so that he decided to write to the author, who had the unusual name of Currer Bell, with his reaction. He could not resist proffering some unsolicited advice that he later described as his 'sermonising' to this first-time author. The letter that Lewes wrote to Currer Bell was the first letter that Charlotte Brontë (for it was indeed her) had ever received from a critic or reader. Excited by the prospect of *Jane Eyre* being reviewed by a London critic and rather anxious about the verdict that Lewes would deliver, on 6 November 1847 Brontë wrote to ask William Smith Williams about Lewes. Paranoid to protect her identity as Currer Bell, she took care to conceal where her letter had been posted:

> Dear Sir, I shall be obliged if you shall direct the enclosed to be posted in London, as at present I wish to avoid giving any clue to my place of residence … Can you give me any information respecting Lewes? What station he occupies in the literary world

and what works he has written? He styles himself 'a fellow-novelist'. There is something in the candid tone of his letter which inclines me to think well of him.

Enclosed was Brontë's first letter, ostensibly from Currer Bell to Lewes, offering a spirited defence to the criticisms he had raised in his opening letter to her:

> You warn me to beware of melodrama, and you exhort me to adhere to the real. When I first began to write, so impressed was I with the truth of the principles you advocate, that I determined to take Nature and Truth as my sole guides, and to follow their very footprints. I restrained imagination, eschewed romance, repressed excitement; over-bright colouring, too, I avoided, and sought to produce something which should be soft, grave, and true.

She then explained that these writing techniques had failed because *The Professor* had been rejected by six publishers due to it lacking 'startling incident' or 'thrilling excitement'. Charlotte then turns to discuss the difference between writing from experience and from imagination, the theme that forms one of the key arguments in their correspondence. Charlotte invites Lewes to reflect:

> You say 'real experience is perennially interesting and to all men.' I feel that this also is true; but dear sir, is not the real experience of each individual very limited? And if a writer dwells upon that solely or principally, is he not in danger of repeating himself, and also of becoming an egotist?

She argues that a novelist must be free to write from imagination:

Then too, imagination is a strong, restless faculty, which claims to be heard and exercised: are we to be quite deaf to her cry and insensate to her struggles? When she shows us bright pictures, are we never to look at them and try to reproduce them? And when she is eloquent, and speaks rapidly and urgently in our ear, are we not to write to her dictation?

Before he had time to reply to this letter from Currer Bell, Lewes received a second one. Picking up his reference that he was a 'fellow novelist', Brontë had bought a copy of his novel *Ranthorpe*. Now lost without trace, *Ranthorpe* tells the story of a young journalist making a living in London. Clearly, Lewes was not straying too far into his imagination. Struggling to find adequate words to praise it, Brontë manages to be unfailingly polite if, for her, uncharacteristically vague:

'I did not know such books were written now. It is very different to any of the popular works of fiction. It fills the mind with fresh knowledge.'

Perhaps hoping that her euphemisms have curried some favour, she braces herself for whatever criticism he would level at *Jane Eyre*:

'You will be severe, your last letter taught me as much.'

Brontë need not have worried quite so much. Lewes's review in *Fraser's Magazine for Town and Country* was entitled 'Recent Novels: French and English'. Like many Victorian critics, Lewes began with a grand statement of his realist literary principles:

What we most heartily enjoy and applaud is truth in the delineation of life and character: incidents however wonderful, adventures however perilous are almost as naught when compared with the deep and lasting interest excited by anything like a correct representation of life. That indeed seems to us to be Art, and the only Art we care to applaud.

Lewes then nails his colours to the mast in this sentence which would have surprised Brontë:

> To make our meaning precise, we should say that Fielding and Miss Austen are the greatest novelists in our language. We have merely to record an individual opinion that great, indeed astonishing as Scott's powers of attraction are, we would rather have written *Pride and Prejudice* or *Tom Jones* than any of the *Waverley* novels.

Eventually he turns to *Jane Eyre* which he praises for its realism, picking up its subtitle *An Autobiography*:

'Reality – deep significant reality – is the great characteristic of the book. It *is* an autobiography – not perhaps in the naked facts and circumstances, but in the actual suffering and experience.'

This was a crucial point for Lewes. The publication of *Jane Eyre* had provoked a frenzy of speculation about the identity of the mysterious Currer Bell. The name was ambiguous but masculine-sounding, and it was assumed that the writer was a man. Relying upon intuition, Lewes disagreed:

'The authoress,' for such, in his view, she had to be, 'is unquestionably setting forth her own experience. This gives the book its charm: it is soul speaking to soul; it is an utterance from the depths of a struggling, suffering, much enduring spirit. *Suspiria de profundis*!'

Taking a wide-ranging and rather personal line, Lewes wonders what experience of life the author might have had: 'Is this experience drawn from an abundant source, or is it only the artistic mastery over small materials?' and asks another personal question: 'Has the author seen much more and felt much more than what is here communicated?'

Lewes concludes his review with some of his characteristic if patronising 'sermonising':

'Keep reality distinctly before you and paint it as accurately as you can: invention will never equal the effect of truth.'

Lewes was clearly a man with strong ideas about the way a novel should be. 'The art of the novelist', he had written, 'is the representation of human life by means of a story,' with the greatest praise going to those novels that managed 'the *truest* representation, effected by the *least expenditure* of means'.

While Lewes had sometimes found fault with *Jane Eyre*, he had also found truth in it, which was why he was so insistent that it must have been written by a woman. He believed that novels should strive to represent reality and they should draw above all not on imagination but on experience. He was certain that the powerful depiction of female unhappiness found in *Jane Eyre* could only be *true* if it was the voice of a woman.

Lewes had given more thought than most nineteenth-century critics to the place of women in literature. Apart from his admiration of Jane Austen, he had also been an early admirer of the novels of Elizabeth Gaskell and a defender of the controversial French novelist George Sand, a woman notorious for dressing in men's clothes. In 1852, five years after the publication of *Jane Eyre*, Lewes would gather these thoughts together in an essay for the *Westminster Review* commissioned by none other than his new acquaintance Mary Ann Evans ('Lewes has written us an agreeable article on lady novelists' she wrote to Sara Hennell on 25 June). Entitled 'The Lady Novelists', it included Charlotte Brontë alongside George

Sand, Elizabeth Gaskell and of course Jane Austen herself as examples of literature's most formidable female writers. Lewes argued that these writers were not great despite being women, they were great *because* they were women and were therefore especially suited to the writing of fiction:

> Of all departments of literature, fiction is the one to which, by nature and by circumstances, women are best adapted ... The domestic experience which forms the bulk of a woman's knowledge finds an appropriate form in novels; while the very nature of fiction calls for the predominance of sentiment which we have already attributed to the female mind.

But Lewes's championing of lady novelists came with strings attached. His insistence on realism meant that a woman novelist had to write within her own experience. Elizabeth Gaskell is praised for approaching a tricky subject 'like a woman, a truly delicate minded woman'. The works of George Sand are admired because they show 'the features of a woman' and in a later article for *Blackwood's Magazine*, Lewes explained that he admired Jane Austen's novels because 'Miss Austen has nothing fervid in her works. She is not capable of producing a profound agitation in the mind.' He concluded: 'Her pages have no sudden illuminations. There are neither epigrams nor aphorisms, neither subtle analyses nor eloquent descriptions. She is without grace or felicity of expression; she has neither fervid nor philosophic comment. Her charm lies solely in the art of representing life and character and that is exquisite.'

If she had read this, Jane Austen might well have felt that she was being damned with the sort of praise that she could have done without.

In the meantime, there was clearly a great deal in Lewes's review of *Jane Eyre* to provide food for thought to Brontë. She immediately wrote to William Smith Williams, worrying about her lack of experience in life: 'The narrow bounds of my attainment, the limited scope of my reading.'

Still digesting the review, Brontë took Lewes's advice to heart. She had never read any Austen and she went to the circulating library and borrowed a copy of *Pride and Prejudice*. This is the moment when their correspondence moved to a different plane. Without her taking this step, Brontë might have just sent Lewes an acknowledgement of his review and their paths would never have crossed again. As she read *Pride and Prejudice*, Brontë would be trying to measure it against Lewes's claim that 'Fielding and Miss Austen are the greatest novelists in our language'. From our perspective today, both *Pride and Prejudice* and *Jane Eyre* would appear in any list of the top twenty greatest English novels ever written, but when Brontë read it over Christmas 1847, this was not clear to anyone – certainly not to her.

What she read in *Pride and Prejudice* triggered a powerful reaction. Lewes might have been expecting a note from Currer Bell to acknowledge his review and possibly even to congratulate him for identifying her as a lady novelist. He must have been deeply impressed and taken aback by the third letter he received dated 12 January 1848. Brontë begins the letter by thanking him for his advice and candidly admits her own limitations:

'I mean to observe your warning about being careful how I undertake new works; my stock of materials is not abundant, but very slender; and, besides, neither my experience, my acquirements, nor my powers, are sufficiently varied to justify my ever becoming a frequent writer.'

She then turns to address his advice, which must have been in his first letter to her because she quotes Lewes back to himself. Her tone turns challenging, because she is not going to take all his advice from one novelist to another, or put another way from the author of *Ranthorpe* to the author of *Jane Eyre*, without question. Her use of italics for key words as she quotes some of his choice words back at him together with inverted commas and with her refusal to commit to change her style betrays a growing sense of indignation and scorn:

> If I ever *do* write another book, I think I will have nothing of what you call 'melodrama'; I *think* so, but I am not sure. I *think* too I will endeavour to follow the counsel which shines out of Miss Austen's 'mild eyes', to finish more, and be more subdued; but neither am I sure of that.

Wrestling with his insistence that writers stick with their depictions of 'real experience', Brontë argues for the freedom to follow inspiration and to break boundaries. The Brontë sisters and their brother, Branwell, had spent their childhood in their family parsonage isolated up on the remote Yorkshire moors, where in their imaginations they had constructed the detailed fantasy world that they called Gondal, complete with four kingdoms and an extensive cast of characters. Given her extraordinary creation of *Jane Eyre*, it now seems strange to hear her arguing this with Lewes, who had himself only written the thinly imagined, obscure novel *Ranthorpe*. Fluent and convincing, she provides a rare glimpse of her own creative process as she sets out her arguments to justify her belief in the power of inspiration that moved her to write:

> When authors write best, or at least when they write most

fluently, an influence seems to waken in them which becomes their master, which will have its own way, putting out of view all behests but its own, dictating certain words and insisting on their being used, whether vehement or measured in their nature; new moulding characters, giving unthought-of turns to incidents, rejecting carefully elaborated old ideas, and suddenly creating and adopting new ones. Is it not so? And should we try to counteract this influence? Can we indeed counteract it?

The real power of the letter bursts out in the next paragraph. She has now read *Pride and Prejudice* and she has not found any such influence or language to admire. Brontë simply cannot understand Lewes's praise of it. Over the last twelve months, Charlotte, Emily and Anne Brontë had created *Jane Eyre*, *Wuthering Heights* and *The Tenant of Wildfell Hall*, all novels of passion, yearning and violence. These were three lady novelists who had broken the mould. In the male characters of Heathcliff and Rochester, they had conjured up two of the most celebrated 'demon lovers' that have ever been created. Now that she had read *Pride and Prejudice*, in the context of her sisters' and her own novels she could not swallow being told to try to write more like Jane Austen. Her anger erupts from the page:

Why do you like Miss Austen so very much? I am puzzled on that point. What induced you to say that you would rather have written *Pride and Prejudice* or *Tom Jones* than any of the *Waverley* novels? I had not seen *Pride and Prejudice* till I read that sentence of yours, and then I got the book and studied it. And what did I find? An accurate daguerreotyped portrait of a common-place face; a carefully fenced, highly cultivated garden with neat borders and delicate flowers – but no glance of a bright vivid physiognomy – no open country – no fresh air – no bonny beck. I should hardly like to live with her ladies and gentlemen in their elegant but confined houses.

These observations will probably irritate you, but I shall run the risk.

Charlotte moves on to compare Austen with George Sand, the French author who was also mentioned by Lewes:

'She has a grasp of mind which, if I cannot fully comprehend, I can very deeply respect: she is sagacious and profound; Miss Austen is only shrewd and observant.'

This letter provoked an immediate response from Lewes, which has been lost. We can guess the tone and pick up some of the words Lewes used from Brontë's next letter that was rapidly sent the following week on 18 January 1848. Once again, Charlotte starts with a low-key agreement over what might have been his riposte about 'influence', which she had mentioned, before she returns to their debate about Austen. Lewes had clearly provided some further advice which Brontë contemptuously throws back in his face:

What a strange lecture comes next in your letter! You say that I must familiarise my mind with the fact that 'Miss Austen is not a poetess, has no "sentiment" (you scornfully enclose the word in inverted commas), no eloquence, none of the ravishing enthusiasm of poetry' and then you add I *must* 'learn to acknowledge her as *one of the greatest artists, of the greatest painters of human character* and one of the writers with the nicest sense of means to an end that ever lived.' The last point only will I ever acknowledge. Can there be a great artist without poetry? What I call – what I will bend to as a great artist, then – cannot be destitute of the divine gift. But by *poetry* I am sure you understand something different to what I do – as you do by 'sentiment'. It is *poetry* as I comprehend the word which elevates that masculine George Sand and makes out of something coarse, something god-like. It is 'sentiment', in my sense of the term, sentiment jealously hidden but genuine, which extracts the venom from that formidable Thackeray and converts what might be only corrosive poison into purifying elixir ... Miss Austen, being as you say without 'sentiment', without *poetry,* may be *is* sensible, real (more *real* than *true*) but she cannot be great.

I submit to your anger which I have now excited (for have I not questioned the perfection of your darling?); the storm may pass over me. Nevertheless, I will, when I can (I do not know when that will be as I have no access to a circulating library) diligently peruse all Miss Austen's works, as you recommend.

What an outburst this is! The letter itself, full of underlinings, italics that emphasise her argument and brackets to cram even more in, is written with all the fervent passion that she has found missing in Jane Austen. The taunt of Austen being his 'darling' still feels raw and even jealous. Brontë knows that she will invoke Lewes's 'anger'. Reading this letter makes us feel immensely close to Brontë – we also feel very close to Austen who, unable to defend herself, has been brought into this fierce argument and is being given such close scrutiny by another novelist.

When Mary Ann Evans later read Brontë's correspondence with Lewes (by then her partner), these perceptive criticisms of Austen might have been like depth charges going off in her mind, charges that provided a view of her work that was different to the unqualified admiration supplied by Lewes. They would have provided a new perspective of what novelists should write about. These three lady novelists would inspire each other. In her future novels as well as in her personal life, as Mary Ann became George Eliot she broke into the psychological territory that was unchartered by Jane Austen but recognised and extensively inhabited by Charlotte Brontë.

Further reading of Jane Austen only strengthened Brontë's opinion. In 1850, Charlotte asked William Smith Williams to send her more Austen novels and he sent her a copy of *Emma*. In her wide-ranging letter of 15 April 1850, Charlotte expanded upon the arguments she had had with Lewes:

> She does her business of delineating the surface of the lives of genteel English people curiously well. There is a Chinese fidelity, a miniature delicacy in the painting. She ruffles her reader by nothing vehement, disturbs him by nothing profound. The passions are perfectly unknown to her; she rejects even a speaking acquaintance with that stormy sisterhood. Even to the feelings she vouchsafes no more than an occasional graceful but distant recognition – too frequent converse with them would ruffle the smooth elegance of her progress. Her business is not half so much with the human heart as with the human eyes, mouth, hands and feet. What sees keenly, speaks aptly, moves flexibly, it suits her to study; but what throbs fast and full, though hidden, what the blood rushes through, what is the unseen seat of life and the sentient target of death – this Miss Austen ignores.

Perhaps thinking of what Lewes might respond, she concludes: 'If this is heresy, I cannot help it.'

The reaction to Brontë's 'heresy' was silence. After her outburst, the correspondence ceased for a year and a half. Both Lewes and

Brontë were engaged in their other writing, but after such a strong disagreement over a subject that went to the heart of their sense of creative imagination, they would also have been reflecting upon what they had each argued and turning it over in their minds. In the meantime, Brontë kept her eye on Lewes and read his second novel *Rose, Blanche and Violet* when it was published in 1848. For Brontë, now writing her next novel *Shirley*, her correspondence with Lewes clearly felt like unfinished business. Writing to William Smith Williams in January 1848, she made the comparison: 'Just as olives are said to taste harshly at first and to become agreeable with custom – the same may in some measure be observed of Mr Lewes's letters.'

Trying to draw the threads together and set out a coherent criticism of Lewes, who with his ebullient and mercurial advice was so difficult to pin down, on 1 May 1848 Charlotte wrote again to William Smith Williams to list exactly what she would say to Lewes if she were to meet him. This is her considered opinion and it is a chastening list for a male literary critic to have to hear about himself from a lady novelist:

> You have sound, clear judgement as far as it goes, but I conceive it to be limited.
>
> Your standard of talent is high, but I cannot acknowledge it to be the highest.
>
> You are deserving of all attention when you lay down the law on principles, but you are to be resisted when you dogmatise on feelings.
>
> To a certain point, Mr Lewes, you can go, but no farther.
>
> Be as sceptical as you please on whatever lies beyond a certain intellectual limit.

> The mystery will never be cleared up to you, for that limit you will never overpass.

History does not record whether Lewes ever saw this letter, but I believe that he did. I believe that William Smith Williams shared it with Lewes, not just because they were friends who shared their commune in Bayswater, but because it was so obviously intended to be passed on to him.

Shirley was published in October 1849 and Brontë's correspondence with Lewes revived. Over the previous thirteen months, both her sisters and her brother had died. She and her father were alone in the parsonage. Charlotte was trying to keep her identity hidden, so that she would not be judged as a lady novelist but as a writer on her merits alone, and this meant keeping Currer Bell as her pseudonym. When *Jane Eyre* had first been published, an impersonator claiming to be Currer Bell attempted to publish another book. Charlotte and her sister Anne had had to dash down to London and make an unannounced visit to William Smith Williams's office in Cornhill, brandishing a copy of his letter addressed to Currer Bell at the Haworth Parsonage as proof of their identity. Now that Anne and Emily were dead, Charlotte was left alone with her writing and she was determined to cling to her literary reputation.

Ominously, after eighteen months of silence Lewes wrote to announce that he would be reviewing *Shirley* for the *Edinburgh Review*. Either tipped off by William Smith Williams or relying upon intuition, Lewes was sure that Currer Bell was a woman. He must have mentioned this in his letter to Currer Bell, because on 1 November 1849 Brontë replied to him:

> It was a pleasure to receive your note. I wish you did not think me

a woman. I wish all reviewers believed 'Currer Bell' to be a man; they would be more just to him. You will, I know, keep measuring me by some standard of what you deem becoming to my sex; where I am not what you consider graceful you will condemn me ... come what will, I cannot, when I write, think always of myself and of which is elegant and charming in femininity; it is not on those terms or with such ideas, I ever took pen in hand: and if it is only on such terms my writing will be tolerated, I shall pass away from the public and trouble it no more.

This letter reads as if she is at the end of her tether. Unlike Eliot a few years later, Brontë had nobody to support her. Her father had become a recluse, mourning his three dead children. It is salutary to think of a genius like Brontë going back to basics and regretting that she 'ever took pen in hand'. Writing is meant to provide creative freedom and being prejudged merely on the grounds of being a woman removed this and destroyed the point of her work. Brontë had already seen reviews of *Jane Eyre* that shouted that 'if *Jane Eyre* had been written by a woman she must be un-sexed'; another described it as 'odious'. If she could remain safely concealed as Currer Bell, there would be no more of these sorts of criticisms. Lewes should have read this plea and taken notice of the challenges that Charlotte was outlining. As soon as female novelists strayed into any territory that was deemed 'unfeminine', such as fantasy or violence – or worse yet sexual fantasy or sexual violence – they were reviled for writing about such 'sordid' subjects. Reviewers stopped reading their writing and just focused on the scandal. Charlotte Brontë's arguments that female novelists were not read with the same objectivity as they deserve were exactly the same arguments that George Eliot was later to use.

Lewes's review of *Shirley* realised Brontë's worst fears. Horrified, she immediately saw that he announced that Currer Bell was a woman. Riding roughshod over all her arguments, he stripped away her dignity and outed her. Worse still, he pontificated about women in general:

> The grand function of woman, it must always be recollected, is and ever must be, maternity: and this we regard not only as her distinctive characteristic, and most endearing charm, but as a high and holy office ...What should we do with a leader of the opposition in the seventh month of her pregnancy? or a general-in-chief who at the beginning of a campaign was 'doing as well as could be expected'? or a chief justice with twins?

In summary Lewes wrote that women had made great names for themselves in literature and that one of the greatest of these was that of Currer Bell who he was able confidently to reveal was a woman and a clergyman's daughter. Her latest novel, however, was not a success. Her first book *Jane Eyre* had been a rather 'masculine' book with a 'vigour that amounts almost to coarseness and is certainly the very antipode to lady-like'. Lewes builds his criticism: 'This same over-masculine vigour is even more prominent in *Shirley* and does not increase the pleasantness of the book.' He provides faint praise for certain 'little touches which at once betray ... the exquisite workmanship of a woman's lighter pencil.'

Quoting a comment by Friedrich Schiller about the novelist Madame de Staël, Lewes concludes with a hammer blow:

'This person wants [lacks] everything that is graceful in a woman and nevertheless the faults of her book are altogether womanly faults. She steps out of her sex without elevating herself above it.'

Given Brontë's anxious request not to be revealed, it is impossible to read this review and maintain sympathy for Lewes. As a freelance journalist, perhaps he thought that the scoop was worth it and did not care about the collateral damage.

Feeling crushed and betrayed, Brontë wrote to William Smith Williams:

'I have received and perused the *Edinburgh Review* – it is very brutal and savage. I am not angry with Lewes, but I wish in future he would let me alone and not write again what makes me feel so cold and sick as I am feeling just now.'

It is such a clear, sad note. 'Cold and sick' are such heartfelt, simple words they cut to the quick. She wrote a single sentence letter, her sixth, to Lewes:

'I can be on my guard against my enemies, but God deliver me from my friends.'

We know Lewes sent a reply, because he later told Elizabeth Gaskell that he had tried to 'remonstrate with her'. Whatever he said, he must have found Brontë's next reply of 19 January 1850 truly sobering:

> I will tell you why I was so hurt by that review in the *Edinburgh* – not because its criticism was keen or its blame sometimes severe; not because its praise was stinted (for indeed I think you give me quite as much praise as I deserve), but because after I had said earnestly that I wished critics would judge me as an author, not as a woman, you so roughly – I even thought so cruelly – handled the question of sex. I dare say you meant no harm, and perhaps you will not now be able to understand why I was so grieved at what you will probably deem such a trifle; but grieved I was, and indignant too.

At the end of the letter Brontë rallies:

'However, I shake hands with you: you have excellent points; you can be generous. I still feel angry and think I do well to be angry, but it is the anger one experiences for rough play rather than foul play.'

Defiantly, she signs herself *Currer Bell*.

That was the last time Brontë wrote to Lewes.

However, this was not the end of their story. In an extraordinary turn of events, they did later meet in person. During a rare visit to London in June 1850, Brontë was introduced to Lewes by William Smith Williams. Remarkably there are three accounts of their meeting, which are each telling in their differences. Lewes recalled:

'I sat by her side a great part of the evening and was greatly interested in by her conversation. On parting, we shook hands, and she said:

"We are friends, are we not?"

"Were we not always, then?" I asked.

"No! Not always." She said significantly, and that was the only allusion to the offending article.'

The second account of the meeting is Brontë's. In a letter to her friend Ellen Nussey, she gave an account of her visit to London, including highlights such as visiting the House of Commons, catching a glimpse of the Duke of Wellington and meeting William Thackeray. She then strikes a note of unexpected poignancy:

> I have seen Lewes too. He is a man with both weakness and sins, but unless I err greatly the foundation of his nature is not bad; and were he almost a fiend in character I could not feel otherwise to him than half-sadly, half-tenderly – a queer word that last, but I use it because the aspect of Lewes's face almost moves me to

tears; it is so wonderfully like Emily, her eyes, her features, the very nose, the somewhat prominent mouth, the forehead, even at moments the expression: whatever Lewes does or says, I believe I cannot hate him.

The last impression of the meeting comes from several years later and is relayed by Eliot:

'Lewes was describing Currer Bell to me yesterday as a little, plain, provincial, sickly looking old maid. Yet what passion, what fire in her! Quite as much as in George Sand, only the clothing less voluptuous.'

Brontë clearly felt far more moved than Lewes. From these three perspectives, it does not appear that Charlotte followed her own stage directions and told Lewes the personal home truths that she had earlier rehearsed. That Lewes reminded her of her sister Emily is unexpected, but that she should feel 'half-tenderly' towards him feels a natural conclusion to their long correspondence in which both of these writers, one a female novelist trying to maintain a male façade, the other a male critic thinking that he was championing female writers, exposed a great deal of their feelings. I believe that as he gathered Charlotte Brontë's letters together and filed them away in his writing desk, Lewes would have learned more than he might initially have admitted or realised.

Soon after this meeting, the relationship between Brontë and Lewes, together with their passionate disagreements over the role of the imagination, the genius or not of Jane Austen and the need to protect the identity of a lady novelist, was over. George Lewes had met another passionate provincial writer: Mary Ann Evans. When he came to give advice on her fiction, this time he was able to encourage and build her prodigious talent rather than to squash it with criticism.

Shortly after her marriage to the local curate, Charlotte Brontë died from the complications of her first pregnancy. The other unspoken truth about lady novelists was that they would have safer and longer lives – and be able to write more novels – if they did not marry and run the risk of childbirth.

* * *

Lewes and Mary Ann's trip to collect seashells at Ilfracombe and Tenby took place the year after Charlotte Brontë died. Without the three Brontë sisters, the numbers of female novelists were diminished. Mary Ann's mind was turning to fiction, but before she could start, she had that one last article to write for the *Westminster Review*. As well as becoming the manifesto for her future writing, 'Silly Novels by Lady Novelists' also defuses the arguments between Lewes and Brontë by treading a line that both Austen and Brontë would have agreed upon. Showing a close reading of Regency romantic comedies and echoing much of the same parody as Jane Austen's *Northanger Abbey*, Mary Ann clearly enjoys herself:

> The heroine is usually an heiress with perhaps a vicious baronet, an amiable duke, and an irresistible younger son of a marquis as lovers in the foreground, a clergyman and a poet sighing for her in the middle distance, and a crowd of undefined adorers dimly indicated beyond. Her eyes and her wit are both dazzling; her nose and her morals are alike free from any tendency to irregularity; she has a superb contralto and a superb intellect; she is

perfectly well dressed and perfectly religious; she dances like a sylph and reads the Bible in the original tongues.

Mary Ann lands some nice touches: 'Rakish men either bite their lips in impotent confusion at her repartees or are touched to penitence by her reproofs' and: 'It is clear that they write in elegant boudoirs with violet-coloured ink and a ruby pen, that they must be entirely indifferent to publishers' accounts and inexperienced in every form of poverty except poverty of brains.'

Her more serious criticism is that most lady novelists do not understand the world beyond their limited existence:

> The fair writers have evidently never talked to a tradesman except from the carriage window, they have no notion of the working classes except as 'dependents' and they think five hundred a year a miserable pittance. Belgravia and baronial halls are their primary truths; and they have no idea of feeling interest in any man who is not at least a great landed proprietor, if not a prime minister ... their peers and peeresses are improbable, but their literary men, tradespeople, and cottagers are impossible; and their intellect seems to have the peculiar impartiality of reproducing both what they have seen and heard, and what they have not seen and heard, with equal unfaithfulness.

Unsparing in her mockery of bad female novelists, we can see some of the themes of her writing being sketched out.

Although the article was published anonymously, there is a personal touch in this comment: 'The standing apology for women who become writers without any special qualification is that society shuts them out from other spheres of occupation. Society is a very culpable entity and has to answer for the manufacture of many unwholesome commodities, from bad pickles to bad poetry'.

Mary Ann had seen enough book reviews to be able to land a blow on the critics who can derail a lady novelist's career, although it is unclear whether she had Lewes's treatment of Brontë in mind:

> No sooner does a woman show that she has genius or effective talent, than she receives the tribute of being moderately praised and severely criticised. By a peculiar thermometric adjustment, when a woman's talent is at zero, journalistic approbation is at the boiling pitch; when she attains mediocrity, it is already at no more than summer heat; and if ever she reaches excellence, critical enthusiasm drops to the freezing point.

Mary Ann was not going to write 'silly novels', and neither was she going to open herself up to sharp male criticism. She was going to write about the broad spectrum of society in as realistic terms as she could, and she was going to conceal her identity as long as she could. In doing all this, she would need help. From their position of isolation in society, the only person who could help her was Lewes the critic, who had almost suffocated Brontë with his insistent advice and then almost broken her confidence by breaking the news of her identity. If Mary Ann was to succeed, Lewes would have to listen carefully to Brontë's long list of personal criticisms and do things very differently.

* * *

Immediately after 'Silly Novels by Lady Novelists' was published, Mary Ann started to sketch out plans for her first fiction. Her journal in 1856 lists her background reading as Edmund Burke's *Reflections on the French Revolution*, Thomas Carlyle's *The French Revolution*, Harriet Martineau's *History of the Peace* and Thomas Macaulay's *The History of England*. Hardly 'silly novels'. And slipped in among them, no doubt recommended by her most persuasive admirer Lewes, was *Mansfield Park*. Mary Ann's journal entry in September 1856 provides this account of how it happened:

> G began to say very positively: 'You must try and write a story' and when we were at Tenby he urged me to begin at once. I deferred it, however, after my usual fashion, with work which does not present itself as an absolute duty. But one morning as I was thinking what should be the subject of my first story, my thoughts merged themselves into a dreamy doze and I imagined myself writing a story, of which the title was 'The Sad Fortunes of the Reverend Amos Barton'. I was soon wide awake again and told G. He said: 'Oh, what a capital title!' and from that time I settled in my mind that this should be my first story.

As soon as Mary Ann finished 'Amos Barton', Lewes swung into action. Naturally taking on the role of her literary agent just as Henry Austen had done for his sister Jane, Lewes sent the manuscript to the publisher John Blackwood. Lewes's covering letter described the writing well and of course – as he was always bound to do – he could not resist bringing in a flattering comparison with Jane Austen:

> This is what I am commissioned to say to you about the proposed series. It will consist of tales and sketches illustrative of the actual life of our country clergy about a quarter of a century ago – but

solely in its human and not at all in its theological aspects; the object being to do what has never yet been done in our literature, for we have had abundant religious stories, polemical and doctrinal, but since the *Vicar of Wakefield* and Miss Austen, no stories representing the clergy like every other class, with the humours, sorrows and troubles of other men.

Succeeding in a literary agent's first job, Lewes chose the right publisher. Immediately recognising the voice of a new talent, Blackwood replied the following week:

'I am happy to say that I think your friend's reminiscences of Clerical Life will do.'

* * *

With the publication of 'Amos Barton', Mary Ann took her first step towards becoming a lady novelist. While Lewes had initially championed the comparison with Austen, writing as George Eliot Mary Ann notably began to veer away from Austen and explore the territory of imagination articulated by Brontë. Her second short story, 'Mr Gilfil's Love Story', could actually have been inspired by aspects of Brontë's own life. Maynard Gilfil is the local curate, a large, solidly built man who loves the tiny, highly strung Caterina (who is so passionate that she wants to murder Captain Wybrow for abandoning her). After the drama of Captain Wybrow's heart failure and natural death, Caterina marries Gilfil, and with immense happiness she very soon conceives. Tragically, she dies in childbirth. It is impossible to prove any link, but it struck me that Reverend Patrick Brontë employed Arthur Nicholls as his curate in Haworth. A large, solidly built man, Arthur fell in love with the tiny, passionate Charlotte and proposed to her. Reverend Brontë abruptly banished Arthur from Haworth, but a year later he returned to make his second proposal. Rather to her surprise, Charlotte found herself happily married and content in her domestic role as an attentive wife. Equally tragically, after just eighteen months of marriage Charlotte died during her pregnancy.

The connections between the lady novelists ran deep.

By her third short story, 'Janet's Repentance', George Eliot moved well beyond Jane Austen's territory and deep into Charlotte Brontë's. Janet Dempster is an alcoholic who is brutally and graphically beaten by her husband. Thrown out of her house in the middle of the night in her nightdress, she eventually begins to find salvation with the evangelical curate Mr Tryan. After a carriage accident, Dempster lies semi unconscious. Although Janet returns to nurse him and forgives him, he rejects her and while hallucinating that her hair is teeming with snakes and that his sheets are swarming with black lice, he dies without offering her the forgiveness she seeks. It is a bleak powerful story. Brutal, shocking and full of psychological insight to a marriage of domestic abuse, none of it could have been written by Jane Austen. George Eliot provided a powerful new voice and *Scenes of Clerical Life* was a publishing triumph.

Lewes could see the popular reactions to these stories and he did not try to lean on Mary Ann to change direction to comply with traditional lady novelists who were writing from their own experience. In due course, they began to talk about another possible story which would involve an even more shocking death, the death of a baby who is murdered by its young, traumatised mother. This story, which was beyond any subject that Jane Austen would have been able to contemplate, would not fit into a short story and would have to be a full-length novel.

As well as supporting Mary Ann as she began to conceive her first novel, *Adam Bede*, Lewes also respected her privacy. Unlike his callous treatment of Brontë, this time Lewes protected Mary Ann's identity. Perhaps he had taken Brontë's painful experience to heart. John Blackwood was curious to meet Eliot and had asked Lewes whether this would be possible. The rumours were that Eliot was a cleric, probably living in the Midlands. Mary Ann stepped in and firmly and wittily replied to Blackwood:

> For several reasons I am very anxious to retain my incognito for some time to come, and to an author not already famous, anonymity is the highest prestige. Besides if George Eliot turns out a dull dog and an ineffective writer – a mere flash in the pan – I, for one, am determined to cut him on the first intimation of that disagreeable fact.

In January 1858, Mary Ann started to wonder if it was time to reveal herself. Charles Dickens had just written to Blackwood praising 'the exquisite truth and delicacy ... the humor and the pathos of these stories'. Dickens had complimented the work for impressing him 'in a manner that I should find it very difficult to describe to you, if I had the impertinence to try'. Mary Ann confided to Sara Hennell that 'the iron mask of my incognito seems quite painful in forbidding me to tell Dickens how thoroughly his generous impulse has been appreciated'. The next month, she made her decision.

In February 1858, Blackwood came to visit Lewes in Richmond. Once again, he asked whether he might meet Eliot in person. At this point, Mary Ann left the room and told Lewes that she 'could be revealed'. It is difficult to know whether Blackwood was surprised. Eliot provides this account in her journal:

Mr John Blackwood called on us. He talked a good deal about the *Clerical Scenes* and George Eliot and at last asked:

'Well, am I to see George Eliot this time?'

G said: 'Do you wish to see him?'

'As he likes – I wish it to be quite spontaneous.'

I left the room and G following me a moment, I told him he might reveal me. Blackwood was kind, came back when he found he was too late for the train and said he would come to Richmond again.

In this moment of high Victorian melodrama, revealed as she walked back into the room like a charade, George Eliot is presented to her publisher, and her literary reality as a lady novelist who would rank alongside Jane Austen and Charlotte Brontë is born.

* * *

To put the significance of Jane Austen, Charlotte Brontë and George Eliot into perspective – these three lady novelists whose works and influences on each other are so interwoven – it is worth considering their global reputations and their long-term impact upon our literary heritage. Today, if any internet search engine is asked to list the best love stories or best romances, *Pride and Prejudice* is their first recommendation, followed by *Jane Eyre*.

When the BBC last conducted an extensive poll of international literary critics in 2015 to provide an objective view of the top twenty-five British novels ever written, the results confirmed how significant these three lady novelists are. Jane Austen occupies three places with *Persuasion* ranked twentieth, *Emma* nineteenth and *Pride and Prejudice* eleventh. Two of the Brontë sisters are ranked in the top ten, Emily's only novel *Wuthering Heights* at seventh, while *Jane Eyre* – Charlotte's first published novel, which prompted Lewes to provide his ebullient if unsolicited advice to the rookie young author Currer Bell – is ranked fifth.

By 1851, when Brontë and Lewes had wound down their correspondence and Mary Ann Evans had walked into William Jeff's bookshop, the novel that would be recognised around the world and considered the finest British novel ever published was yet to be written. It was written twenty years later in 1871 and it still invariably tops any literary chart – it is *Middlemarch* by George Eliot, the third lady novelist.

* * *

CHAPTER 3

LOVE AND MARRIAGE

If Jane Austen's most famous opening line, 'It is a truth universally acknowledged, that a single man in possession of a good fortune must be in want of a wife', is true, then the opposite might also apply: a single woman must be in want of a husband. Although the search for love and marriage is the bedrock of all her novels, Jane Austen wrote with the objectivity of someone who was herself perhaps only briefly in love and never married.

Austen's private correspondence reveals that in her early twenties, she was wholeheartedly engrossed in the Hampshire marriage market and eyeing up potential husbands. Her letters to her sister Cassandra, full of the *joie de vivre* of writing to a sister who is on exactly the same wavelength as her, keenly scrutinise possible partners and judge their prospects.

Austen's first preserved letter to Cassandra is written on her 23rd birthday, 9 January 1796. Jane herself had just turned twenty-one and without pause for breath she opens with: 'In the first place I hope you will live twenty-three years longer,' before exuberantly plunging into an account of the previous evening's drama: 'After this necessary preamble I shall proceed to inform you that we had an exceeding good ball last night...'

The letter is so intensely private and immediate that it feels as if we are reading it over Cassandra's shoulder. It takes a moment to realise that this is the authentic voice of Jane Austen speaking directly, just as if she were speaking to Cassandra. Of course, she wants to entertain Cassandra, so there is some flourish and some performance, but this is her true, unedited voice. Jane lists the guests and teasingly confides to her sister:

> I am almost afraid to tell you how my Irish friend and I behaved. Imagine to yourself everything most profligate and shocking in the way of dancing and sitting down together. I can expose myself only once more because he leaves the country soon after next Friday, on which day we are to have a dance at Ashe after all. He is a very gentlemanlike, good-looking, pleasant young man, I assure you.

With her emphatic underlinings, this conspiratorial letter could have been written from Elizabeth Bennet to her older sister Jane. Austen's novels set out the fleeting opportunities that the leading ladies must take to secure their partners in the marriage market and this letter reinforces this sense of pent-up sexual attraction and urgency. Jane's meticulous compilation for Cassandra of the list of men lining up to be her dancing partner, with the invisible question marks hanging over their heads as to which of them might also become her husband, illustrates both how limited the options were and how pressing time was.

In this scene which could have come straight out of any of her novels, the 'gentlemanlike, good-looking young man' who was behaving in just as giddy a fashion as Austen was Tom Lefroy. The ball which she describes took place at Manydown Manor, where the Bigg family, who were neighbours and old family friends of the Austens, lived. As Jane danced and misbehaved in such a 'profligate and shocking' manner (what can they have been doing?) she might have been watched with awe and admiration by Harris Bigg-Withers, at that time a shy teenage boy with a stammer. We shall hear more from him later.

After the dizzying series of Christmas balls, Jane Austen was half expecting a marriage proposal from Tom Lefroy. The following week she writes to Cassandra: 'I look forward with great impatience to [the next ball to be held at Ashe], as I rather expect to receive an offer from my friend in the course of the evening.' She adds: 'I shall refuse him, however, unless he promises to give away his white coat.' This is a playful reference to Lefroy wearing the same coat as Henry Fielding's hero Tom Jones, for Lefroy is a 'great admirer of Tom Jones and therefore wears the same coloured clothes'. It is very revealing that Austen and Tom Lefroy were discussing *Tom Jones*. Many years later in his pious eulogy of Jane, her brother Henry would try to claim that Jane had found *Tom Jones* immoral and distasteful. Yet here she is as a 21-year-old discussing it in detail with a young admirer, sending a clear and daring signal that she had read and enjoyed an adult book with several sex scenes in it. This would have given Lefroy plenty to think about as he eyed her up and they flirted and danced together. Love and marriage were progressed with such small signals.

Whether Austen was really in love or just momentarily infatuated, sadly for her after the Christmas season Tom Lefroy abruptly left the Hampshire neighbourhood. She never saw him again. We should probably be grateful that Lefroy returned to Ireland, where in due course he married, became an MP, fathered seven children and was eventually appointed Lord Chief Justice. If Tom Lefroy had proposed to Austen (and assuming that she put aside her misgivings about his white coat and accepted him), we would almost certainly never have heard of the novelist Jane Austen. She would have been spirited away to Ireland and as wife to an ambitious and successful politician and mother to seven children, she would have struggled to find the time to write any of her novels.

In a more immediately tragic disappointment the following month after the Manydown Manor ball, Cassandra's fiance Tom Fowle left for service as a military chaplain in the West Indies where he promptly caught yellow fever and died. Far from the happy fictional ending of *Pride and Prejudice*, with both sisters embarking on their married lives, Austen and her sister Cassandra were in danger of missing out on the marriage market.

In her early twenties, Jane had clearly been sought after as a dancing partner. Recounting another Christmas ball in 1798, she proudly writes to Cassandra:

'There were twenty dances and I danced them all and without any fatigue. I was glad to find myself capable of dancing so much and with so much satisfaction as I did.'

There is even a ghostly forerunner of a moment that might have inspired the first dance in *Pride and Prejudice* where Elizabeth meets Darcy. As she lists the men present, Austen mentions a Mr Calland, who

> appeared as usual with his hat in his hand and stood every now and then behind Catherine and me to be talked to and abused for not dancing. We teased him however into it at last. I was very glad to see him again after so long a separation and he was altogether rather the genius and the flirt of the evening.

However, as time passes there are fewer mentions of balls and dancing in her letters, and we find no more lists of available gentlemen and potential partners lining up to secure Jane as their dancing partner. In 1801, their father Reverend George Austen retired and passed his parish living to his eldest son, James. The Austen family, now reduced to the elderly parents and their two dependent daughters Cassandra and Jane, moved to Bath. A household of a genial and elderly vicar with two highly spirited, unmarried daughters could be the opening premise for a Jane Austen novel, but despite their visits to the Pump Room and the teeming social scene at Bath, still no love and no potential marriage partners were forthcoming.

Then, in an astonishing surprise in December 1802, Austen received an unexpected marriage proposal. She and Cassandra went to stay at Manydown Manor with their friends the Biggs. They had grown up with the three Bigg daughters, Alethea, Elizabeth and Catherine. Unbeknown to Jane, their younger brother Harris had fallen in love with her. Aged just twenty-two, Harris was five years younger than Jane, but he bravely asked her to marry him. Jane accepted him on the spot and the family apparently spent the evening celebrating. However, something happened overnight and by the morning Jane had changed her mind. She withdrew her acceptance and in some confusion she and Cassandra left the Biggs and returned home. Although Harris was later described by Jane's niece Caroline as 'very plain in person – awkward and even uncouth in manner' this seems to miss the point. He was of absolutely the right society and went on to marry happily, inherit the large Manydown estate and father ten children. Perhaps Jane and Cassandra had spent the night debating the situation and came to the same conclusion as Jane Bennet would in *Pride and Prejudice*:

'Oh Lizzy! Do anything rather than marry without affection.' Or perhaps something else had gone wrong.

As with Tom Lefroy, had Austen accepted Harris's proposal then her life and the whole body of English literature would have been very different. If Austen had wanted to marry, this was a risky rejection. Jane was twenty-seven, which was the same age that Marianne, the impulsive heroine of her first novel *Sense and Sensibility*, would choose to ridicule: 'A woman of seven and twenty can never hope to inspire affection again.' Jane would then later defiantly choose it as the age for Anne Elliot, who at the opening of her last novel *Persuasion* is apparently destined to remain a spinster. In Hampshire, the marriage market appears to have closed for the two Austen sisters. By the end of 1802, the Austen girls had been dropped from the invitation lists to the balls and thereafter Jane Austen was destined for life as a single woman.

* * *

Almost fifteen years later, when Jane Austen was a published author and spending some time in London, her letters seem to refer to at least two opportunities for her to have some kind of romantic affair. There may have been other men who do not appear in her letters, and I might be misreading these two references, but I detect a seductive invitation from Reverend James Clarke, the Prince Regent's librarian who had arranged for *Emma* to be dedicated to the Prince Regent. As they met and discussed the dedication, Austen clearly caught his eye and attracted him beyond the realms of the library. In his letter to her of 21 December 1815, at first he appears simply as no more than pompous and vainglorious in the manner of the absurdly snobbish Mr Collins in *Pride and Prejudice*:

On Monday I go to Lord Egremont's at Petworth where your praises have long been sounded as they ought to be. I shall then look in on the Party at the [Brighton] Pavilion for a couple of nights and return to preach at Park Street Chapel Green Street on the Thanksgiving Day.

But the parties James Clarke is going to are very different from Mr Collins having tea with Lady Catherine de Bourgh. Lord Egremont's stately home at Petworth was described by a contemporary as being 'like an inn', by which I take it that he meant that there were a great many visitors and a great many very busy bedrooms – Lord Egremont kept at least fifteen mistresses, many in the house at the same time and one of whom he married after having seven children with her. He is acknowledged to have fathered over forty illegitimate children. The Prince Regent had built the Brighton Pavilion as his pleasure dome and a two-day Christmas party there was not for the god-fearing or faint of heart. The company that James Clarke was keen to let Austen know that he was keeping was aristocratic, royal and highly decadent. His final paragraph contains this coded message:

Pray, dear Madam, remember that besides my cell at Carlton House, I have another which Dr Barne procured for me at Number 37 Golden Square where I often hide myself. There is a small Library there much at your Service – and if you can make the cell render you any service as a sort of Halfway House, when you come to Town – I shall be most happy.

Such a loaded invitation in Regency England seems a clear attempt at seduction. Austen dexterously deflected both his suggestions for her narrative and his invitation to come and make him happy in his 'Halfway House'.

Around the same time, Austen was also enjoying a flirtation with her brother's apothecary, Charles Haden. This time it seems that Jane was making the running. Writing to Cassandra, Jane announces with pointed enthusiasm: 'Tomorrow Mr Haden is to dine with us – There's Happiness! We really grow so fond of Mr Haden that I do not know what to expect.' The dinner party seems to have been a great success, as Jane later writes: 'It is Mr Haden's firm belief that a person not musical is fit for every sort of wickedness. I ventured to assert a little on the other side, but wished the cause in abler hands.'

As with discussing *Tom Jones* with her younger admirer Tom Lefroy, there is a significant clue in this apparently incidental detail, which I think was a message to Cassandra that she would have immediately understood. I believe that this sparring conversation is a veiled allusion to a scene between Lorenzo and Jessica, the runaway lovers in Shakespeare's *The Merchant of Venice*. Jane is recalling the moment when Lorenzo declares to Jessica that 'The man that hath no music in himself ... is fit for treasons. Let no such man be trusted.' The lovers have eloped together. The previous year, there had been an Austen family gathering when Edward and his wife Fanny had been in London, along with Jane and Cassandra. Henry had organised a large Austen family outing to see Edmund Kean playing Shylock in *The Merchant of Venice* in Drury Lane. As ever with Austen, it is the tiny details that count and I wonder whether Austen and Charles Haden were speaking in code across the table, confident that their reference to the Shakespearean lovers would not be picked up by the other dinner guests. In this letter, Jane might have been sending her sister a secret message that perhaps Mr Haden was her last chance to have her own Lorenzo.

As Jane's stay in London was extended, more supplies were sent up from Hampshire and her letters approvingly note the delivery of pheasants, a hare and four rabbits. Mr Haden kept his foot in the door and his place at their table as Jane relays to Cassandra in her letter two days later on 26 November 1815: 'And what is to be fancied next? Why that Mr Haden dines here again tomorrow. Mr H is reading *Mansfield Park* for the first time and prefers it to *P&P*.'

I cannot help but think this perverse opinion is the most conclusive proof of Charles Haden's affection. Could anyone really prefer *Mansfield Park* to *Pride and Prejudice*? Austen herself did not. Perhaps Charles Haden was playing a wily game and thought that it would be tactically astute and flattering to an author to prefer her most recent book.

Early in December 1815, Charles Haden is still the centre of attention:

> To make his return a complete Gala, Mr Haden was secured for dinner – I need not say that our evening was agreeable. But you seem to be under a mistake as to Mr H – you call him an Apothecary; he is no Apothecary; he has never been an Apothecary – he is a Haden, nothing but a Haden, a sort of wonderful nondescript creature on two legs, something between a man and an angel.

With the repeated use of his name (just as she repeated Tom Lefroy's name all those years ago) as well as his semi-celestial positioning, Austen's description either reads as mock heroic or as a somewhat self-conscious infatuation. Certainly she never gave such praise to Mr Perry, the Highbury apothecary in *Emma*.

Without warning Charles Haden disappears from Austen's life. Her last known letter to him is on 14 December 1815 when she tells him: 'I leave Town early on Saturday and must say "Good-bye" to you.'

Despite their implicit role-playing as Lorenzo and Jessica and her strong hints of attraction, it is unknown whether Austen and Haden ever met to say goodbye. Just as Tom Lefroy and Harris Bigg-Withers vanished from her life in Hampshire, so did the two older London admirers James Clarke and Charles Haden.

This succession of unfulfilled love stories leaves an emotional void. There is an uneasy sense of unfinished business in her personal life where Austen did not find love or marriage. If they were not to be found in her personal life, the place where she knew that she could conjure up love and marriage was, of course, her fiction.

* * *

Unlike Jane Austen, George Eliot found love in both her personal life and her fiction. The personal love was complicated because it was with Lewes who could not marry her. Nevertheless, they shared a lifelong, fulfilling relationship that she proudly and defiantly called a marriage, frequently referring to herself as Mrs Lewes. We can trace her growing feelings for Lewes through her letters and journals. Until they broke cover and left for the Continent, she was very circumspect. After the first fleeting mention of meeting him in Jeff's bookshop as a miniature Mirabeau, he is mentioned at the theatre and then in this letter to the Brays of 1852, when she provides this account of her happy and busy life in the offices of *The Westminster Review*:

> The fact is, both callers and work thicken – the former sadly interfering with the latter. I will just tell you how it was last Saturday

and that will give you an idea of my days ... My task was to read an article of Greg's in the 'North British' on taxation, a heap of newspaper articles, and all that J. S. Mill says on the same subject. When I had got some way into this *magnum mare*, in comes Mr Chapman with a thick German volume: 'Will you read enough of this to give me your opinion of it?' Then of course I must have a walk after lunch ... When I had sat down again, thinking that I had two clear hours before dinner, rap at the door – Mr Lewes, who of course sits talking till the second bell rings. After dinner another visitor...

For Lewes to drop in like this and monopolise her attention indicates how relaxed they had become in each other's company.

The first hint that she is in a secret relationship, though, is her letter to Cara Bray of 28 December 1853: 'Spent Christmas Day alone at Cambridge Street. How shall I thank you enough for sending me that splendid barrel of beetroot, so nicely packed?'

Presumably if she were not in a relationship, she would have accepted an invitation to spend Christmas Day with friends or perhaps headed north to see the Brays. I assume that she is alone because she had made plans to spend part of Christmas with Lewes, who could only see her for part of the day because he had his other family with Agnes.

By 1854, she is more open about spending time with Lewes. In April, she let Cara Bray know:

'Poor Lewes is ill, and is ordered not to put pen to paper for a month; so I have something to do for him in addition to my own work.' She gaily admits that she will not go out without him: 'No opera and no fun for me for the next month!'

Then of course there was the three-line bombshell: '*Poste Restante*

Weimar for the next six weeks and afterwards Berlin' and everything changed.

After they returned from their eight-month stay in Germany, the complications rose to meet them. If Eliot had hoped that she might at least be able to keep her friendships with Cara and Sara, she would be disappointed. She tried to argue that her relationship with Lewes was a marriage, but Cara and Sara were never persuaded:

'I do not wish to take the ground of ignoring what is unconventional in my position,' she wrote to Cara. 'I have counted the cost of the step that I have taken and am prepared to bear, without irritation or bitterness, renunciation by all my friends. I am not mistaken in the person to whom I have attached myself. He is worthy of the sacrifice I have incurred.'

It is surprising that Cara should have held such disdain for Lewes, since Cara and Charles had an unconventional marriage themselves. Cara was involved in a long affair with Edward Noel and Charles Bray fathered six children with another woman, possibly because Cara was unable to bear children of her own. Eliot refers quite overtly to Noel in a letter, perhaps to remind her friends that their situations were not so different:

'If Mr Noel comes to see us – and we shall be very happy if he will do so – we hope you will impress on his memory that he must ask for *Mrs. Lewes* and not for Miss Evans, for a misunderstanding on this matter would be very painful.'

In defiance of society, Eliot did not believe that marriage needed to be legal to be real. She expressed as much in a letter to Cara in 1855, confiding happily:

'It is a great experience – this marriage! I can't tell you how happy I am in this double life which helps me to feel and think with double strength.'

When *Adam Bede* was published in 1859, Eliot dedicated it to the man she steadfastly viewed as her husband:

'To my dear husband, George Henry Lewes, I give the manuscript of a work which would never have been written but for the happiness his love has conferred on my life.'

Although society did not recognise their marriage, Eliot had no doubts that it was the binding and most fulfilling relationship of her life. Neither she nor Lewes wavered or appeared to compromise.

Writing from this different personal position, George Eliot took an opposite attitude from Jane Austen towards exploring love and marriage in her fiction. Rather than seeking them as the satisfying conclusions of her novels, George Eliot generally arranges for her heroines to believe that they are in love and to marry at the beginning of the stories. As their love and their marriages are examined, that is where the drama starts.

* * *

As the opening line of *Pride and Prejudice* so confidently implies, Jane Austen's ladies want to love and marry 'gentlemen', ideally ones that allow them to 'marry up' and secure more wealth. George Eliot's ladies, meanwhile, make broader, more radical choices. Eliot's heroines readily choose impoverished husbands rather than those who can provide good fortunes and sometimes, most radical of all, they end the novels as single women.

Jane Austen would be baffled by the narrative choices made for Eppie in *Silas Marner*, Esther in *Felix Holt* and Dorothea in *Middlemarch*. Whether they are being naive, headstrong or idealistic, these three heroines each decide to turn down wealth and the offer of a country estate together with its pre-eminent position in society in favour of marrying a gardener, a watch repairer and a hopeful politician. When Will Ladislaw stretches out to pick up his hat and leave her, Dorothea speaks for these choices:

> 'Oh, I cannot bear it – my heart will break,' said Dorothea ... 'I don't mind about poverty – I hate my wealth.' In an instant Will was close to her and had his arms round her, but she drew her head back and held his away gently that she might go on speaking ... 'We could live quite well on my own fortune – it is too much – seven hundred a year – I want so little – no new clothes – and I will learn what everything costs.'

Like Eppie Marner and Esther Lyon, Dorothea explicitly rejects wealth, and it is a realistic appraisal of her future, as well as a deeper recognition of what carries true value in life, that she will 'learn what everything costs'.

Austen's leading ladies are typically poorer than the gentlemen. They are generally daughters of 'gentlemen', but (with the single exception of Emma Woodhouse) they have not inherited any money. Accordingly, the ladies have fewer cards to play and fewer opportunities to play them, yet despite these restrictions they manage to pull off some stunning marriages. Once they have made their choice, Austen conjures up sufficient money for them to never have to worry about learning 'what everything costs'.

Emma is Austen's only novel where two equal partners marry: Emma Woodhouse and Mr Knightley are both socially and financially equal. Unusually, we do not hear Mr Knightley's wealth measured, but Emma has her own capital of £30,000 and their respective estates can be readily joined together. Hartfield estate which Emma will inherit from her aged father is described as 'an incursion into

Donwell' which is Mr Knightley's estate. To Highbury society, their marriage would have been the obvious marriage all along. After the torrid sequence of misunderstandings, Emma and Mr Knightley marry as equals – although perhaps not quite. Mr Knightley awkwardly touches upon what they will call each other:

'Mr Knightley ... it is formal. I want you to call me something else, but I do not know what.'

'I remember once calling you "George" in one of my amiable fits, about ten years ago. I did it because I thought it would offend you.'

'And cannot you call me George now?'

'Impossible! I never can call you anything but Mr Knightley.'

While lightly touched upon in this exchange, the underlying point is sharp: when Emma becomes his wife, she will have to forfeit all her wealth to Mr Knightley. The marriage of two social and financial 'equals' actually leads to the woman giving up a great deal of independence and freedom. Love might be equal, but marriage is not.

Since most of the marriages take place at the end of her narratives, in the interests of tying the plot up neatly Austen ducks this issue and gives herself no time to explore this. When we hear that Emma will always call Mr Knightley 'Mr Knightley', it casts a different light upon their relationship. I can't help but wonder whether in *Pride and Prejudice* Elizabeth Bennet will call Darcy 'Fitzwilliam', or in *Persuasion* Anne Elliot will call Captain Wentworth 'Frederick'. It is an uncomfortable fact that is glossed over by Austen: as love crystallises into marriage, a woman has to give up her social status and forfeit her independence and all her property and money to her husband. A married woman falls wholly under the control of her husband.

This may be glossed over by Austen, but it recurs and is examined much more painfully in Eliot's novels, where the reality of the heroine's loss of control within a marriage is a long way from the gentle banter about how Emma might address Mr Knightley.

Janet's Repentance explores a brutal story of domestic abuse within a marriage. In a candid and surprisingly modern way, she describes how women such as Janet Dempster come to terms not only with physical brutality and endure horrific beatings, but also how they feel the shame of them. She touches upon why women might cover up their husbands' violence, to what extent they might collude in it for fear of life outside marriage and then why they might return to forgive their husbands. Janet's attempted suicides and her drinking addiction are described with a sympathy that feels more contemporary than Victorian. Along with this story of an abusive marriage is the growing love that Janet begins to feel for the local evangelical curate Mr Tryan. Their relationship falls outside marriage, but – like Eliot's own relationship with Lewes – Janet's and Tryan's love is held up as a 'true marriage'. *Janet's Repentance* is Eliot's first attempt to confront and explore many aspects of a fractured, brutal marriage, something she returns to in greater detail and depth throughout her writing.

Love and marriage are seen in a fundamentally different light by Austen and Eliot. For Austen, marriage is the triumphant closing note of a well-designed plot. For Eliot, a first marriage is invariably a catastrophic mistake that reveals a woman's vulnerability, her loss of authority and painfully shreds her self-esteem. Only after their first marriages have been thoroughly assessed and dismantled, twice violently and each time involving deaths, can Eliot's later heroines

– notably Romola, Dorothea and Gwendolen – re-establish their sense of themselves and contemplate how to proceed towards a happier future.

In Jane Austen's world, while marriage often ties up the plot, the opportunity for a desired marriage is a narrow and quickly closing window. It is seen as a prize to be reached out for and won. The competition is intense and determined, partners and time are limited and the stakes are high. Each of Austen's heroines understands (Emma only just in time) that the window of the marriage market is limited. The timing of marriage opportunities is fleeting and the results are binary. If the heroines were to fail, then their futures would be desolate. Austen's heroines are greatly restricted because they are given few occasions to make the right move and even fewer available men. They have to make decisions and take what restricted action they can. In *Pride and Prejudice* Charlotte Lucas is very self-aware and recognises that her options are limited. Charlotte is considered plain; she is not rich and therefore unlikely to attract a husband. Knowing that Mr Collins has been turned down by both Jane and Elizabeth Bennet, she watches out of her window for Mr Collins to walk down the lane and then walks out 'accidentally' to intercept him. Seizing her only available opportunity, with that single decisive move, Charlotte succeeds. She answers Elizabeth's incredulous reaction with this pragmatic justification:

'I am not a romantic you know. I never was. I ask only a comfortable home; and considering Mr Collins's character, connections, and situation in life I am convinced that my chance of happiness with him is as fair as most people can boast on entering the marriage state.'

Charlotte Lucas and Mr Collins provide the first wedding in *Pride and Prejudice* and it is a salutary warning about the compromises that might be necessary. Looking at herself and her position dispassionately, Charlotte realises that, despite his obvious flaws, Mr Collins represents her best chance to marry and secure her position in society. Charlotte has scant illusions about romance. She is prepared to come to terms with physical distaste and compromise her repulsion concerning Mr Collins because she sees that despite his off-putting manners, he is not bad, deceitful or evil – merely painfully honest, absurdly correct, snobbish and pompous. Besides, due to the 'entailment' of the Longbourne estate to Mr Collins, it will not be long before he inherits the Bennets' house and estate. Charlotte comes to terms with Mr Collins's grotesque and snobbish manners because they are ultimately harmless compared to the esteemed place in society she will secure as his wife – and because the alternative social situation for Charlotte as a single woman would be so bleak. For Charlotte, marriage without love is a much better result than no marriage at all.

Unlike Charlotte Lucas, in *Persuasion* Louisa Musgrove dramatically overplays her hand. When she first jumps into Captain Wentworth's arms on the Cobb at Lyme Regis, she has already virtually won his affections, certainly enough to make everyone assume they will shortly become engaged. To prove her point, Louisa dashes back to the top of the steps and impetuously throws herself down at him a second time. This time, Captain Wentworth is unprepared and she crashes to the ground. As Louisa is knocked unconscious, the accident prompts Captain Wentworth to turn to Anne for help. In this moment, the plot swivels. The love that was Louisa's for the taking vanishes. Anne moves centre stage to manage the crisis and in doing so rekindles Captain Wentworth's love. Austen's characters might succeed, as with Charlotte Lucas's simple walk out into the lane to lasso Mr Collins, or they might crash and burn, as with

Louisa, but one way or another the prospects for love and marriage can turn in an instant.

As Austen was keenly aware herself, if a woman missed her moment whether in a lane, at a dance or on the Cobb then their age would remorselessly start counting against them. Perhaps making a barbed joke at herself and her own rejection of Harris Bigg-Withers's blurted marriage proposal when she was twenty-seven, Austen gives Marianne in *Sense and Sensibility*, her youngest heroine at sixteen, these provocative lines:

> A woman of seven and twenty can never hope to inspire affection again, and if her home be uncomfortable, or her fortune small, I can suppose that she might bring herself to submit to the offices of a nurse for the sake of the provision and security of a wife … In my eyes [that] would be no marriage at all … to me it would seem only a commercial exchange, in which each wished to be benefited at the expense of the other.

As a determinedly comic writer who was just as ready to laugh at herself as at anyone else, Austen would have known that this would trigger a smile from Cassandra who had been with her that evening in Manydown Manor when Harris had made his move. Whether this smile would have turned into a rueful smile of regret by the time *Sense and Sensibility* was published nine years later in 1811 when Jane was in her mid-thirties is difficult to say. Austen never showed any self-pity and she never looked backwards. Writing much later when she was aged forty, in *Persuasion* she contrives a brilliant answer to Marianne's jejune criticism. At first it looks obvious to everyone, including herself, that Anne Elliot – who at twenty-seven is the oldest of Austen's heroines by six years – will prove Marianne right. But then, gradually and thrillingly over the course of the novel, Austen restores Anne's bloom, vitality, beauty and sexuality and gloriously proves Marianne wrong. With William Elliot and Captain Wentworth both vying for her, by the end of the novel Anne has received more marriage proposals (four, if you count Charles Musgrove and William Elliot) than any other Jane Austen heroine.

During the marriage manoeuvring, the respective manners need careful scrutiny. The heroines need to be sure that the men are really attracted to them and genuinely in love. As well as signifying apparent admiration and devotion, manners can equally be used to conceal deceit. The constant use of plausible manners to disguise their real intentions is embodied in such villains as Willoughby in *Sense and Sensibility*, Wickham in *Pride and Prejudice*, Henry Crawford in *Mansfield Park* and William Elliot in *Persuasion*. These villains do not love the heroines, but their guile often deceives and threatens to ensnare them into committing to a relationship that would prevent them from turning to anyone else. The plots hinge on the timing of the discovery of this latent treachery. Marianne is nearly destroyed by Willoughby's deceitful pretence of love that he had no intention of fulfilling; Elizabeth Bennet comes very close to falling in love with the treacherous Wickham and any kind of liaison with him would forfeit any future with Darcy; Anne Elliot is flattered by William Elliot's attention, which her mentor Lady Russell encourages and her friend Mrs Smith worries has crossed a line; only Fanny Price remains impervious to Henry Crawford's attempted seduction and withstands the pressure applied by both Edmund and her uncle Sir Thomas Bertram to accept him.

Sometimes the revelations that unmask the villains come from unlikely sources, such as the housekeeper at Pemberley or the invalid

Mrs Smith cooped up on the wrong side of Bath. The ensuing springback from this revelation sets the scene for the happy ending by enabling the heroine to love and be loved by the genuine lover, and of course the final page can then sign off with the happy marriage.

The quest for marriage shapes all Jane Austen's novels and is the prime end and purpose of each unmarried character – and of any mother with an unmarried daughter. Almost every scene is dictated by the implications it provides for the heroines to advance their love stories, and at every turn these are loudly and gratuitously commented on by a wide range of friends, relations and neighbours who helpfully – or most often unhelpfully – interfere. Love and marriage seem to be everyone's business. Austen enjoys looking at relationships just as much through a heroine's eyes as through the boisterous comic gossips such as Sir John Middleton or Mrs Jennings, who is

> a good humoured, merry, fat elderly woman who talked a great deal, seemed very happy and rather vulgar. She was full of jokes and laughter and before dinner was over had said many witty things on the subjects of loves and husbands; hoped that they had not left their hearts behind them in Sussex and pretended to see them blush whether they did or not.

Predictably, Mrs Jennings infuriates Marianne.

As her writing career progresses Jane Austen becomes increasingly sophisticated and ambitious in her ability to achieve multiple weddings. In her first published novel, *Sense and Sensibility,* Austen juggles the prospective marriages of the two sisters Elinor and Marianne with the two side marriages of the villains of the book, Willoughby to the rich heiress Sophia Grey and Lucy Steele to

Robert Ferrars. In *Pride and Prejudice*, Mrs Bennet feels the pressure of her five unmarried daughters weighing on her, heightened by the ticking time-bomb of Mr Bennet's estate being entailed to Mr Collins. Unless the daughters marry well, when their father dies they will be left impoverished. By the end of the novel, Mrs Bennet has successfully married off three daughters and Charlotte Lucas's pre-emptive marriage to Mr Collins brings the number of weddings to four.

Austen continues to build her narrative skills until by *Emma* she reaches the top number of weddings: five. To pull off five weddings – ten partners – is a masterpiece of choreography and plotting. The book opens on the day of Miss Taylor's wedding to Mr Weston, so one marriage is already in the bag. This still leaves four further marriages to arrange, and along the way each partner is waylaid by other prospective partners. Austen shifts from the simple love triangles of *Sense and Sensibility* (Elinor, Edward Ferrars and Lucy Steele in one triangle and Marianne, Willoughby and Colonel Brandon in the other) to building a revolving pattern of four men and four women. In this complex sequence, each pairing is misplaced in succession: Harriet and Mr Elton; Mr Elton and Emma, then Mr Elton finds Augusta. In parallel, there is the phantom pairing of Emma and Frank Churchill; Emma's fantasy about Harriet and Frank Churchill and finally the revelation that all along it was Jane Fairfax and Frank Churchill. Then just when we think we have got it all straight, Mr Knightley is thought to be in love with Jane Fairfax, then Harriet, but all along he is in love with Emma. Finally, of course, Harriet reverts to Robert Martin to close the circle. This is a dizzying sequence of marriage options that sustains the narrative tension. The giddy misunderstandings proliferate because time and again Emma fools herself. The enveloping farce is only fully cleared up when she recognises a stunning and unexpected feeling: 'It darted through her with the speed of an arrow that Mr Knightley must marry no one but herself!' This blast of emotion is an imperative. The various strings are pulled together and the remaining couples are united in marriage. As Emma and Harriet and the circle around them become ever more ensnared by their own spurious and misconstrued marriage plots, we echo Puck's wry observation in that other great farcical marriage story, *A Midsummer Night's Dream*: 'Lord! What fools these mortals be!'

As well as marrying off the good characters, at the ends of her novels Jane Austen is invariably generous enough to allow even the disgraced characters – the schemers, the rogues, the villains – to be partially redeemed. In *Sense and Sensibility*, Willoughby is well settled with a rich wife (and his dogs and horses) and with exquisite irony the scheming Lucy Steele parlays a loveless impoverished affair with Edward into a loveless lucrative marriage with his younger brother Robert Ferrars, to whom Edward has forfeited his Norfolk estate. Seen through the sharp eyes of Lucy Steele, life has been extremely good as she plays the meagre hand of cards that she was dealt superbly well. In *Pride and Prejudice*, Wickham and Lydia do not come out so very badly with their £10,000 marriage settlement and their posting up north (and we expect they will keep slipping back to borrow money off Jane and Bingley and perhaps even brazenly visit Elizabeth and Darcy at Pemberley). The Crawfords disappear, Henry separates from Maria Bertram, and the pair are effectively airbrushed out of the final line-up of *Mansfield Park*. Even William Elliot, the villain of *Persuasion*, is potentially rewarded with the scheming Mrs Clay, which is not that unhappy an outcome for him as he will also inherit the title, as of course will she if indeed they do marry. If the novels had been written from their perspective, we could yet see Lucy Steele and Mrs Clay as opportunistic heroines in the vein of Becky Sharp of *Vanity Fair*. However, with two such scheming and selfish pairs as Lucy Steele and Robert Ferrars and Mrs Clay and William Elliot, it might be that, without any love, their weddings will fail to provide the mutual happiness that we are assured will be the result of the heroines' marriages.

While the marriages of the leading ladies and their partners appear set for sustained happiness, some of the marriages of the older generation are presented as compromised. The marriage between Mr and Mrs Bennet is superficially presented as a comedy, and we enjoy Mr Bennet's dry witticisms and the crass insults that, in her ignorance, Mrs Bennet aims at Darcy. However, beneath this comedy a rather desolate relationship exists, because we understand that Mr Bennet has lived to regret his marriage. Throughout the novel, Mr Bennet maintains a perpetual veneer of detached irony – after Mary's excruciating piano performance: 'You have delighted us long enough' – but when Darcy asks him for Elizabeth's hand in marriage, he invites her into his library and abandons this posture:

'He is rich to be sure, and you may have more fine clothes and fine carriages than Jane. But will they make you happy?'

He warns Elizabeth of his concerns that she is in danger of marrying a partner she would not respect:

> I know your disposition, Lizzy. I know that you could be neither happy nor respectable unless you truly esteemed your husband; unless you looked up to him as a superior. My child, let me not have the grief of seeing *you* unable to respect your partner in life. You know not what you are about.

This is the only time when Mr Bennet speaks with urgency and honesty. Implicitly confessing his lack of respect for Mrs Bennet and acknowledging their own compromised marriage, he is trying to ensure that Elizabeth does not fall into this trap. Putting aside all Darcy's wealth, which he points out will not sustain a relationship, Mr Bennet is alarmed and determined to have a candid and emotionally intelligent conversation with Elizabeth. Only when Elizabeth manages to 'conquer his incredulity and reconcile him to the match' does he accept the situation. It is then safe for him to revert to his usual role of assumed laconic irony: 'If any young men come for Mary or Kitty, send them in for I am quite at leisure.'

The marriage of Sir Thomas and Lady Bertram in *Mansfield Park* is another compromise. Rather than providing detailed insight into their relationship, Austen emphasises the languid selfishness of Lady Bertram and the well-meaning but obtuse efforts of Sir Thomas to try to persuade Fanny to marry Henry Crawford. The real evidence of the failure of their marriage is provided by the moral collapse of their children. Without moral guidance from their parents, three of their children flounder. It is only thanks to the beacon of Fanny to guide him that the fourth child Edmund survives.

Across Jane Austen's novels, many of the older generation have lost a partner so their marriages are not examined. Unlike the two compromised marriages of the Bennets and the Bertrams, the one dynamic marriage between an older couple is that of Admiral and Mrs Croft, whose joint carriage driving in *Persuasion* is a lively metaphor for their marriage. Picking up Anne and squeezing her beside them in their gig, with Mrs Croft adroitly taking the reins to 'give a better direction', they manage to avoid gate posts, ruts and even a dung cart by a whisker: 'My dear Admiral, that post! We shall certainly take that post.' They will become role models for Anne when she becomes a sailor's wife.

In Jane Austen, then, the good end up with true love, a happy marriage and lots of money, and the bad end up – well, in not such a bad place as they deserve.

* * *

Not so with George Eliot.

Eliot presents a totally different perspective on marriage. Many of Eliot's marriages disappoint, and many are damaging and destructive. In *Romola*, *Middlemarch* and *Daniel Deronda*, the wives are rapidly and brutally taught that within the confines of marriage they are to suffer total loss of independence, loss of control over their movements, their property and their bodies. The marriages across Eliot's novels unflinchingly document domestic abuse, violence, emotional and physical bullying, growing hatred, forced sexual relations and predation. Very quickly after the initial rush of impulsive attraction, which is mistaken for love, the ensuing compromises that the women have to make – and it is always the women – are extremely painful.

From the start of George Eliot's first novel, *Adam Bede*, we see all the differences in her world from that of Jane Austen. The first proposed marriage is between Adam and Hetty. When Adam and Hetty become engaged, he knows that Arthur Donnithorne, scion of the local landowner, has flirted with her (and on this basis he has knocked Arthur down in a bare-knuckle fight), but he does not know the full extent of her seduction. When Adam was helping Arthur to recover from the fight in the Hermitage, he failed to notice that Arthur had retrieved a 'slight thing' (Hetty's 'little pink silk neckerchief') and surreptitiously hidden it in the bottom of the waste-paper basket. Not only have they had sex, but Hetty is pregnant. As the pressure mounts leading towards their wedding date and her still undetected pregnancy advances, Hetty abandons Adam to try to find Arthur with his regiment in Windsor.

This journey is the first of many painful journeys that Eliot will provide of unwanted pregnant women, or unwanted women with unwanted babies who are trying to return to their lovers or husbands. Unable to find Arthur, Hetty staggers back towards the Midlands and tries to find an appropriate pond in which to drown herself. The desolate landscape where Hetty fails to kill herself but then gives birth to her baby and kills it forms the backdrop to the tragic consequences of her love affair with Arthur and her aborted marriage to Adam. When at the end of the book Adam marries Dinah, they acknowledge that they will have to carry the shared memories of Hetty and her dead baby, of the night in the prison cell before Hetty's expected execution and of the tragic life of Arthur with them. The first marriage that Eliot sets out in her first full-length novel starts with the deep-rooted sadness of carrying the tragedy of the past. After his early infatuation with Hetty, Adam builds a new and strong marriage with Dinah. While it is built upon the past 'sorrow upon sorrow', as Dinah describes, Eliot presents this marriage as one that will endure.

After the all-enveloping destruction caused by Maggie Tulliver, no marriage is possible in *The Mill on the Floss*. The only marriage in the novel takes place in the conclusion, which is set long after the end of the story and opens with: 'Nature repairs her ravages.' Five years have passed and we learn that two men regularly visit Maggie's tomb 'who both felt that their keenest joy and keenest sorrow were forever buried there' and then 'one of them visited the tomb again with a sweet face beside him – but that was years after'. This apparently married couple is unnamed, but we assume that it is Stephen Guest and Lucy. If it is them, and the 'sweet face' sounds as if it must be Lucy, their lives and their marriage carry the heavy baggage of the destruction. Far from a glorious Jane Austen marriage to wrap up the narrative, the damage incurred in *The Mill on the Floss* has made it impossible for the married couple even to be named let alone celebrated. The 'sweet face' has had to come to terms with Stephen's deceit and betrayal.

The three central marriages set out in *Romola*, *Middlemarch* and *Daniel Deronda* are yet more excoriating and tragic. Each early bride – Romola, Dorothea and Gwendolen – has to endure a cruel relationship – with Tito, Casaubon and Grandcourt – which is often deceitful and violent. Only once they have survived the deaths of their first husbands can they find redemption. While the frail but mendacious Casaubon dies quietly and unmourned on a garden bench as he waits for Dorothea to promise that she will devote her life to his pointless work, Tito and Grandcourt die violently and graphically. These three husbands each die without our pity.

Like Austen, Eliot includes several marriages within each book and she uses them to provide contrasts to each other. In *Middlemarch*, Sir James Chettam initially proposes to Dorothea. To his surprise, his rather bone-headed approach is flatly rejected because Dorothea has decided to devote herself to what she believes is the profound intellectual quest of Edward Casaubon. Sir James is redirected towards her younger sister Celia who he is assured is a better match since she lacks the 'dose of Methodism' that makes Dorothea such an awkward proposition. Celia proves Mrs Cadwallader correct, ostensibly agreeing with Sir James yet easily manipulating him whenever she wishes to. Their marriage lends a gentle comedy to the wider drama:

'Of course men know best about everything,' Celia comments

to Dorothea with unanswerable logic. 'Except what women know better.'

Meanwhile, the marriage of Fred Vincy, son of the mayor of Middlemarch, to his childhood sweetheart Mary Garth is the mirror image of the disastrous marriage of Fred's sister Rosamond to the ambitious doctor Tertius Lydgate. Unlike the beautiful Rosamond, Mary is the 'plain brown girl' who would 'pass unnoticed along a street'. Mary is diametrically opposed to Rosamond in every way – down-to-earth, pragmatic and unfailingly generous as she gives her life's savings to her father when Fred fails to repay his loan. Mary and Fred's path to their happy marriage is complicated and Fred has to change his approach to life significantly before Mary accepts him. The Vincy family are socially ambitious and both Fred and Rosamond want to climb the social ladder. It has become common knowledge that Fred has been made the heir to the old miser Peter Featherstone's fortune. Lazy and complacent, Fred aims to become a 'gentleman' simply by inheriting Peter Featherstone's fortune rather than doing any work. Mary is called in to nurse the dying miser, but afraid to breach any legal protocol she refuses Featherstone's dying instruction to burn his second will. When it is read out, the second will gives all Featherstone's fortune to a distant relative and Fred's prospects are ruined. With no money and no more prospects of having money, Fred is forced to reinvent himself. Helped by Mary's father, Caleb, he becomes a surveyor and learns that trade is honourable. Earning his own living paves the way to earning Mary's respect and love.

Rosamond's ambition to marry up in society focuses upon Lydgate, with his superior family connections. Theirs will be a marriage of mutual ambition and at their first meeting the omens of who will wield the power are clear. As Rosamond goes to leave, she heads across the room to pick up her riding whip:

'Lydgate was quick in anticipating her. He reached the whip before she did and turned to present it to her.'

As Rosamond manipulates Lydgate towards their marriage, there is little sense of any love between them:

> To Rosamond it seemed as if she and Lydgate were as good as engaged ... It is true, Lydgate had the counter-idea of remaining unengaged. Circumstance was almost sure to be on the side of Rosamond's idea which had a shaping activity and looked through watchful blue eyes, whereas Lydgate's lay blind and unconcerned as a jellyfish which gets melted without knowing it.

Inevitably, Rosamond prevails. As a marriage partner, Rosamond is an imperturbable monster who with her voice 'that fell and trickled like cold waterdrops' remorselessly gets her own way:

'I never give up anything that I choose to do.'

Unyielding in her selfishness, Rosamond destroys Lydgate:

'Lydgate's hair never became white. He died when he was only fifty.'

Despite Rosamond's callous treatment of Lydgate, the only woman whose marriages provoke disgust and outrage across Middlemarch society is Dorothea herself. Her sister Celia is the voice of reason and she neatly sums up:

> You would have Mr Casaubon because he had such a great soul and was so old and dismal and learned; and now to thinking of marrying Mr Ladislaw, who has got no estate or anything. I

suppose it is because you must be making yourself uncomfortable in some way or other.

The prospect of Casaubon as a husband for Dorothea disgusts society because of his age: 'He's no better than a mummy ... Look at his legs!'

Another reason for repulsion is that Casaubon's will explicitly set the condition that if Dorothea were to marry Ladislaw, then she would forfeit her inheritance. Dorothea and Ladislaw face censure from all sides:

> Sir James never ceased to regard Dorothea's second marriage as a mistake; and indeed this remained the tradition concerning it in Middlemarch, where she was spoken of to a younger generation as a fine girl who married a sickly clergyman old enough to be her father, and in little more than a year after his death gave up her estate to marry his cousin – young enough to have been his son, with no property and not well-born. Those who had not seen anything of Dorothea usually observed that she could not have been 'a nice woman' else she would not have married either the one or the other.

It is telling that from her own ostracised position living with Lewes, Eliot is content to leave her leading lady outside of mainstream society. Dorothea and Will are marginalised, whereas after being mentored and redeemed by Caleb Garth (poignantly a gentler and more understanding version of Eliot's own father), it is Fred and Mary who are universally approved and take up central roles in the town: 'On sunny days the two lovers who were first engaged with the umbrella-ring may be seen in white-haired placidity at the open window from which Mary Garth, in the days of old Peter Featherstone, had often been ordered to look out for Mr Lydgate.'

Their marriage is a triumph of middle-class society. The clue is in the title. Set in the Midlands of Eliot's childhood, *Middlemarch* is a story of 'Middle England' that shines a light across the breadth of English society of 1832. In this age of the Reform Act, love and marriage are measured in political and social terms. Eliot concludes that Lydgate's zeal for social reform will implode with his marriage and financial stress. Dorothea's aristocratic idealism for reform will be thwarted by her first marriage and eventually diluted and marginalised by her second marriage. The love and marriage that will endure is the marriage which has been hard-earned by Fred and Mary.

Of the many marriages across George Eliot's novels, the only one which could have been contemplated by Jane Austen is the marriage between Celia and Sir James Chettam. While all of Austen's heroines happily head towards their weddings, two of Eliot's heroines, Romola and Gwendolen, end up alone. Their brutal and scheming husbands have both violently died, which has provided them with a freedom, yet unlike the other young widow Dorothea they have no new partner to turn to. They face a solitary future. Gwendolen has been blocked from turning to Daniel Deronda for support by his marriage to Mirah, so she is going to have to recreate herself. As her mother watches over her, she takes her first steps: 'Don't be afraid. I shall live. I mean to live.' When Romola returns to Florence effectively reborn as a 'Madonna', she finds that her husband Tito is dead. She is free. Taking charge of his second wife Tessa's impoverished household and educating Tito and Tessa's children is Romola's first step towards her new life.

When Charlotte Brontë wrote to Lewes: 'I think I will endeavour to follow the counsel which shines out of Miss Austen's "mild eyes", to finish more, and be more subdued; but neither am I sure of that,' one possible reading is that she was referring to the way in which Jane Austen finishes her novels with such neat endings. To an extent, she is questioning how the demands of the plot for each happy marriage effectively 'subdues' the characters. In Brontë's opinion, the imperative to 'finish more' by giving each character a neatly resolved ending sucks some of the oxygen out of them.

I think that George Eliot absorbed Charlotte Brontë's approach particularly in *Romola* and *Daniel Deronda*, in which she gave her heroines open endings that involved a future with no love and no marriage. Whether determinedly confident as with Romola or realistically faltering as with Gwendolen, by contemplating their future life as single women George Eliot breaks open Jane Austen's assumption that a good marriage is the essential element of a happy ending.

* * *

CHAPTER 4

FORTUNES AND FINANCE

The theme of money runs through all of Jane Austen's and George Eliot's novels like the watermarks on a stack of banknotes. Who has it? Who wins it? Who loses it? These are vital questions which preoccupy every character and determine their actions. If a family is financially sound, then money does not need to move very much and life is normal – but 'normal' is not enough to set the pulse or the plot racing for a novelist. In order to build up pressure and precipitate the action, both Austen and Eliot use the same plot device – they both invent heroines who are grappling with the loss of a parent. With the exception of Elizabeth Bennet, whose family has lost their inheritance, each Jane Austen heroine has lost a parent – Elinor and Marianne Dashwood's father has died, Emma Woodhouse and Anne Elliot have both lost their mothers, Fanny Price and Catherine Morland are removed from their impoverished families. The financial strain triggered by these fractured families and absent parents places the heroines under extraordinary stress, kick-starts the action and accelerates the plots.

As well as the heroines, a surprising number of leading men also have no parents to guide them. These men have either inherited money like Colonel Brandon, Darcy, Bingley, Henry Crawford and Mr Knightley in which case they are secure but then they themselves are sought after as marriage partners (the price on their backs makes Bingley and Darcy especially targeted), or they have no money and urgently need to find it like Willoughby, Wickham, Frank Churchill and William Elliot in which case they are the predators. George Eliot follows the same pattern. With the exception of Mary Garth, every single George Eliot heroine – Dinah, Maggie, Eppie, Romola, Esther, Dorothea, Gwendolen, and Mirah – has lost one or both of her parents. Their fortunes are inextricably tied to their finances.

Both authors had personal experience of the destabilising effect that a fractured family could have on the family fortune and in turn what that had meant for their own lives. Eliot was sixteen when her mother died, forcing her to take on the domestic duties of managing the household. While her father was alive, she enjoyed financial security, but this was materially reduced when he passed the house and his job to her brother Isaac. When he died, she inherited a small settlement of £2,000. Assuming the prevailing rate of interest of 5 per cent, this settlement would produce £100 a year for her, which would barely cover the £90 annual rent for board and lodgings in John Chapman's London house – a long way short of securing her independence.

Jane Austen was twenty-nine when her father died. With no obvious inheritance, Jane lived together with Cassandra and their mother for the rest of her life. Unlike Eliot, Jane and Cassandra enjoyed the generosity of their brothers, who all sent money to their mother to support their household at Chawton (although quite how they might have reacted to Jane if she had accepted James Clarke's offer and moved in with him at his Halfway House in Soho was never tested).

Jane Austen was keenly aware of the plight of the older, solitary, impoverished woman. In her letter to Cassandra of April 1805, she describes their ageing, widowed neighbour:

'Poor Mrs Stent! It has been her lot to be always in the way; but we must be merciful for perhaps in time we may come to be Mrs Stents ourselves, unequal to anything and unwelcome to everybody.'

The spectre of Mrs Stent haunted Austen, who later invented Miss Bates, the genteel but impoverished spinster aunt of Jane Fairfax in *Emma*. When Emma declares to Harriet that she does not intend to marry, Harriet is aghast and hits upon a deeper truth than she might realise when she baldly points out what her future might look like:

'But then, to be an old maid at last like Miss Bates!'

Beyond Harriet's dismay at the status of being an unmarried 'old maid', Miss Bates is chronically poor and clings to the edge of Highbury society. Mr Knightley's careful gifts of salted pork and his winter's store of dried apples make a material difference to her. In a poignant revelation of her own miniscule budget, Miss Bates confides to Emma that she is amazed by the scale of the governess pay that her niece Jane Fairfax would receive, which is £12 a year. From the perspective of her poverty, Miss Bates thinks this is a handsome sum. Given her own wealth of £30,000, which at 5 per cent would provide an annual income of £1,500, Emma must have squirmed with embarrassment. Emma answers Harriet's attempt to put her in the same category as Miss Bates by pointing out the difference between a rich old maid and a poor one:

> It is poverty only which makes celibacy contemptible to a generous public. A single woman with a very narrow income must be a ridiculous, disagreeable old maid – the proper sport of boys and

girls; but a single woman of good fortune is always respectable, and may be as sensible and pleasant as anybody else.

Austen was aware that family fortunes could change on a whim. The prospect of becoming 'the proper sport of boys and girls' would have been a constant and latent threat in her life as she remained unmarried and dependent upon her family. I believe that the fear of this potential humiliation, the dread of becoming 'ridiculous and disagreeable', was the single most important inspiration for her to keep writing and try to earn her own money.

In the opening scene of *Sense and Sensibility*, John Dashwood is in the process of deciding how much of his generous inheritance to pass to his half-sisters Elinor, Marianne and Margaret, who have been excluded from their grandfather's will but whom their father asked John to look after. John Dashwood initially decides to give each of them £1,000: 'Yes, he would give them three thousand pounds. It would be liberal and handsome! It would be enough to make them completely easy.' With excruciating comic effect, when his grasping wife hears of this plan, she negotiates him down from his initial proposal of £1,000 to £500 each: 'Five hundred pounds would be a prodigious increase to their fortunes!' then to a suggested annuity to his step-mother, then to a present of fifty pounds 'now and then' and eventually to the conclusion that he should give them nothing at all:

'As to your giving them more, it is quite absurd to think on it. They will be much more able to give *you* something.'

'Upon my word,' said Mr Dashwood, 'I believe you are perfectly right.'

With two of her brothers on active service in the Royal Navy, Austen knew that the next letter home could just as easily contain a gleeful account of the capture of a wealthy enemy ship as a condolence note signed by the ship's captain and framed with a funereal black border. Her brother Edward had inherited two estates, one in Godmersham, in Kent, and the other in Chawton, in Hampshire. Edward had become truly wealthy, but even his generosity might be distracted if his wife intervened. In her fiction, Austen could control the narrative and engineer an escape for these sisters, but in the reality of her life in Hampshire she and her sister were dependent upon the support of her brothers and – like Miss Bates – would gratefully accept presents of any pheasants, partridges and rabbits that they shot and dropped off with her.

Until the last five years of her life, when she finally began to earn the *pewter* that she desperately coveted, Austen's life would have had the undercurrent of her possibly ending up 'always in the way' like Mrs Stent, or as poor and having to be as eternally grateful for every kindness as Miss Bates. Managing money and making it go further were key to eking out a more comfortable life. Although she did not manage the household finances, Austen was highly financially literate and alive to the prices of everything. She delighted in discussing money.

George Lewes may have fantasised that Jane Austen was most like her dazzling, sexy heroine Elizabeth Bennet, but I am struck by the fact that so many of the Austen family chose the miserly Mrs Norris in *Mansfield Park* as their favourite character. I wonder whether this could have been a veiled reference to the similarity of her character with their sister Jane's. It is Mrs Norris who leaves the outing to Sotherton Court having managed to wangle some cream cheese and four pheasant eggs from the housekeeper, the only contented person on the way home. Again, it is Mrs Norris who in the nick of time whips away the green baize curtain from the theatrical production which the Bertram family are putting on when their father so disastrously makes his surprise return home. In her letters, Austen details how she and her mother are reworking their clothes for mourning:

> My mother is preparing mourning for Mrs E.K. – she has picked her old silk pelisse to pieces and means to have it dyed black for a gown – a very interesting scheme. How is your blue gown? Mine is all to pieces – I think there must have been something wrong in the dye for in places it divided with a touch. There was four shillings thrown away and to be added to my subjects of never failing regret.

Exactly echoing this enthusiastic frugality, Mrs Norris also knows the value of everything and how to make tiny but vital savings. After the makeshift stage is dismantled and all the props removed, the green baize that she had cut up to make the stage curtain 'with a saving by her good management of full three quarters of a yard' reappears in her cottage 'where she happened to be particularly in need of green baize'.

If love and marriage are the obvious romantic themes of her novels, the question of money is the pervasive undercurrent. To be a 'single man in possession of a good fortune' is to be blessed with a serene and unassailable privilege, essentially to have won the Jane Austen lottery of life. In the eyes of the neighbourhood mothers, such a man was of almost mythical status – as if a unicorn had walked into the room. Regency society was a world where fortunes were visible to everyone and openly discussed. When Bingley arrives in the Netherfield neighbourhood it is immediately rumoured and confirmed that he has an income of between £4,000 and £5,000 a year. When his friend Darcy arrives, it is immediately whispered that he enjoys an annual income of £10,000, news that takes only 'five minutes' to confirm. Even the hapless Mr Rushworth in *Mansfield Park* is known to have an annual income of £12,000, which is the largest income of any Jane Austen hero and the only thing which prevents him from being 'a very stupid fellow'.

Each of the leading characters has their price attached. In *Emma*, we are told that Emma Woodhouse has capital of £30,000, Jane Fairfax's friend Miss Crawford has capital of £12,000 and Mr Knightley correctly estimates that Mr Elton is looking for a bride with £10,000. By wilfully ignoring this financial reality, Emma ensures that her matchmaking plans for Harriet and Mr Elton collapse in chaos. Sure enough, once Mr Elton has been rejected by Emma he leaves Highbury and finds a suitable bride: 'The charming Augusta Hawkins, in addition to all the usual advantages of perfect beauty and merit, was in possession of an independent fortune, of so many thousands as would always be called ten.'

Even Marianne Dashwood, the impetuous 'sensibility' to her sister Elinor's practical 'sense', can put an exact price on what her ideal lifestyle would cost. The unerring accuracy of her financial forecasts undermine her apparent idealism and reveals her as more like a champagne socialist:

'What have wealth or grandeur to do with happiness?' asked Marianne.

'Grandeur has but little,' said Elinor, 'but wealth has much to do with it.'

'Elinor, for shame!' said Marianne; 'money can only give happiness where there is nothing else to give it.'

Elinor challenges her to be explicit:

'Come, what is your competence?'
'About eighteen hundred or two thousand a year; not more than *that*.'
Elinor laughed, '*Two* thousand a year! *One* is my wealth!'
'And yet two thousand a year is a very moderate income. A family cannot well be maintained on a smaller. I am sure I am not extravagant in my demands. A proper establishment of servants, a carriage, perhaps two, and hunters, cannot be supported on less.'
'Hunters!' repeated Edward. 'But why must you have hunters? Everybody does not hunt.'
Marianne coloured as she replied, 'But most people do.'

As the plot of *Sense and Sensibility* speeds up, financial calculations come thick and fast. With hindsight, we realise that the Willoughby and Marianne storyline is not a love story based on mutual romantic interests and passion and love at all; it is a story about deceit and the manipulation of money. Everything else is a smokescreen. Without his own capital, Willoughby is driven by the need to obtain money. Willoughby later confessed to Elinor the reason why he had abandoned Marianne for an heiress:

'But I am talking like a fool... in honest words, her money was necessary to me.'

By refusing to acknowledge this and airily assuming that she will share his money, Marianne is blindsided. When she discovers the truth at the London ball, she collapses. When she resurfaces, it is a bruising awakening for her.

Meanwhile as Marianne is sidelined in her sickbed, the finances keep spinning. As the lines of the plot are drawn tighter together, financial negotiations take over at a rapidly accelerating speed. In fury at his secret engagement to Lucy Steele, Edward Ferrars's mother starts to negotiate:

'His mother explained to him her liberal designs, in case of his marrying Miss Morton; told him she would settle on him the Norfolk estate, which, clear of land-tax, brings in a good thousand a-year; offered even, when matters grew desperate, to make it twelve hundred.'

When Edward stands firm by Lucy, Mrs Ferrars cuts him off and gives his inheritance to his younger brother. Edward is left impoverished by his furious mother: 'His own two thousand she protested should be his all.' At 5 per cent, this £2,000 of capital would yield a paltry £100 a year, which was then about half the annual income of a church curate.

Elinor and Marianne's brother John Dashwood is excitedly trying to keep up with these whirling financial negotiations. Dashwood even begins to quantify the change in value of Marianne's altered looks:

> She was as handsome a girl last September as any I ever saw; and as likely to attract the men. There was something in her style of beauty to please them particularly ... I question whether Marianne *now* will marry a man worth more than five or six hundred a year, at the utmost, and I am very much deceived if *you* do not do better.

The marriage market has a value and John Dashwood is like an options trader making a market in spread betting. This was the height of the Regency period when every night gambling fortunes were made and lost up and down the clubs of St James's. Bets were notoriously taken on anything. One evening in 1816, when they had run out of other ideas, two Regency dandies in White's Club bet £3,000 on which of two raindrops trickling down the dining room windowpane would be the first to reach the bottom. In this manic atmosphere, it is perfectly understandable for John Dashwood to be putting a value on anything, even gambling on the sadly altered looks of his poor sister.

Jane Austen's most blatant account of the financial value of a marriage is set out in *Pride and Prejudice*. Charlotte Lucas has been eyeing up Colonel Fitzwilliam as a possible husband for Elizabeth. They are attracted to each other and in order to understand the viability of any relationship, Elizabeth has to clarify what an Earl's son – crucially, an Earl's younger son – would be looking for. At first they circle each other warily, but Elizabeth needs to cut to the chase. When Fitzwilliam comments that 'a younger son you know must be inured to self-denial and dependence', Elizabeth challenges him:

'The younger son of an Earl can know very little of either. Now, seriously, what have you known of self-denial and dependence? When have you been prevented by want of money from going wherever you chose, or procuring anything you had a fancy for?'

Fitzwilliam tries to deflect this:

'These are home questions – and perhaps I cannot say that I have experienced many hardships of that nature. But in matters of greater weight, I may suffer from the want of money. Younger sons cannot marry where they like.'

'Unless where they like women of fortune, which I think they very often do.'

'Our habits of expense make us too dependent and there are not many in my rank of life who can afford to marry without some attention to money.'

Given Elizabeth's lack of money, this amounts to a confession that Fitzwilliam cannot consider her as a potential wife. Elizabeth is very alive to this: '"Is this," thought Elizabeth, "meant for me?" and she coloured at the idea.'

With great candour and perhaps because she is riled by this subtle, albeit honest, rejection, Elizabeth brings the money question to a head and speaks for all Jane Austen heroines – and her readers – who might need this blunt yet helpful clarification:

'And pray, what is the usual price of an Earl's younger son? Unless the elder brother is very sickly, I suppose you would not ask above £50,000.'

With nothing to lose because Colonel Fitzwilliam has told her that she is unacceptable to him, Elizabeth is talking brass tacks. What started as a teasing conversation has taken a more serious turn and with £1,000 to her name, which would provide just £50 of income a year, Elizabeth is on the wrong side of the maths. The conversation reads like a memo to herself as to the prevailing price of a dowry without the intervention of a Darcy. Elizabeth's precarious financial position places the marriage proposal by Mr Collins in context – most ladies would not have gambled upon a unicorn like Darcy appearing with a better offer, and they would have been right.

As she wrote her first four novels, Austen was in the same position as Elizabeth. She was a gentleman's daughter, but not rich.

She enjoyed dealing with money and many of her letters contained accounts of ribbons or material bought, dresses being reconfigured and the exact prices she paid for materials. Once *Sense and Sensibility* and *Pride and Prejudice* had been published and sold their first editions, Austen suddenly had the experience of having some money in her own name. For the first time, she could behave like one of her more monied characters. When she is staying with her brother Henry in London, she is thrilled by the chance to go on a shopping spree. Clearly exhilarated, on 24 May 1813 she provides this heady account of Regency life in the fast lane. Her delight and her fantasy about how the married Bennet sisters might have appeared if their portraits had been painted is infectious:

> Henry and I went to the exhibition in Spring Gardens. It is not thought a good collection, but I was very well pleased, particularly (pray tell Fanny) with a small portrait of Mrs. Bingley, excessively like her... She is dressed in a white gown, with green ornaments, which convinces me of what I had always supposed, that green was a favourite colour with her. I dare say Mrs. D. will be in yellow.

Breathlessly, she recounts shopping sprees to buy gloves, gowns and some dimity (a hard-wearing woven cotton) for Fanny and a gold locket for Cassandra, providing the detailed account:

> I gave 2s 6d for the dimity. I do not boast of any bargains but think both the sarsenet and dimity good of their sort. I have bought your locket but was obliged to give 18s for it, which must be rather more than you intended. It is neat and plain and set in gold.

Unlike any of her heroines, and unlike virtually all the women of her time, Austen had made her money herself and was for the first time revelling in the giddy experience of living off her own, earned income. It was clearly an intoxicating sensation and as she bowled about London in the open barouche on that bright early summer day, she gives the sense that she had to pinch herself to prove that it was all real:

> I had great amusement among the pictures and the driving about, the carriage being open it was very pleasant. I liked my solitary elegance very much and was ready to laugh all the time at my being where I was. I could not but feel that I had naturally small right to be parading about London in a Barouche.

Later that same year in July, Austen was still on a high. Writing to her brother Francis, she describes how Henry is faring after the death of his wife Eliza. Never one to dwell on sad news, she is cheerfully pragmatic:

> Upon the whole his spirits are very much recovered. If I may so express myself, his mind is not a mind for affliction. He is too busy, too active, too sanguine. Sincerely as he was attached to poor Eliza moreover and excellently as he behaved to her, he was always used to be away from her at times, that her loss is not felt as that of many a beloved wife might be, especially when all the circumstances of her long and dreadful illness are taken into the account.

The really pressing news that she is bursting to tell Francis is held back until the postscript, which, written upside down on the top of the front page, would have been the first thing to catch his eye. She proudly announces:

> You will be glad to hear that every copy of S. and S. is sold and that it has brought me £140 – besides the copyright, if that should ever be of any value. I have now therefore written myself into £250 – which only makes me long for more. I have something in hand – which I hope on the credit of P. and P. will sell well, tho' not half so entertaining.

Jane Austen's passion for earning money and her enjoyment of spending it is palpable. Nobody sums up the ecstatic feeling of having more money than they ever dreamed of better than Mrs Bennet:

> Goodness gracious! Lord bless me! Only think! Dear me! Mr Darcy! Who would have thought it! Oh! My sweetest Lizzy! How rich and how great you will be! What pin-money, what jewels, what carriages you will have! A house in town! Everything that is charming! Three daughters married! Ten thousand a year!

Eventually she runs out of exclamation marks and just collapses in a heap:

'Oh, Lord! What will become of me. I shall go distracted.'

As Jane Austen cavorted around Berkeley Square in the open barouche, Mrs Bennet would have been great company for her.

* * *

At exactly the moment when Jane reached the peak of her fortune, the Austen family suffered a financial calamity. Jane had just seen

Emma published, she had grown used to staying in London with Henry and she had enjoyed a flirtation with her secret Lorenzo, Charles Haden. All these pleasures were destroyed when Henry's bank, Austen & Maunde, collapsed in March 1816. Interestingly, there are no surviving letters between Jane Austen and her brother Henry – they were all destroyed. With her keen interest in finance, I wonder what she would have thought of the inner workings of the private bank Austen & Maunde and the kinds of men Henry had been lending money to who never repaid him.

In the classic pattern of bankruptcies, the collapse of Austen & Maunde started slowly and then happened all at once. By the time *Emma* was published in December 1815, Austen & Maunde was already irrevocably holed beneath the surface. Henry had set up two banks, Austen, Gray & Vincent, which he had co-founded in Alton Hampshire in 1806, and Austen & Maunde, a London bank which alongside making its own loans also underwrote the loans of the Hampshire bank. In November 1815, Henry had realised that his Hampshire partners at Austen, Gray & Vincent were making dangerously unsecured loans. In 1815, the end of the Napoleonic Wars had caused high unemployment. The economic downturn was exacerbated by the terrible weather caused by the eruption of Mount Tambora in Indonesia, when the ash from the volcano blotted out the sun and caused crop failures around the world. First wheat and barley farmers and then millers and maltsters began defaulting on their loans. A number of regional banks failed, and in Hampshire, Austen, Gray & Vincent was among them. In order to keep the London bank solvent, Henry turned to his brother Edward, who provided a capital injection of £10,325. As the winter of 1815 turned to spring of 1816, it looked as if the Hampshire crisis had been contained. Unfortunately, this was wishful thinking.

By February 1816, it was clear that the London bank Austen & Maunde was in serious trouble. The root of the problem was that back in 1813, the bank had been appointed as the Receiver General of Taxes for Oxfordshire. The taxes received in this coveted role only had to be passed on to the Crown Tax Office two years later. In the meantime, the cash received could be used to provide more bank loans to earn more income. Effectively, Henry was borrowing short-term money from the Crown Tax Office and lending long-term unsecured loans on a handshake to Regency swells up and down St James's Street. Whether they were honest barley maltsters, flour millers caught by the recession or aristocratic dandies gambling on raindrops trickling down the windowpanes in White's, Henry's list of bad debts began to add up. As the bank's debtors began to default in 1815, the monies owed to the government were escalating and the deadline to pay them was approaching. The jaws of a financial trap were closing around him.

The worst of the debtors was Lord Moira, the Marquess of Hastings. A flamboyant Regency figure and a massive gambler, if Lord Moira had featured in one of Jane Austen's novels, he would have been the richest, most aristocratic and best connected of all her characters, with at least twice the income of Darcy. 'Moira and I are like two brothers,' the Prince Regent apparently boasted. 'When one wants money, he puts his hand in the other's pocket.' As his gambling partner, the Prince Regent certainly put his hand in Lord Moira's pocket, but he repaid him with only favours and influence. Apparently, Lord Moira was in debt of more than £100,000, an impossible sum ever to repay. Yet his powerful influence in royal and political circles meant he remained an attractive prospect for bankers like Henry Austen.

To begin with, Henry's strategy worked. Although Lord Moira's debts to Austen & Maunde were rising, his introductions secured more business and also advanced the careers of Henry's two younger brothers in the Royal Navy. In 1807, Austen approvingly mentions the First Lord's promise to Lord Moira 'that Captain A should have the first good frigate that was vacant'. In an echo of this, in *Mansfield Park* Fanny Price later approves of Henry Crawford putting in a good word at the Admiralty to secure her brother William's promotion. But as Lord Moira's debts ballooned, his credit began to be exhausted and his bankers began to agitate for repayment. A promissory note with Lord Moira's signature was clearly no longer worth the paper it was written on.

On 11 November 1812 with his financial downfall looming, Lord Moira wrong-footed all his creditors by abruptly accepting an appointment as Governor-General of India. The Prince Regent had saved him. Effectively, Lord Moira was fleeing the country. Just weeks before he set sail, Lord Moira borrowed an additional £6,000 from Austen & Maunde with no collateral other than his word as a gentleman. 'Mr Austen,' he said at their last meeting, 'be under no anxiety; I would rather cut off my right hand than permit you or anyone to lose a farthing by me.'

As well as the offer of his right hand, Henry might also have been attracted by the steep interest rates he applied to the loan and even the opportunities to do business in the new economy of India. But if Henry Austen had dreams of following in the gilded footsteps of Clive of India, who had famously responded to questions about his ill-gotten fortune with 'My God, Mr. Chairman, at this moment I stand astonished at my own modesty', they vanished in 1813 when Lord Moira's ship set sail from Portsmouth. It was the last that Henry or any British banker would see of Lord Moira or his money.

Amidst the mounting threat to his bank, Henry managed to pull off one last significant deal. In the early months of 1816, he went to visit Richard Crosby, who was himself suffering financial hardship as the recession bit and the craze for gothic novels waned. Without telling him the true identity of Mrs Ashton Dennis, Henry bought back the manuscript of *Susan* for the original £10. His nephew James Edward Austen's memoir triumphantly notes the family's satisfaction at this: 'When the bargain was concluded and the money paid, but not till then, the negotiator had the satisfaction of informing him that the work which had been so lightly esteemed was by the author of *Pride and Prejudice*.'

Henry and Jane had little time to enjoy the satisfaction of having *Susan* back in their ownership. Austen would have barely had time to blow the dust off the manuscript, let alone start thinking about editing it, when Henry's bank received its death blow. On 15 March 1816, Austen & Maunde received notification from the Crown that the bank must make the payment of £22,743.8s.10d owing from the taxes which it had collected. With their debtors unable to repay any of their loans, and this time well beyond the reach of his brother Edward's ability to bail out, Austen & Maunde ceased trading. The following day, 16 March 1816, the *London Gazette* listed Austen & Maunde as bankrupt.

Henry himself was declared personally bankrupt. He was allowed to keep £200, but all his possessions from the bank's premises in Covent Garden and his house at Hans Place were seized and auctioned. Jane Austen knew the furniture well – the dining table and blue and white china dinner set with which they had recently entertained Mr Haden with the pheasants and rabbits supplied from Hampshire; the mahogany writing desk that she had used to check the proofs of *Emma* and write parts of her next novel.

It all went under the hammer. Along with the inevitable blow to the family reputation and pride, Henry's bankruptcy shattered the bustling, prosperous and above all happy London life which Henry and Jane Austen had enjoyed together.

As well as financial loss, Jane Austen suffered a loss of self-confidence which comes across in her last letter to her publisher, John Murray. Just the previous December, she was impatiently urging him to an early publication of *Emma*: 'I wish you would have the goodness to send a line by the bearer stating the day on which the set will be ready for the Prince Regent.' Austen's next and last recorded letter to him dated 1 April 1816 strikes a forlorn note. John Murray had managed to arrange for Sir Walter Scott to review *Emma* in the *Quarterly Review*. Scott was one of Austen's literary heroes, but the review was not especially flattering and sales faltered, with John Murray recording that just 150 copies of *Emma* were sold over the next six months. Austen seems deflated and resigned:

'The Authoress of *Emma* has no reason I think to complain of her treatment in it – except in the total omission of *Mansfield Park*. I cannot but be sorry that so clever a Man as the Reviewer of *Emma* should consider it as unworthy of being noticed.'

Her other reason for feeling dejected emerges in the last paragraph:

In consequence of the late sad Event in Henrietta Street, I must request that if you should at any time have anything to communicate by Letter, you will be so good as to write by the post directing to me (Miss J. Austen) Chawton, near Alton – and that for anything of a larger bulk, you will add to the same direction by Collier's Southampton Coach.

The 'late sad Event in Henrietta Street' is the closest Jane Austen can come to acknowledging the collapse of Henry's bank and his financial implosion. Her need to put her name in brackets 'me (Miss J. Austen)' feels like a crisis of self-confidence, as does the acknowledgment that her fast-paced life in the city is over. Jane Austen never visited London again.

* * *

The Austen family lost significant money in the collapse of Henry's bank. They also lost some local reputation because Austen, Gray & Vincent was well known in Hampshire, where its banking offices were in the market town of Alton. After Henry's assets were sold and his creditors received the proceeds, he was discharged from bankruptcy and went away to Switzerland to consider his next move. When he returned to England, Henry announced that he would become a clergyman and entered the church on the lowly apprentice rank of curate. Their eldest brother, James, who had inherited two parishes from their father, gave him a curate's living in Steventon.

Showing tremendous resilience and forgiveness, the Austen family closed ranks and swung behind Henry. They knew that he had helped secure lucrative positions in the Royal Navy for Francis and Charles and, sharing Jane's attitude, the rest of the family chose not to dwell on anything that was 'odious'. In Jane Austen's letter of 24 January 1817 to her old friend Alethea Bigg (there is no mention of her brother Harris), she reports that she is rather nervously waiting for Henry's first sermon:

Our own new Clergyman is expected here very soon, perhaps in time to assist Mr Papillon on Sunday. I shall be very glad when

Jane Austen by her sister, Cassandra. This is the only confirmed likeness of Jane, the single member of the Austen family apart from her epileptic brother not to have a formal portrait painted. With her chin resolutely high, mouth set straight and arms defensively folded, Jane looks determined, observant, shrewd and independent – perhaps a daunting woman to propose marriage to. Despite her energetic dancing and caustic wit – 'Imagine to yourself everything most profligate and shocking in the way of dancing and sitting down together' – the right proposal never came.
© National Portrait Gallery

Cassandra's earlier portrait of Jane was airbrushed by the Victorians in 1869 to match their sanitised version of her life, following the insistence of the Austen family that their Aunt Jane led a scrupulously uneventful 'spinster' existence – a myth that has prevailed. By popular vote in 2013, Jane Austen was chosen to feature on the back of the £10 note. She would have enjoyed using one of these notes to buy back the copyright of her early novel *Susan*, which was posthumously published as *Northanger Abbey*.
Via PhotoEdit / Alamy Stock Photo

Jane Austen regularly stayed with her brother Edward after he inherited Godmersham Park. Here, she recognised that she was something of a poor relation, writing long letters to Cassandra: 'I am all alone. Edward is gone into his woods. At this present time I have five tables, eight and twenty chairs and two fires all to myself.' She also noted her social role shifting with her age: 'By the bye, as I must leave off being young, I find many douceurs in being a sort of chaperon for I am put on the sofa near the fire and can drink as much wine as I like.'

Via Universal Art Archive / Alamy Stock Photo

162 letters of Jane Austen survive, some 100 addressed to her sister, Cassandra. Intimate, theatrical, gossipy and catty, they provide a vivid insight into her character.

© Jane Austen's House / Bodleian Libraries

The Austens were a good-looking family and, with the tragic exception of Jane, generally long-lived. The brothers, with the exception of George, also had large families – Jane and Cassandra were aunties to thirty-one children.
© Jane Austen's House

BURLINGTON ARCADE.

ABOVE Mary Ann Evans and George Lewes met at William Jeff's bookshop in Burlington Arcade in 1851. While many of the ground-floor shops still appear similar today, in 1851 the first floor comprised a line of brothels, where the prostitutes advertised their availability by hanging black stockings out of the upstairs windows.

LEFT George Lewes, a dazzling raconteur, actor and freelance journalist, was celebrated as both 'the ugliest man in London' and 'the most amusing little fellow in the whole world'. He captivated the more serious Mary Ann Evans when they met in 1851 and they became lifelong partners. Taking his first name, George, and adding 'Eliot' gave Mary Ann her pen name. Her colossal advances and royalties not only funded their lifestyle but also provided financial support to his wife and sons.
© National Portrait Gallery

This unfinished portrait by Charlotte Brontë's brother, Branwell, captures her intensity. Her first published novel, *Jane Eyre*, attracted the attention of George Lewes. His unsolicited advice to 'write more like Jane Austen' prompted her to read *Pride and Prejudice* (which she had never heard of) and triggered a passionate correspondence in which they vehemently disagreed over virtually all aspects of writing. George Lewes kept these letters, and I believe they profoundly influenced George Eliot when she started to write her novels.
© National Portrait Gallery

After her father died in 1849, Mary Ann Evans travelled to Switzerland to consider her future. This portrait by François D'Albert Durade shows her on the cusp of a life-changing decision. She decided to 'pack up her carpet-bag', leave her family home in the Midlands and try her hand as a freelance journalist in London.
© National Portrait Gallery

Sight unseen, in 1862, Smith, Elder & Co. offered £10,000 to purchase *Romola* – an unprecedented publishing deal and 'the most magnificent offer ever yet made for a novel', as George Lewes noted. George Eliot thought that this was too high and asked the publisher to reduce it.

© British Library

Portrait of George Eliot by Sir Frederic Burton. Painted at a time when she was widely revered and celebrated as the leading author of her day, Eliot appears serene and thoughtful. Her recurring lack of self-confidence can perhaps be detected in the slight tilt of her head. Her calm and penetrating gaze is clearly conveyed and we pick up a sense of her empathy, which made men queue up to sit beside her at her tea parties and admit with some surprise that they had fallen in love with her. This painting hung in George Lewes's study.
© National Portrait Gallery

the first hearing is over. It will be a nervous hour for our Pew though we hear that he acquits himself with as much ease & collectedness as if he had been used to it all his Life.

It was a tense moment. Perhaps Jane Austen worried that in the congregation there might be aggrieved customers of the bank who had lost their savings, but Henry gave a polished performance and all was well.

After the bankruptcy, Austen's attitude to money shifted decisively. Retrieved from the shelves of Richard Crosby, the thirteen-year-old manuscript of *Susan* was now hers to edit. The original manuscript has been lost, so it is impossible to know what final changes she made, but Austen certainly had to change the name of the heroine from Susan to Catherine Morland. It seems too much of a coincidence that the hero had already been called Henry. In this highly fraught time when she wanted to show the utmost support for her brother who was reinventing himself as a church curate, I suspect that she also changed the name of the fine young hero who is embarking on a career in the church to Henry. Henry Tilney is an exemplary hero who will make a model vicar. More than that, he stands up to his mercenary, bullying father and proposes to the impoverished Catherine Morland because he loves her. Catherine will make a charming if rather ditzy parish wife.

Inevitably, money plays a crucial role in the plot. When Henry's tyrannical father General Tilney first hears from John Thorpe that Catherine is a rich heiress, he invites her to Northanger Abbey. Absurdly, General Tilney is taken in by the delusional John Thorpe, a serial liar who was simply boasting about Catherine because he himself entertained romantic hopes for her. When General Tilney meets him again this time, bruised by his rejection by Catherine,

Thorpe tells him that Catherine's family is poor: 'They were in fact a necessitous family, numerous too almost beyond example, by no means respected in their neighbourhood; a forward bragging race.' Horrified by his mistake, General Tilney rushes back to Northanger Abbey and sends Catherine home in disgrace. Just when Catherine is at her lowest ebb and her mother has scolded her ('you always were a sad little shatter-brained creature'), Henry Tilney is announced. Henry has come with just one question on his mind that he is burning to ask – and of course, Catherine accepts him. *Northanger Abbey* is a resoundingly upbeat and life-affirming message that wealth and poverty, or even bankruptcy, are two sides of the same coin – life and love are to be enjoyed and celebrated whether you are rich or poor.

Austen might have made a few such personal changes to *Susan* in light of the bankruptcy, but that manuscript was otherwise completed, and after gathering dust on Richard Crosby's shelves for thirteen years it was ready to go. For the rest of 1816, she was focused upon her next novel, which was to become *Persuasion*. This time, Austen presents wealth very differently. The fortunes and finances of the Elliot family dominate the story. In her earlier books, the wealthy characters stayed wealthy and their money was presented as permanent. There is no concept that Darcy, Bingley, Colonel Brandon or Mr Knightley could conceivably speculate or lose their money. Heroines might aspire to marrying them and inheritances might be withheld by capricious parents or frustrated by rich relations living too long, but the money itself was safe capital and was invested at the prevailing rate of 5 per cent to provide a steady income. In the shocking aftermath of Henry's bankruptcy, Austen presents money with a totally different slant. She now understood more about Henry's white-knuckle ride as a banker, and she might have looked more critically at some of his debtors – like Lord Moira – and wondered at their wild swings of fortune which had caused Austen & Maunde's collapse and lost the family so much money.

Ultimately, *Persuasion* is a story about risk. Austen identifies and explores risk both in terms of fortune and finance, and equally in terms of love. For the first time, she presents an aristocratic family with a magnificent house, the sort of family who would have appeared impregnable in her earlier novels, as facing imminent bankruptcy. Sir Walter Elliot has to take the drastic action of renting out Kellynch Hall to restore his finances. Money is now presented as much more fluid, a powerful current that can sweep family fortunes both upwards and downwards. Money has left families like the Elliots and is now owned by people who have made their fortunes themselves. The new tenant of Kellynch Hall is the down to earth Admiral Croft, who has made his fortune in the Royal Navy. He is a no-nonsense man and the first thing he does in Kellynch Hall is to remove all the many mirrors – he has money, but no vanity. There is also another naval officer who is about to reappear in the neighbourhood: Captain Wentworth. Eight years earlier as a young officer setting out on his career, Frederick Wentworth had fallen in love with Sir Walter's daughter Anne. With some temerity he had proposed to her, but because he had no money or social standing Anne had been persuaded to reject him. That was eight years ago, when Anne was only nineteen. Now with a fortune earned from capturing French and Spanish ships, Frederick has been promoted to Captain Wentworth. Does Anne still love him? Will he even remember her? At twenty-seven is Anne just too old? Rising to answer these questions and combining love with money, the plot is sprung.

Admiral and Mrs Croft set the background for this new theme of risk, which combines the emotional with the financial. Unlike

Anne Elliot, who held back from marrying a young officer, Mrs Croft made an emotional commitment. During Admiral Croft's various postings, they survived tempestuous times together and with her by his side he made his fortune. Mrs Croft has sailed with her husband across the Atlantic four times, and she has also gone to Lisbon, Gibraltar and even India. When asked if she had ever felt unwell, she retorts that the only time was when her husband, then the young Captain Croft, was in the North Sea and she was left behind on shore. With her earlier failure to accept the then junior officer Wentworth's marriage proposal, Anne had baulked at embracing similar risk. The clear message of Anne's rebirth from the state of virtual paralysis which she had inhabited since she rejected Captain Wentworth is the imperative to bounce back and embrace risk. If grasped in this way, as Mrs Croft has done, then not only love but life fulfilment will follow and, true to Austen's core desires, also a healthy fortune.

Mrs Croft sums up this new zeitgeist: 'We none of us expect to be in calm waters all our days.'

As love and fortune are successfully combined, *Persuasion* reads as a message of hope. It is a message of hope for Henry that he can rise again from his bankruptcy; I also read it as a message of hope for Jane Austen herself. By showing how her oldest heroine can rekindle her youth and attract Captain Wentworth, with whom she can unite to face a risky world, Austen might be reassuring herself that no matter how ill she was beginning to feel, she too would recover her looks and her health. She had only recently left London where she had enjoyed dinner parties with Charles Haden, and she may well have wanted to believe that all this was possible again. If Anne Elliot could do it, then perhaps some of that magic could rub off on the author who created her.

* * *

George Eliot had a completely different relationship with money from Jane Austen, one which stemmed from her earlier life as Mary Ann Evans. Unlike Austen, who scrimped and saved so that she could buy ribbons and trimmings for her bonnets, Mary Ann was uninterested in fashion. She was reluctant to make a fuss of herself, determined not to attract attention to her appearance and tended to focus on her academic reading. As she grew older and moved to London, Mary Ann arrived as a freelance journalist, then – as now – a notoriously precarious, low-paid existence and not one for someone looking to make serious money. Mary Ann was more interested in participating in London literary life than earning *pewter*. When she was together with Lewes, they funded their early life by muddling through with income from their journalism and Lewes's own published books, such as *Goethe* and *Seaside Studies*.

'The Fortunes of Amos Barton' was the title of Eliot's first story. Although in this context, 'fortunes' had little financial association and related to Barton's life story, it did raise the question of money with Eliot both because it provided an immediate commission of fifty guineas – significantly more than her magazine articles paid – and it was an instant critical success. This clearly made them both pause and think. Eliot wrote to the publisher John Blackwood to acknowledge the debt she felt:

> Your letter has proved to me that the generous editor and publisher – generous both in word and in deed – who makes the author's path smooth and easy is something more than a pleasant tradition. I am very sensitive to the merits of cheques for 50 guineas, but I am still more sensitive to that cordial appreciation

which is a guarantee to me that my work was worth doing for its own sake.

Each December, Eliot would sum up the personal events of the year in her journal. As 1857 drew to a close, she looked back with self-effacing pride on the ongoing success of Lewes's writing. She noted that his *History of Philosophy* had been reprinted and that he had written *Seaside Studies*, which had been accepted by Blackwood 'and [is] now on the verge of being published with bright prospects'. She took pleasure in noting that '*Goethe* has passed into its third German edition and best of all, G's head is well'.

Finally, she turned to herself: 'I have written the *Scenes of Clerical Life* – my first book; and though we are uncertain still whether it will be a success as a separate publication, I have had much sympathy from my readers in Blackwood.' Touchingly, she does not imagine her future success in financial terms but compares it to planting primroses: 'I feel a deep satisfaction in having done a bit of faithful work that will perhaps remain like a primrose root in the hedgerow and gladden and chasten human hearts in years to come.'

In the final sentence, she slipped in: 'I am writing my new novel.' The new novel – her first full-length work – was *Adam Bede*. Just two months later in February 1858, Eliot noted in her journal:

'I gave Blackwood the MS of my new novel, to the end of the second scene in the wood. He opened it, read the first page and smiling said: "This will do."'

'This will do' were the exact same words he had written to Lewes in his response to reading *Amos Barton*: 'I am happy to say that I think your friend's reminiscences of Clerical Life will do.' Back then he had been struck by the brilliant introduction to Shepperton Church and its vicar Amos Barton:

'The walls are as smooth and innutrient as the summit of the Rev Amos Barton's head after ten years of baldness and supererogatory soap.'

In February 1858, the first words of *Adam Bede* that Blackwood would have read when he opened the manuscript were this arresting image:

'With a single drop of ink for a mirror, the Egyptian sorcerer undertakes to reveal to any chance comer far-reaching visions of the past' followed by the promise: 'This is what I undertake to do for you, reader.'

John Blackwood was the first in a long line of readers who gave themselves up to the magic held in the drop of ink at the end of Eliot's pen and the far-reaching visions of the past that she conjures up with it. As an experienced publisher, he must have immediately recognised the genius of the novel. His deliberate understatement 'this will do' was proved right. Sure enough, *Adam Bede* was a stunning success. In its first year alone, it was reprinted seven times and sold over 16,000 copies. This was the moment when Eliot's earnings took off.

Yet despite her bestseller status, Eliot constantly suffered from a corrosive self-doubt. As an author, she was always mindful that nothing was created until it was written down. It is salutary to read her comment in a letter to Blackwood as she struggled to write *Middlemarch*:

'I am thoroughly comforted as to the half of the work which is already written; but there remains the terror about the *un*written.'

As her career progressed, rather than finding her writing and her outward life easier to manage, Eliot suffered increasingly greater depths of despondency and self-doubt. Her early success provided her with no assurance that she would continue to succeed; indeed, the fear of failure grew with each novel. The self-deprecation and wry humour of her early journal entries gave way to extensive crises of self-confidence. Perhaps the ultimate cause for her sense of despondency and corrosive self-doubt was the fear she expressed to Blackwood in her letter of 11 September 1866:

'And yet I sicken again with despondency under the sense that the most carefully written books lie, both outside and inside people's minds, deep undermost in a heap of trash.'

Happily for Eliot, both Lewes and Blackwood grew to understand how best to help alleviate this depression. Both men appreciated the colossal earning power of each book, and their care ensured that these novels were delivered. Lewes was available to support her on a daily basis, and although he busied himself with many other journalistic and literary endeavours, he was well aware of the implications there would be of any failure and he managed her self-confidence and her finances flawlessly. Acting as her constant sounding-board, his judgement proved infallible. Careful never to trespass upon her correspondence with Blackwood, Lewes encouraged her with each new work. It was as if he had taken each of Charlotte Brontë's earlier criticisms of him and reinvented himself.

Over her writing career, Eliot was to earn more money than any other woman in the country, enough to rent and buy a succession of large houses, to travel extensively around the spa towns of Europe and to look after Lewes and his family. Eliot also paid for his wife Agnes and her growing family – Agnes was still with the impecunious Thornton Hunt and she went on to have eight children in all.

Despite her steeply growing royalties, Eliot's attitude to the money she received never really changed. She remained dispassionate, and after a few initial tense negotiations she was invariably generous in her lifelong correspondence with Blackwood, who provided her royalties. She passed the management of her finances to Lewes, perhaps because she was focusing upon her writing or perhaps because that was the traditional role that a Victorian husband was expected to play, and more than anything she insisted that George was her 'husband' and rejoiced in that definition.

The only sense of any disagreement between them came when she was writing *Romola*. Lewes was discussing possible terms with Blackwood when a rival publisher, Smith, Elder & Co. (who had published *Jane Eyre*), made a dramatic unsolicited offer. Without even reading the manuscript, Smith, Elder & Co. offered £10,000 for the copyright of *Romola*. In Victorian times, this was a life-changing amount of money. To provide some context, it was more than Charles Dickens had ever been offered. Today it would be worth around £1 million, broadly what a top international author or film star would receive. As Lewes noted in his journal, it was 'the most magnificent offer ever yet made for a novel'. But for Eliot, who essentially viewed money as a moral issue – she wanted money fairly to represent the work which earned it – it was simply too much. To Lewes's consternation, she asked him to turn the amount down before accepting a reduced offer. She explained herself to Blackwood: 'I don't want the world to give me anything for my books except money enough to save me from the temptation to write only for money,' and whether slightly boasting or just to note the fact, she wrote to Sara Hennell: 'I have refused the highest price ever offered for fiction'.

After *Romola* was published by Smith, Elder & Co. in 1862, Eliot returned to publish her last three novels (*Felix Holt*, *Middlemarch* and *Daniel Deronda*) with Blackwood. She could have sold her novels for more money to other publishers, but for her money was not the driving imperative. Unlike Jane Austen's determination to earn *pewter*, which involved her chivvying John Murray and coming up to London to arrange dedications and create some buzz around the publications of her books, after Eliot delivered each manuscript she and Lewes would immediately leave for the Continent to escape from the reviews. With her fragile self-confidence, Eliot was vulnerable to criticism and so Lewes would intercept any reviews to stop them from upsetting her. Eliot explained how it worked to her friend Elma Stuart:

> Mr Lewes carefully protects me from reading about myself, and as soon as I know that there is an article on me in any periodical I wait till it is cut out before I take up the print for other reading. But Mr Lewes reads everything about me that comes his way.

Eliot's correspondence with Blackwood centred less on her royalties and more on her self-confidence and her ability to write. Eliot was not oblivious to the importance of earning her living, but she valued a deeper relationship with a publisher and this lay at the heart of the support that Blackwood provided for her. After the soaring sales of *Adam Bede*, she wrote to him in May 1859:

> Thank you: first for acting with that fine integrity which makes part of my faith in you; secondly for the material sign of that integrity. I don't know which of those two things I care for most – that people should act nobly towards me, or that I should get honest money. I certainly care a great deal for the money as I suppose all anxious minds do that love independence and have been brought up to think debt and begging the two deepest dishonours short of crime.

* * *

FORTUNES AND FINANCE

George Eliot's personal life was financially secure. I believe that, like so many of her heroines who chose a future life of poverty rather than wealth, Eliot would have been truly happy with whatever level of money she earned, as long as she felt that it was fair, and as long as she and George were together. As it happened, she could afford to travel to Germany, Switzerland, Italy and France and she could rent or buy any house she chose, whether in the suburbs of London, Surrey or their final mansion on Cheyne Walk in Chelsea overlooking the River Thames.

In her novels, though, money is a much more threatening force. Like Austen, Eliot uses money as a vital accelerator of her plots. But where in Jane Austen's novels money provides the bedrock of a happy future and all her heroines end up with wealthy husbands, George Eliot's characters find money difficult to trace and secure. Many of her heroines ultimately choose a path that leads them away from money. In Eliot's fictional world, money is not as simple or as certain as a reward to cement a marriage. Money does not mean steady capital and steady income; rather, it is mercurial and elusive. Money might have concealed origins and present a trap to ensnare them, or most alarmingly it might vanish without warning.

In *Middlemarch*, the town banker Nicholas Bulstrode at first appears to be a devoutly Christian bastion of civic life, but when his wealth is revealed to have come from the widow of a London pawnbroker who may have dealt in stolen goods, his money becomes toxic. His offer of money to Will Ladislaw is thrown back in his face. Separately, Silas Marner only leaves his cottage door unlocked for a moment, but it is enough for Dunstan to slip in and steal his life savings of gold coins.

For Eliot, wealth can be won and lost in an instant. In the opening scene of *Daniel Deronda*, Gwendolen is gambling in the casino.

At first she wins, but when her luck turns she obstinately stays until she has lost all her winnings. When she returns to her hotel bedroom, a letter from her mother is waiting for her. It is a bombshell:

'Grapnell & Co. have failed for a million and we are totally ruined.'

Gwendolen knows exactly what she must do – she takes her turquoise necklace to the pawn shop and heads home to secure a rich husband.

Romola opens on the morning of 9 April 1492 with a shipwreck survivor waking up on the streets of Florence. Sleeping rough, Tito is in possession of just three things: his ring, his charm and his secret. Later that morning, he is taken to the barber's shop and begins his climb in Florentine society. Within days, Tito is lifted into a position of power and the prospective wealth of marrying Romola.

Even in those cases where wealth is secure, it can still paralyse its owners. In *Middlemarch*, the dying miser Peter Featherstone is grimly enjoying the queue of hard-up relatives downstairs who are vying to inherit from him. He has written two wills and he treasures his secret – he intends to burn one of them. But he leaves it too late. He cannot get out of bed to reach the desk where the wills are so he dies impotently clutching his moneybox in bed with him, viciously trying to throw his stick at Mary because she refuses to put his second will in the fire. Featherstone's deathbed scene is reminiscent of medieval morality Flemish paintings, where misers die surrounded by their strong boxes and with devils snapping at their souls. For George Eliot, money was always a moral issue.

When money is expected, it often fails to materialise. Fred Vincy's expectations are dashed over Featherstone's will and the knock-on effect is that Caleb Garth's debt is called in and he can no longer pay for his children's education. Even when characters try to give money away, as with Dorothea's idealistic charitable plans to fund a new hospital, problems arise and politics interfere. Money is no guarantee of happiness and even when provided in comfortable excess as it is to Romola, Mrs Transome, Dorothea or Featherstone, money is at best a source of worry that leads to unfulfilled ideals. At worst, it is a trap and a burden.

George Eliot's happiest characters are those who explicitly turn down the offer of money in favour of love and family, as do Dorothea, Eppie and Esther. A large crowd turns out to witness Esther's marriage to the penniless radical Felix Holt and the bride who turned down her inheritance. Their neighbour Mr Wace says to his wife:

'It's wonderful how things go through you – you don't know how. I feel somehow as if I believed more in everything that's good.'

* * *

Despite George Eliot's radical approach to fortune and finance, the advances and royalties for her novels made her extremely wealthy. If there had been a *Sunday Times Rich List* in the 1860s, Mary Ann Evans would have topped the list of women earning the highest income (the richest woman of property would have been Queen Victoria). Way beyond her fond imagination that she had simply 'planted a primrose root in the hedgerow which would gladden some human hearts', George Eliot became a literary superstar.

Eventually George Eliot's wealth and success bought her way back into Victorian society and Lewes was able to arrange Sunday soirées where guests (mainly men but increasingly also some women) would queue up in order to sit beside her. Queen Victoria let it be known that she admired *Adam Bede* and had commissioned two paintings to depict scenes from the novel. Fortune and finance worked their magic in Victorian society and brushed over Eliot's earlier radical and scandalous relationship with Lewes. When George Lewes died, Eliot promptly married the only other man in her life, John Cross. In a perfect blend of money and love, he was her financial advisor.

Jane Austen's financial reckoning looked very different. As her health deteriorated towards the end of her life, she drew up a final measure of what she had earned as an author. She titled it 'Profit from my Novels over and above the £600 in the Navy Fives' and recorded her earnings since March 1816. The 'Navy Fives' were government bonds with a 5 per cent coupon. Her invested capital of £600 had provided three coupons since March 1816 (the coupon was paid half-yearly) that accounted for £45 in her new Hoare's bank account, which she had opened after Henry's bankruptcy. She notes the £13.7s of royalties from *Mansfield Park* as 'remaining in Henrietta Street', which represents the money that had been lost with Austen & Maunde. Additional profits from her other books were put at £71.6s, but this is somewhat confusing because these appear to be profits since March 1816 so she does not account for earlier income which had either been spent along the way or – if deposited at Austen & Maunde – lost in the bankruptcy.

Whereas George Eliot ended up marrying her financial advisor, Jane Austen's financial advisor was her brother Henry, who as we know went bust. Perhaps scarred by his financial ruin, in his preface to the posthumous editions of *Northanger Abbey* and *Persuasion* Henry Austen tried to explain how his sister Jane had become an author:

'She became an authoress entirely from taste and inclination. Neither the hope of fame nor profit mixed with her early motives.'

Sounding as if he is reading from somebody else's biography, this was the start of the misinformation which the Austen family would sustain about Jane. From everything I have read about Jane Austen, I believe that she emphatically liked fame and profit. I think that she would have ridiculed Henry for these comments as merrily as she ridiculed James Clarke's suggestion to write about the House of Saxe-Coburg. She might have retorted to him as she did to their niece Fanny:

'Tho' I like praise as well as anybody, I like what Edward calls *pewter* too.'

Over the next 200 years, the sales of Jane Austen's six novels and their royalties would have represented *pewter* beyond her wildest aspirations.

By popular vote conducted by the Bank of England, in 2017 Jane Austen's portrait was reproduced on the back of the British £10 note, a perfect combination of fortune and finance with her literature.

I like to imagine how much Jane Austen would have enjoyed sitting opposite Richard Crosby in his publishing office at Stationer's Court and being able to answer his request to buy back her manuscript of *Susan* for the original £10. Unable to keep a poker face, I see the smile playing at the corners of her mouth and spreading across her face as she pushes the £10 note across the table towards him. As he picks up the £10 and turns it over, she leans forward and shares her secret:

'You see Mr Crosby, I'm not really Mrs Ashton Dennis. I hope you like the cap.'

* * *

CHAPTER 5

GENTLEMEN AND TRADE

Both Jane Austen and George Eliot invent characters who perfectly capture the spirit of their times. The changes in nineteenth-century society from the Regency era of the 1800s to the Victorian period of the 1850s are unerringly reflected by the changes in the choices of their leading characters.

With the exception of *Romola*, which is set in Renaissance Florence, all of their novels are rooted in England. Both authors highlight and explore the divisions across English society, where they unpick the dynamic shift in the balance of power between the older inherited wealth and authority of 'gentlemen' and the growing prosperity and influence of those in 'trade'. A great deal of the narrative tension derives from the complex way in which these two powerful forces both attract and depend upon each other but equally clash and repulse each other.

As the respective daughters of a Regency gentleman vicar and a consummate Victorian tradesman, Austen and Eliot spin their stories from the fabric of their own lives. Both authors create drama by placing their characters across the spectrum of society. The headline story might tell how these men and women meet, fall in love and try to bridge the gulfs that divide them. The deeper narratives, though, lie within the portrayal of a shifting society where every relationship, every decision and every intended action is under pressure, questioned and redefined – this is as true for a recently rich Regency family trying to organise a dinner party in Highbury as for a newly qualified doctor trying to open a hospital in Middlemarch.

In Jane Austen's Regency world, the focus is almost exclusively upon those who are 'Gentlemen'. Austen's own family certainly considered themselves of 'Gentlemen' class and her fictional worlds keep within this boundary. Across her six novels there is barely a male character with a speaking part below this defined rank. While wealth is an important attribute for a gentleman it is not the absolute definition. Very little is known about her disabled brother George Austen, who lived in a nursing home all his life, but when he died in 1838 his death certificate carried the description 'Gentleman'.

In fact, there was some dissension within the Austen family about their social standing. Sometime after Austen died, her great-nephew Edward Austen-Leigh asked his cousin Fanny Knight to contribute some memories of their Aunt Jane for the biography that he was writing. To the everlasting dismay of both Edward Austen-Leigh and generations of Jane Austen fans, Fanny replied:

> Aunt Jane from various circumstances was not so refined as she ought to have been from her talent, and if she had lived 50 years later she would have been in many respects more suitable to our more refined tastes. They were not rich and the people around with whom they chiefly mixed were not at all high bred or in short anything more than mediocre, and they of course, tho' superior in mental powers and cultivation, were on the same level as far as refinement goes – but I think in later life their intercourse

with Mrs Knight (who was very fond and kind to them) improved them both and Aunt Jane was too clever not to put aside all possible signs of 'common-ness' (if such an expression is allowable) and teach herself to be more refined, at least in intercourse with people in general.

Fanny went on to conclude:

Both the Aunts [Cassandra and Jane] were brought up in the most complete ignorance of the World and its ways (I mean as to Fashion etc.) and if it had not been for Papa's marriage which brought them into Kent and the kindness of Mrs Knight who used often to have one or the other staying with her, they would have been tho' not less clever and agreeable in themselves, very much below par as to good Society and its ways. If you hate all this, I beg your pardon, but I felt it at my pen's end, and it chose to come along and speak its truth.

This account feels genuine and there is a truth to the expression 'I felt it at my pen's end'. As Fanny anticipated, many Jane Austen readers did indeed 'hate all this' and ever since they have tried to ignore, excuse or refute this account, citing Fanny's old age or the Victorian principles of 1869 that surely made her too snobbish for her opinion to be taken seriously. Edward Austen-Leigh left this commentary out of his 1870 biography, presumably because it tarnished the image he wanted to project of his 'blameless' Aunt Jane. Personally, I prefer the idea that Aunt Jane was not as refined as she might have seemed. It moves her a little closer to the Mrs Norris figure who was so admired by the Austen family and it might have helped to make her analysis of social rank even sharper because there is nobody who understands and unpicks the nuances of social hierarchy more adroitly than someone who was sitting just beneath the class they are scrutinising.

Famously, in *Pride and Prejudice* Lady Catherine de Bourgh tries to pull rank on Elizabeth Bennet when she asks what is to stop Darcy, one of the richest men in Jane Austen's novels and with Pemberley and his independent fortune perhaps the ultimate 'gentleman' (that is until Elizabeth corrects his manners), from marrying her own daughter. Lady Catherine seeks to reinforce the social hierarchy and tries to warn Elizabeth off with a rhetorical question:

> What is to divide them? The upstart pretensions of a young woman without family, connections, or fortune. Is this to be endured! But it must not, shall not be. If you were sensible of your own good, you would not wish to quit the sphere in which you have been brought up.

Elizabeth tartly points out to Lady Catherine that this is not a point of difference:

'In marrying your nephew, I should not consider myself as quitting that sphere. He is a gentleman; I am a gentleman's daughter. So far we are equal.'

Elizabeth's indignation rings true – and Jane Austen could have said this of herself. Through these words we might even sense her own relationship with her father and some of the time they might have spent together in his library. Reluctantly and with bad grace, the indignant aristocrat has to concede this point:

'True, you are a gentleman's daughter. But who was your mother? Who are your uncles and aunts? Do not imagine me ignorant of their condition.'

Earlier, Elizabeth has been anxious about her mother's relations and how Darcy would interact with them, but the walk along the trout stream at Pemberley with Darcy enthusiastically pointing out the rising trout and inviting her uncle to come back to fish for them shows that Darcy can bridge this gap. Elizabeth's uncle Edward Gardiner is in 'trade'; he lives in London within sight of his warehouses. We do not hear what these warehouses contain – textiles, machinery, sugar, wool? Imports from the Caribbean? Is slave labour involved? Austen is silent on this. Perhaps in the glow of Darcy's attraction for Elizabeth, Edward Gardiner passes as a gentleman. He is the only character of any significance across all Austen's novels who is in trade. All the other main male characters, whether rich or poor, are classified as gentlemen. Austen is careful to illustrate that the real issue is not their wealth, because that can be provided to them by marriage or inheritance, but their manners and ultimately their morals, which are the true currency of the gentleman. Initially drawn to and fro between Darcy and Wickham and too easily hoodwinked by Wickham's plausible patter, Elizabeth fails to distinguish a true gentleman from a rogue. However, whatever mistakes she makes she is nevertheless confident that she herself is a 'gentleman's daughter'. This cast-iron certainty is sufficiently powerful to weather Lady Catherine's criticism of the rest of the Bennet family's compromised background and the scandal surrounding Lydia's elopement with Wickham:

'Are the shades of Pemberley to be thus polluted?' Lady Catherine scornfully (and ridiculously) laments.

Indeed, they are.

Elizabeth is stringently observant about the necessary manners of a 'gentleman'. In Darcy's first spectacularly misconceived marriage proposal, she pinpoints his social blunder: 'You are mistaken,

Mr Darcy, if you suppose that the mode of your declaration affected me in any other way than as it spared me the concern which I might have felt in refusing you had you behaved in a more gentleman-like manner.'

It is this criticism that he had not behaved like a gentleman rather than the rejection itself that stings Darcy: 'She saw him start at this, but he said nothing.'

Once they have become happily engaged, a gentleman and a gentleman's daughter, they later reflect on this criticism and joke about it:

> The recollection of what I then said, of my conduct, my manners, my expressions during the whole of it, is now, and has been many months, inexpressibly painful to me. Your reproof, so well applied, I shall never forget: 'Had you behaved in a more gentleman-like manner.' Those were your words. You know not, you can scarcely conceive, how they have tortured me.

Like Elizabeth Bennet, all of Jane Austen's heroines must discover for themselves that some gentlemen are true; others are false. Some display manners that are genuine; others are deceitful and treacherous. Some gentlemen have money; others need it. Throughout all her novels, various lovers must navigate these obstacles to bridge the gap between subtly different class layers and different expectations to secure their marriage partners. The risk surrounding these moves, the antics of competing rivals and the resistance put up by society opposition to these changes add tension and suspense to the unfolding drama. Only someone who can correctly interpret the manners, morals and sincerity of each Jane Austen character can predict where the storylines will lead.

The plot of *Emma* hinges on Harriet Smith, an illegitimate girl placed by her unknown father at Mrs Goddard's boarding school. Harriet is 'the natural daughter of somebody' and when she finishes at the school, the 'somebody' pays for her to stay on with Mrs Goddard as a parlour-boarder, an arrangement which can only be finite. Described as very pretty, with a beauty that 'happened to be of a sort which Emma particularly admired' (presumably because it contrasts with her own), Harriet is 'short, plump and fair'. Aged seventeen, 'sweet', 'docile' and with a 'fine bloom', in fact Harriet is in a highly vulnerable position – she is on the cusp of the marriage market and her choice will define her future. With no family, no money and few prospects, Harriet cannot afford to make a mistake. *Emma* opens on the wedding day of Emma's governess Miss Taylor. Miss Taylor has left Emma's home at Hartfield and successfully secured her place in Highbury society by marrying Mr Weston. Her absence creates a vacuum, which Emma decides to fill by adopting Harriet as her companion. This is an undefined role somewhere between a friend and a protegee, and it provides Emma with undue influence.

With the approval of Mr Knightley, who is the major landowner in Highbury, Robert Martin, one of his well-respected tenant farmers, proposes to Harriet. Having reviewed his farming accounts to ensure that Robert can afford to marry, Mr Knightley agrees that this is a very satisfactory proposal for Harriet which would secure her place in society. Left to her own devices, Harriet would have happily accepted him. However, now in a position of influence, Emma decides (in the absence of any evidence) that Harriet is a 'gentleman's daughter' and should therefore marry into a different social circle. Mr Knightley and Emma fundamentally disagree over this potentially life-changing move which has repercussions for all the characters in the novel. When he hears that Harriet has refused

Robert Martin's marriage proposal, Mr Knightley is astonished and outraged. 'Red with surprise and displeasure' and in 'tall indignation', he exclaims of Harriet: 'She is a greater simpleton than I ever believed her. What is the foolish girl about?' Mr Knightley soon understands that Emma has been pulling the strings and their ensuing argument sheds light on the complex layers of social rank that recur throughout Jane Austen's novels, revealing how her characters often find themselves on opposite sides of society's fault-lines.

Emma argues: 'Mr Martin may be the richest of the two, but he is undoubtedly her inferior as to rank in society. The sphere in which she moves is much above his. It would be a degradation.'

There is wishful thinking by Emma and in due course she is proved wrong when Harriet's father is revealed to be in trade, but even taking Emma's argument at face value Mr Knightley indignantly refutes it:

'A degradation to illegitimacy and ignorance, to be married to a respectable, intelligent gentleman-farmer!'

Emma pushes back:

'That she is a gentleman's daughter is indubitable to me ... She is superior to Mr Robert Martin.'

Emma overplays her hand, making a remark which will later return to haunt her:

'Oh! Harriet may pick and choose! Were you yourself ever to marry, she is the very woman for you.'

Mr Knightley and Emma's argument illustrates some of the hairline cracks which run through the definition of a gentleman. Robert Martin is a 'gentleman farmer' according to Mr Knightley but a 'yeoman farmer' according to Emma. Emma's claims that Harriet is a 'gentleman's daughter' are speculative, but she sticks to her argument that Harriet is now above the station of a farmer:

'[Harriet] knows now what gentlemen are; and nothing but a gentleman in education and manner has any chance with Harriet.'

In the absence of proof, Mr Knightley explodes:

'Nonsense, errant nonsense, as ever was talked! Robert Martin's manners have sense, sincerity, and good humour to recommend them; and his mind has more true gentility than Harriet Smith could understand.'

Mr Knightley is concerned that both Harriet's and Robert Martin's lives will be ruined by what he sees as Emma's social engineering. His perceptive verdict is that:

'Vanity working on a weak head produces every sort of mischief.'

To Emma's eventual mortification, Mr Knightley's warning that 'you have been no friend to Harriet Smith, Emma' is of course proved right. The 'mischief' of Emma's social engineering will engulf everyone in the novel and causes all the twists and turns of the plot. In *Emma*, Austen builds upon the more obvious class distinctions of her earlier novels and seems to delight in creating tiny sub-classes of society. Many of these fractional differences are now opaque to us, but Emma becomes obsessed by them. As each marriageable person is sucked into Emma's matchmaking schemes, she ties herself in knots trying to unpick their social standing and their manners so that she can set about trying to orchestrate the right pairing.

The first casualty is Mr Elton, a gentleman vicar who is identified by Emma as a suitable husband for Harriet. Mr Elton, who has to marry into money and therefore cannot conceive of marrying Harriet, understandably assumes that it is Emma herself who is sending signals to him. Fuelled by 'Mr Weston's good wine', Mr Elton deliriously proposes to Emma. Horrified at the misunderstanding and smug with her private wealth of £30,000, Emma feels insulted that he has so egregiously overstepped the social boundaries. Mr Elton in turn feels insulted that Emma ever thought that he could address Harriet. Stung and bruised, Mr Elton has to leave Highbury to find his bride.

The next partner under scrutiny is Frank Churchill, Mr Weston's son. Frank has been adopted by the wealthy and otherwise childless Churchill family and has taken their surname just as Austen's brother Edward was adopted by the wealthy Knight family, took their surname and inherited their estates. When Frank eventually arrives in Highbury society, he is widely feted and considered to be a gentleman. Emma is rather more attracted to him than she expected. However, watching his behaviour closely Mr Knightley suspects that Frank does not have the manners of a gentleman. Perhaps envious of Emma's initial attraction to Frank, Mr Knightley concludes: 'Just the trifling, silly fellow I took him for.'

The role of 'gentleman' is so constantly and minutely appraised that when describing the scene of the ball at The Crown inn, Austen even invents a new definition: 'Now the highest purpose was to accommodate a whist club established among the gentlemen and half-gentlemen of the place.' The gently mocking term 'half-gentlemen' shows how the social nuances are becoming increasingly incremental and verging on the ludicrous.

Even minor characters such as the Coles family create a frisson of uncertainty. Although they have made their money in trade, they are now on entertaining terms with the gentlemen of Highbury: 'The Coles had been settled some years in Highbury, and were very good sort of people – friendly, liberal and unpretending; but, on the other hand, they were of low origin, in trade, and only moderately genteel.'

In an example of how scrambled and confused the social order is becoming in her mind, Emma desires an invitation to their supper party but only so she can decline it. This is on the grounds that 'the Coles were very respectable in their way, but they ought to be taught that it was not for them to arrange the terms on which the superior families would visit them'.

As Emma pursues her quest to manipulate Harriet into a contrived position in society, she loses her moral compass. Her flawed thinking grows increasingly entrenched and blind. When Emma arrives at the Coles's supper party, she sees that Mr Knightley has arrived in his carriage and she welcomes this: 'This is coming as you should do … like a gentleman.'

She then congratulates Mr Knightley upon how he enters a room:

'Now you have nothing to try for. You are not afraid of being supposed ashamed. You are not striving to look taller than anyone else. Now I shall really be very happy to walk into the same room with you.'

'Nonsensical girl' was his reply, but not at all in anger.

Despite his smile, Mr Knightley's judgement of Emma is correct: she is 'nonsensical', because, blinded by her determination to re-interpret the rules of society, Emma has failed to appreciate the real reason Mr Knightley has taken his carriage. It is not for social display, but so that on a cold winter evening – Christmas Eve – he can provide Miss Bates and Jane Fairfax with a safe and comfortable ride to the Coles. This is the action of a 'true' gentleman and contrasts sharply with the selfish Frank Churchill, who is among those who demand that Jane Fairfax sing another song despite the risk to her throat. Again, it is Mr Knightley who takes control of the situation to protect Jane:

> Mr Knightley grew angry. 'That fellow', said he, indignantly, 'thinks of nothing but showing off his own voice. This must not be.' And touching Miss Bates, who at that moment passed near – 'Miss Bates, are you mad, to let your niece sing herself hoarse in this manner? Go and interfere. They have no mercy upon her.'

Emma fails to see the difference between these two apparent gentlemen. As Emma is progressively fooled by Frank Churchill, she grows less gentlemanly herself. She begins to lose her manners and becomes vindictive in her treatment of Jane Fairfax and of Miss Bates. At the Coles's dinner party, she mimics Miss Bates:

"'So kind and obliging! – but he had always been such a very kind neighbour!" and then fly off, through half a sentence, to her mother's old petticoat. "Not that it was such a very old petticoat either – for still it would last a great while."'

'For shame, Emma! Do not mimic her,' Mrs Weston chides.

In her folly, Emma sides with Frank Churchill and speculates cruelly that Jane Fairfax is enjoying a love affair with her friend's husband, Mr Dixon. Emma's treatment of Jane grows increasingly vicious, and Frank Churchill colludes with it to hide his secret engagement to Jane. When their engagement is finally revealed, Emma condemns this deception. She understands that Frank Churchill can never be a gentleman:

'I shall always think it a very abominable sort of proceeding. What has it been but a system of hypocrisy and deceit – espionage and treachery?'

By misconstruing the worlds of gentleman and trade and trying to change the natural order of Highbury society, Emma loses both her moral compass and her manners. When she only focuses upon Mrs Elton's flaws and fails to give her the respect which is due to her as the new vicar's wife, even her father rebukes her:

'My dear, you do not understand me. This is a matter of mere common politeness and good-breeding and has nothing to do with any encouragement to people to marry.'

Emma has crossed a line of manners and judgement which will later cause her great shame. Until she learns to recognise her true feelings and accept reality, she is lost in a moral maze. Her failure to distinguish between a true gentleman and a false one wreaks havoc in Highbury society. It is only when she acknowledges the truth of an emotional imperative ('Mr Knightley must marry no one but herself!') that she is redeemed and the rest of the plot falls into place. It is only when Harriet's background is revealed and she is 'proved to be the daughter of a tradesman, rich enough to afford her the comfortable maintenance which had ever been hers, and decent enough to have always wished for concealment' that Highbury society can finally revert to its natural order.

Amidst the densely packed debates about social definitions, occasional flashes of clear insight appear. At the Coles's dinner party, Austen shows how two aligned minds can cut through all the confusion and social tension if they reach out, listen and trust each other. As the guests emerge from their meal on Christmas Eve, they realise that heavy snow has been falling, which might prevent them from travelling home. There is gridlock because all the guests are paralysed in their differing social positions. Nobody can take a decision. In a triumph of brevity and speaking the same language as gentlemen, Emma and Mr Knightley turn to each other and cut across all the noise:

>   Mr Knightley and Emma settled it in a few brief sentences: thus –
>   'Your father will not be easy; why do not you go?'
>   'I am ready, if the others are.'
>   'Shall I ring the bell?'
>   'Yes, do.'
>   And the bell was rung.

In these four lines of dialogue, Austen shows two minds working perfectly together. For the first time, Emma and Mr Knightley are not correcting each other or arguing about class distinctions and manners; rather, they combine to be dynamic, decisive and pragmatic. They understand each other. This dialogue shows Emma at her best and opens the path to her marriage with Mr Knightley.

Until Emma can use such clear language and understand such simple truths, she is lost in a labyrinth of different class definitions and she continually misjudges character. The number of syllables in each line are progressively reduced as they cut out all the extraneous noise – the beat grows simpler and simpler, thirteen; nine; five (dropping by four syllables each line) until with the final two syllables, 'Yes, do,' it feels like a heartbeat.

Perfectly distilled, it reads like a marriage proposal.

* * *

Trade was socially unacceptable for Jane Austen, who ignored it for her fiction. Drawn from a country society that had its roots in the eighteenth century, Austen's characters include local landowners, vicars, officers either retired or on leave from the army or navy and young Regency squires vying to marry or inherit money with no intention of ever working beyond vaguely 'managing' an estate.

Despite her brother setting himself up as a banker, there are no bankers in her fiction and only fleeting references to lawyers. The doctors who attend are not given speaking roles, even if they might be enthusiastically quoted by Emma's father, Mr Woodhouse.

Jane Austen was on far firmer ground when it came to the higher classes. Any one of her leading men and women could easily have walked out of the dining room of one house in one novel and into the sitting room of another house in another novel and been instantly at home with the company they found. Colonel Brandon, Mr Darcy and Mr Knightley would have greeted each other with a firm handshake and recognised each other as the gentlemen they were. Keeping well apart from those genuine gentlemen, Willoughby, Wickham, John Thorpe and Henry Crawford would have recognised each other as the rogues they were, secretly sympathised with each other's skullduggery and coveted each other's curricles.

* * *

George Eliot, however, saw trade as central to society and therefore to her novels. Right from the opening scene of her first novel, *Adam Bede*, Eliot's focus is upon working men. We are taken straight into the carpenter's workshop where Adam is working. To heighten the sense of realism, we are given the date, 18 June 1799 (just when in real life Austen was starting to write about Darcy and Elizabeth), and as she immerses us in this scene of trade Eliot activates each of our senses: the smell of the pine planks, the touch of the soft wood shavings and the banter of the carpenters.

These are men at work. As she walked around her village, Austen herself would have passed by carpenters' workshops and also smelt the wood shavings and heard similar broad accents and Hampshire dialect around her, but she saw no glory in any of this and they form no part of her literary references. Throughout George Eliot's novels, the work of tradesmen is held up as an honourable human endeavour and consequently she casts them as the leading men. Eliot's heroes are Adam Bede, a carpenter; Maggie Tulliver, a miller's daughter; Silas Marner, a weaver; Caleb Garth and Fred Vincy, estate managers; Felix Holt, a watch repairer. None of these trades feature in Austen's work, but by the time of Eliot these tradesmen form the core of middle-class society and with the fast-changing technology of the nineteenth century, this section of society was growing in influence and power.

George Eliot draws the landowners and squires in a different light to her tradesmen. These gentlemen include Arthur Donnithorne, Sir James Chettam, Mr Brooke, Sir Maximus Debarry and Grandcourt, all of whom are at best amiable and vague and at worse seducers and bullies. This different perspective would partially have been driven by the changing time and society around her. Eliot was writing during the 1860s when the industrial revolution had dramatically shifted the economic power from the traditional landowning aristocracy to the new industrial and commercial classes. Manufacturers, merchants and professionals were amassing significant wealth through industry rather than through land ownership. Probably rather like her readers who were buying her novels in mass printed serialisations, Eliot has scant sympathy for the landed gentry. When Dorothea's uncle, the genial and easily distracted Mr Brooke, seeks public endorsement as a reforming MP in *Middlemarch*, he is ridiculed at the hustings. Mr Brooke's own land reforms are exposed as hopelessly inadequate and the condition of his own estate is lamentably dilapidated and poorly invested. In *Felix Holt*, the inheritance of Transome Court and its estate, which would have been a prize for any Jane Austen heroine, is at stake. Esther Lyon has a binary choice: she can either inherit Transome Court and become a wealthy lady with a country estate, or she can marry the impoverished Felix Holt. Eliot presents it as a cause for celebration that Esther chooses love in a Midlands town with an impoverished watch repairer over the prospect of a 'comfortable' life as a landowner.

Other estate owners cast a more ominous shadow. In *Daniel Deronda*, Henleigh Grandcourt is initially presented as a gentleman with magnificent estates who is the obvious match for Gwendolen. There is a warning when he is introduced and commands his 'friend' and *homme d'affaires* Thomas Lush to silence a howling dog and we later see him with Lush in his study. Without deigning to move, Grandcourt says:

'Oblige me by pushing that pen and paper here, will you?'

It is the all-encompassing mastery of a gentleman over his social junior:

'No thunderous, bullying superior could have exercised the imperious spell that Grandcourt did. Why, instead of being obeyed, he had never been told to go to a warmer place, was perhaps a mystery to those who found themselves obeying him.'

At first, Gwendolen is attracted to Grandcourt. She shamelessly covets the gentleman's lifestyle that he will provide with his property and magnificent horses. It is a trap. Too late she sees that 'the cord which united her with this lover and which she had heretofore held by the hand was now being flung over her neck.'

Eliot describes how Grandcourt explicitly desires to dominate and destroy:

'He had no taste for a woman who was all tenderness to him,

full of petitioning solicitude and willing obedience. He meant to be master of a woman who would have liked to master him, and who perhaps would have been capable of mastering another man.'

Where men with a trade are honourable, honest and hardworking – the beating heart of George Eliot's novels – her gentlemen tend to be callous in their privilege and treacherous to the women. They seek to suffocate and destroy the women. They might do so inadvertently, like the oblivious Mr Brooke or Romola's blind father Bardo, or more deliberately, like Casaubon who seeks to undermine Dorothea to try to protect his fading reputation. Like Arthur Donnithorne, they might see no harm in a casual, illicit love affair with the pretty Hetty, or like Grandcourt or Dempster they might abuse their wives with premeditated brutality and systematic cruelty. The wealthy powerful gentlemen in Eliot's novels are invariably dangerous.

While Austen's true gentlemen emerge as trustworthy enough to win the hand of the leading ladies, Eliot's gentlemen abuse their positions and are excluded as leading romantic heroes. The only gentleman who escapes censure by Eliot is the benign if rather bone-headed Sir James Chettam in *Middlemarch*, who embodies the class of landed privilege. Although Sir James is neither a sinister nor a bullying figure, he is still inadequate. His prime ambition is to combine his and Dorothea's estates, which sit alongside one another. In the eyes of Austen, this would make him a prime candidate for a leading man, but for Eliot he remains a minor and rather foolish character. When he tries to flatter Dorothea with 'you have your own opinion about everything, Miss Brooke, and it is always a good opinion', he never really recovers from Dorothea's supercilious reaction: 'What answer was possible to such stupid complimenting?' Without losing too much face, Sir James promptly settles for a match with Dorothea's pragmatic sister Celia. Secure in his comfort and privilege, he avoids the politics of Middlemarch and in the heady period of the 1832 Reform Bill his only contribution is to improve the cottages on his estate.

Although the lines between gentlemen and trade had begun to blur, in the era of Eliot they were still terms of reference which carried real social weight. *Middlemarch* was published in 1871 but set forty years earlier in 1832. In this year of the Reform Act, we are rather surprised to hear that Mr Brooke, who views himself as a reformer, still draws this distinction:

'The Miss Vincy who had the honour of being Mr Chichely's ideal was of course not present; for Mr Brooke, always objecting to go too far, would not have chosen that his nieces should meet the daughter of a Middlemarch manufacturer, unless it were on a public occasion.'

By extending the voting electorate, the 1832 Reform Act shifted the balance of power away from the landed gentry and towards the rising middle class. The town of Middlemarch embodies the changes taking place across the country. Eliot shows how class barriers are being challenged by the town's leading tradesmen who, sometimes with self-righteous zeal and sometimes with slightly pompous wishful thinking, are beginning to view themselves as gentlemen. Eliot recognises that actual social change cannot be brought about immediately by an Act of Parliament but is complex and incremental. She shows this with great comic touch when two ladies, Mrs Cadwallader and Lady Chettam, discuss the new surgeon:

> 'Tell me about this new young surgeon, Mr Lydgate. I am told he is wonderfully clever, he certainly looks it – a fine brow indeed.'
>
> 'He is a gentleman. I heard him talking to Humphrey. He talks well.'

'Yes. Mr Brooke says he is one of the Lydgates of Northumberland, really well connected. One does not expect it in a practitioner of that kind. For my own part, I like a medical man more on a footing with the servants; they are often all the cleverer.'

George Eliot's wit is often overlooked in favour of her realism, but as she unpeels the layers of society she can be just as witty as Jane Austen. Unlike Austen, though, Eliot's wit is often laced with foreboding. This dialogue lays the ground for Lydgate's tragic downfall because part of Rosamond's attraction for him stems from his perceived superior class and family connections, which are later found to be worthless. Lydgate might try to be radical and try to implement intellectual research, but he is ensnared by Rosamond. Her determination that he should live in the style of a gentleman rather than a tradesman ultimately ruins him. Lydgate's final assessment of his marriage with Rosamond is that he is her 'basil plant':

'When she asked for an explanation, he said that basil was a plant which had flourished wonderfully on a murdered man's brains.'

Despite his intellectual aspirations and gentleman-like qualities, Lydgate is destroyed and turned into mush, acknowledging that his brain has simply ended up as plant food. Of course, even this damning assessment bounces off Rosamond, who 'had a placid but strong answer to such speeches ... and thus the conversation ended with the advantage on [her] side'.

For Lydgate, the status of 'gentleman' comes at a fatal cost; he dies at the age of fifty. Having devoured and buried Lydgate, Rosamond entrenches her place in society by marrying a second, richer husband.

Eliot enjoys poking fun at the traditional English social order and their aversion to intellectual progress. When Lydgate's new ideas are discussed, Middlemarch opinion rejects his medical expertise:

> 'Lydgate has lots of ideas, quite new, about ventilation and diet, that sort of thing,' resumed Mr Brooke.
> 'Hang it, do you think that is quite sound? – upsetting the old treatment, which has made Englishmen what they are?' said Mr Standish.

As a doctor, if Lydgate had been in one of Jane Austen's novels he would have remained offstage or would have only been given a non-speaking comic role. In *Middlemarch*, Lydgate plays a pivotal role. On the positive side he is an intellectual, idealistic reforming doctor who becomes involved in every aspect of Middlemarch society, from issues of health to town politics; on the negative side he is also a social climber who accepts a loan from Bulstrode to secure his social status. A scandal surrounding this conflict of interest precipitates both Bulstrode's and his own downfall.

In Middlemarch society, the divisions between trade and gentlemen appear broadly to follow the town and country divide – the town characters are trade, and the Brooke side of the story comprises the landed estates and the obvious gentlemen. Several characters are able to bridge this divide: as a doctor, Lydgate visits patients across society, as a vicar Mr Farebrother has access across Middlemarch and as an estate manager Caleb Garth can work for both Mr Brooke and Mr Bulstrode.

The role of Will Ladislaw is more complicated. Perhaps mindful of George Lewes's own exotic background and his ability to dazzle anyone he met across the full spectrum of society, George

Eliot provides Ladislaw with a mixed heritage including a Polish grandfather. This makes him an outsider to the traditional social order. Unlike Austen, Eliot often gave her leading men complex or undefinable family backgrounds – as well as Ladislaw, both Tito and Daniel Deronda have opaque origins which are fundamental to their characters and their storylines. In an improbable – if classically Victorian – twist of the plot, Will Ladislaw turns out to be related to both sides of Middlemarch society. As a cousin of Casaubon, Ladislaw should have been accepted as a gentleman. However, as he has been left out of the inheritance which Casaubon has received, he can exist only on the margins, acting as a companion to Dorothea on her honeymoon in Rome while Casaubon busies himself in the library. In another implausible plot twist, it materialises that Ladislaw's grandmother had married a Jewish pawnbroker and then after his death had married none other than Bulstrode. This sort of mixed heritage could never feature in a Jane Austen leading man.

Bulstrode had cut Ladislaw's mother out of her inheritance and when he seeks to make amends and pass money to Will, Will defines himself as a gentleman and refuses to take it:

> I have to decide whether I will have transactions with you and accept your money. My unblemished honour is important to me. It is important to me to have no stain on my birth and connections. And now I find there is a stain which I can't help. My mother felt it, and tried to keep as clear of it as she could, and so will I. You shall keep your ill-gotten money ... What I have to thank you for is that you kept the money till now, when I can refuse it. It ought to lie with a man's self that he is a gentleman. Goodnight, sir.

Bulstrode's reputation is destroyed by the revelations that he was involved in pawnbroking, which in the nineteenth century was assumed to be closely linked to handling stolen goods. As the gossip circulates through Middlemarch, Bulstrode is ostracised. As well as Will refusing Bulstrode's money, Caleb Garth resigns on principle from working for him. As Will demands of Bulstrode:

'And was that business, or was it not, a thoroughly dishonourable one, nay, one that, if its nature had been made public, might have ranked those concerned in it with thieves and convicts?'

Bulstrode fails to deny this and the slur gathers pace. The rumours spread in town, washing around the tradesmen at The Tankard in Slaughter Lane. In this unmasking and condemnation of a perceived 'gentleman' who is in fact a fraud and possibly a crook dealing in stolen goods, Eliot is careful to list each trade of the tradesmen who give their verdict: Mr Limp, the meditative shoemaker; Mr Crabbe, the glazier; Mr Dill, the barber; Mr Jonas, the firm-voiced dyer; Mr Baldwin, the tax-gatherer; and Mr Byles, the butcher. Bulstrode's ambition to reinvent himself as a gentleman has been destroyed, and it is notable that it is the tradesmen who are the judges. The rumours of Bulstrode's past life, Raffles's suspicious death (which itself is at the heart of the conflict of interest between Lydgate and Bulstrode) and Bulstrode's loan of £1,000 to bail out Lydgate reach the ears of the town's officials. At the Town Hall meeting, the simmering resentment of Bulstrode's evangelical Christianity and his use of his money to buy political control of the town provokes Frank Hawley to attack Bulstrode. Hawley asks to 'speak on a question of public feeling, which not only by myself, but by many gentlemen present, is regarded as preliminary'.

The once-solid definition has morphed: the town tradesmen now view themselves as gentlemen.

Hawley's attack on Bulstrode is devastating:

> I am speaking with the concurrence and at the express request of no fewer than eight of my fellow-townsmen, who are immediately around us. It is our united sentiment that Mr Bulstrode should be called upon – and I do now call upon him – to resign public positions which he holds not simply as a taxpayer, but as a gentleman among gentlemen.

Hawley continues:

> There are practices and there are acts which, owing to circumstances, the law cannot visit, though they may be worse than many things which are legally punishable. Honest men and gentlemen, if they don't want the company of people who perpetrate such acts, have got to defend themselves as they best can.

Hawley asks Bulstrode to defend himself, to withdraw from 'positions which could only have been allowed him as a gentleman among gentlemen'.

Bulstrode staggers out, assisted by Lydgate, and his destruction at the hands of the town's tradesmen is complete.

Will Ladislaw is caught up in Bulstrode's disgrace and that same set of Middlemarch tradesmen decide to reject Ladislaw as a gentleman, albeit for different reasons:

> So our mercurial Ladislaw has a queer genealogy! A high-spirited young lady and a musical Polish patriot made a likely enough

stock for him to spring from, but I should never have suspected a grafting of the Jew pawnbroker. However, there's no knowing what a mixture will turn out beforehand. Some sorts of dirt serve to clarify.

'It's just what I should have expected,' said Mr Hawley, mounting his horse. 'Any cursed alien blood, Jew, Corsican or Gypsy.'

Neither Middlemarch society as represented by the tradesmen nor country society as represented by Sir James and Lady Chettam can accept it:

> 'It is difficult to say what Mr Ladislaw is, eh, James?'
>
> Sir James gave a small grunt, which was less respectful than his usual mode of answering his mother.
>
> 'It must be admitted that his blood is a frightful mixture!' said Mrs Cadwallader. 'The Casaubon cuttle-fish fluid to begin with, and then a rebellious Polish fiddler or dancing-master, was it?'
>
> 'Nonsense, Elinor,' said the Rector, rising. 'It is time for us to go.'

In the end, despite his compromised social position and in defiance of universal prejudice, Dorothea chooses love over wealth and marries Ladislaw. As she will later do with *Daniel Deronda*, Eliot casts a man of fluid social standing with complex origins as her romantic lead.

Just as Eliot sets out to prove that it is not the institution of the Church that necessarily represents the core of Christianity but the people who enact it, so too with the presentation of Will Ladislaw she sets out how it is individual actions which define a gentleman, rather than the assumed class. In an echo of George Lewes, who was never publicly described as a gentleman but rather 'the most amusing little fellow in the whole world', Will Ladislaw is rejected publicly as a gentleman and only accepted privately by Dorothea. Initially, they are ostracised from society, a form of exclusion that Eliot understood from her own life with Lewes. When Celia eventually inveigles Sir James to allow her to see her sister, the exclusion begins to thaw. If Eliot was sending a private message to her family in the Midlands, it went unreciprocated.

Like *Middlemarch*, *Felix Holt* is set during the time of the Reform Act of 1832. While the focus of the novel, which has the subtitle *The Radical*, is upon who is truly radical and what constitutes radical behaviour, there is also a telling insult when the simmering tension between the Transome family lawyer, Mr Jermyn, and Harold Transome, recently returned from India to run the estate and run as a radical MP for Parliament, boils over into a fight. Harold hits Jermyn across the face with his riding whip while Jermyn grabs him by the throat. Sir Maximus Debarry intervenes. Sir Maximus, who has not heard Jermyn's astounding revelation 'I am your father', chooses to help Harold the landowner rather than Jermyn the lawyer:

> 'Leave the room, sir!' the Baronet said to Jermyn, in a voice of imperious scorn. 'This is a meeting of gentlemen.'
> 'Come, Harold,' he said, in the old friendly voice, 'come away with me.'

Eliot's characters are frequently caught like this, at a moment when their very identity is in question thanks to the collision of personal relationships, social hierarchy and the currents of political change.

By the time of *Daniel Deronda*, written in 1876 and set around 1865, the term gentleman was used much more fluidly. Although the story revolves around Daniel's identity, his class is much less important than his heritage. At first, Daniel refutes Mordecai's suggestion that he might be Jewish, saying: 'I am an Englishman!' As he gradually discovers, this does not exclude him from being Jewish. By the end of the book, it seems that George Eliot has used the changing role of the English gentleman to question the whole idea of national identity, asking whether it should be based on actions and morals rather than ethnicity or inheritance. Perhaps anticipating the twenty-first century, she invites her readers to consider a more inclusive and morally grounded vision of English society where gentlemen and trade are blended together.

* * *

Although gentlemen and tradesmen generally do not interact in Jane Austen's novels, there are two professions which straddle both worlds with which she was very familiar: the clergy and the military.

With two of her brothers serving in the Royal Navy, Jane Austen had a soft spot for naval officers, which emerges time and again in her novels. In *Persuasion*, Anne Elliot notices the camaraderie between the officers and poignantly reflects that if she had married Captain Wentworth eight years earlier, she would have been party to that mutual respect and affection. Austen would have heard her brothers' naval stories, whether at the dinner table or from their letters, she would have witnessed their affection and loyalty to their fellow officers and perhaps she might even have wished to be the wife of a naval officer herself. Army officers were also considered viable marriage material. As Lydia Bennet rightly if tactlessly points out in *Pride and Prejudice*, if she had taken all her Bennet sisters to follow the regiment to Brighton she could have 'secured husbands for them all'.

Outside of the officer class, in her early novels Austen also considered the clergy a suitable profession from which to draw her romantic heroes. The Church of England was a bastion of her life and it is noteworthy that there is no hint of any Methodists, Dissenters or Catholics in her novels. Brought up in her father's secure and lucrative Church livings in Steventon, which her eldest brother James inherited, Austen saw at first hand the role a vicar played in a country parish. In Regency England, the clergy were often landed gentry and were looked to as social figures just as much as spiritual leaders. Austen's clergymen reflect this, with many of them appearing more interested in their own social standing than in their parishioners. While the Church provides a decent, 'respectable' living for honourable men such as Henry Tilney, Edward Ferrars and Edmund Bertram, it also attracts pompous social climbers such as Mr Collins and Mr Elton. Indeed, a church living with few responsibilities can also offer the opportunity for a downright scam for a rogue such as Wickham, who extracts money from Darcy by trading the promise of a church living for a cash settlement.

As her novels progress, Austen's view of the role of the Church changes significantly. Part of the difficulty with a church living is that it does not pay quite enough. In Austen's time, the annual church living for a curate was some £200, which was enough to support a single man but not enough to afford the trappings of a family with servants, horses and a carriage. Even if we take a pinch of salt with Marianne Dashwood's assertion that £2,000 is necessary to live in secure comfort, there was still a huge financial gap between a curate's salary and his possible social aspirations.

After her first young clergyman, the exemplary Henry Tilney, Austen's subsequent vicars become increasingly flawed. In *Sense and Sensibility*, Edward Ferrars starts off as an apparently solid and reliable figure, not obsessed by money and apparently all set to propose to Elinor by the third chapter. But by the end of the novel, Edward has been revealed as compromised. His poor judgement and his continuing silence to Elinor about his prior engagement to Lucy Steele borders on deceit. Despite now feeling nothing but contempt for her, Edward doggedly follows his principles of honour and stands by Lucy, for which he is duly disinherited by his mother. While this triggers Colonel Brandon's admiration for his steadfastness, we cannot help feeling that when his younger brother Robert secures his inheritance Edward looks rather foolish. Edward's passive dependency upon Lucy to make the break and then on Colonel Brandon to finance him with a church living represent two material failures. Edward lacks the characteristics of a leading man or a romantic hero like Darcy, who we would not expect to be outwitted in any sense either in love or in money. We would prefer Edward to be honourable, smart and to stay rich. Appearing foolish, mulish and being outwitted by his feckless brother damages his reputation and his credibility as a leading man. But more than anything we want Edward to be honest with Elinor – his lack of honesty corrodes our respect for him.

In her subsequent books, Jane Austen's vicars become increasingly mercenary, pompous, weak, confused, hypocritical and grasping. Mr Collins is a figure of much ridicule in *Pride and Prejudice*, although he is no fool. He readily calculates exactly what his financial worth is, as well as (rather more ominously) the value of the Bennet estate, which is entailed to him. Wickham's play for a church living not only reveals him as wholly without principle but also sheds light on how positions in the church were so often in the gift of those who might be swayed for personal reasons.

In *Mansfield Park*, Austen lampoons the hypocrisy, complacency and pomposity of the Church and the easy livings which it provides. Dr Grant is ridiculed for his luxurious diet. His is one of only two deaths in Jane Austen's novels and is gloriously unmourned, mentioned only in passing while the narrative is wrapped up: 'Dr Grant had brought on apoplexy and death by three great institutionary dinners in one week.' His death allows Edmund to take on his living. Fanny will of course be a model vicar's wife, but by the end of *Mansfield Park* it feels as if Austen's sympathy for Edmund and Fanny has faltered. When they finally come together, their marriage takes place offstage and – as Austen's family commented to her when they read the first edition – the love between them appears 'cold'.

We have struggled to maintain our respect for Edmund, who starts the novel as a figure of moral authority and clarity when he mentors Fanny but becomes increasingly flaccid, passive and confused as the novel progresses. Edmund forfeits our respect as he vacillates between decisions, unsure of what to do with his career and painfully obtuse about Mary Crawford's lack of moral compass. His final rejection of Mary is far from decisive – our last view of Mary is of her calling Edmund back with a 'saucy, playful smile' on her face as she stands by an open door. Edmund manages to walk away from her and in the last move of the final chapter he turns to Fanny. Punctured by Edmund's weak moral judgement, which does not bode well for his role in the Church, it is a limp rather than a resounding ending.

Jane Austen's final incarnation of a vicar is Mr Elton in *Emma*. Initially, Mr Elton is defined as a gentleman. Emma considers him a worthy husband for Harriet and Mr Elton considers himself a worthy husband for Emma. He is keenly aware that a marriage with Harriet would be a financial catastrophe, so it never crosses his mind that this is Emma's scheme. It should have been no surprise that Mr Elton misunderstands Emma's signals and proposes to her; he would only be marrying up, as so many vicars needed to do. In this light, Emma's judgement of him is harsh. She never allows him to recover from his mistake of falling in love with her and fancying that it is reciprocated.

The ensuing ridicule of Mr Elton is led by Emma. As the reader, we are invited to share this mockery, which we do both because Emma is our heroine and Mr Elton is snobbish and mean, but we should bear in mind that he is not ridiculed by the wider Highbury society. Mr Knightley continues to have many meetings with him and after Mr Elton marries Augusta Hawkins and returns to Highbury, the newlyweds become an important element of every social event. Until Emma is married, Mrs Elton would lead the formation of any dance and lead ladies into the dining room, a role with high social status. This role could be conducted with grace and good manners, but at each turn Mr and Mrs Elton show themselves to be crass and snobbish. Mrs Elton boasts of her brother's wealth and her aristocratic acquaintances, the couple share pompous expressions ('*caro sposo*') and their snobbery is held up to ridicule. Augusta Elton is the second daughter of a Bristol merchant, and by marrying Mr Elton she is making good her move into the gentleman class. Mr Elton is exposed as not having the manners of a gentleman, which is the most damning criticism that Austen can make. He is unforgivably disdainful of Harriet at the ball in The Crown inn, when he refuses to offer to dance with her and leaves her standing alone. Showing the manners of a true gentleman, Mr Knightley steps in and asks her to dance.

By the time Jane Austen wrote her final novel *Persuasion*, the clergy have disappeared altogether. For a vicar to be a viable love interest, he needs to be seen as a good catch. As her writing career progresses, Jane Austen seems to decide they can no longer hold down their corner of a romantic plot but must instead be consigned to the margins where they are caricatured, lampooned and attract mockery. Mary Crawford has many of the best lines in *Mansfield Park* and although rather heartless she distinguishes between the officers and the clergy:

'The profession, either navy or army, is its own justification. It has everything in its favour; heroism, danger, bustle, fashion. Soldiers and sailors are always acceptable in society. Nobody can wonder that men are soldiers and sailors.'

She goes on to dismiss the clergy:

'Indolence and love of ease ... make men clergymen. A clergyman has nothing to do but be slovenly and selfish – read the newspaper, watch the weather and quarrel with his wife. His curate does all the work and the business of his own life is to dine.'

During the Regency, in the time of Trafalgar and Waterloo, both officers and clergymen were an integral part of society. Ladies could choose between the glamorous officers or the worthy vicars, and if their need for additional capital could be met, then all could be managed. Over the next twenty or thirty years, as the time of Jane Austen passed into the time of George Eliot, the status of both of these figures diminishes. The gap between the prospects of an officer and the prospects of other trades expands. As the military grew increasingly mechanised, the officers became marginalised as picturesque but irrelevant. As other trades flourished, wealthy merchants became more visible and influential in the marriage market. As to the clergy – they cease to be such an attraction for a bright dynamic heroine, but at least the vicar will always be there at the altar to conduct the weddings.

* * *

George Eliot's clergymen play an altogether different role. Her novels are less interested in the traditional figure of the Church of England country vicar than in the intellectual pursuit that underlies the profession. She explores the intellectual and social friction between the traditional Church of England and other more evangelical branches such as Methodists and other Dissenters, as well as the radical and the conservative wings of the Catholic church in *Romola* and the Jewish faith in *Daniel Deronda*. As an author who spent two years translating *Das Leben Jesu* and followed this with the translation of *Das Wesen des Christentums* (*The Essence of Christianity*) by Ludwig Feuerbach, George Eliot was interested in the specific role of the individual within the Church, rather than the role of the institution.

One of her minor characters Rufus Lyon, Esther's adopted father in *Felix Holt*, reveals Eliot's interest in pragmatic churchmen. Rufus Lyon is an unworldly dissenting preacher, very different from the fashionable, fastidious Esther who delights in 'silk stockings [and] irreproachable nails' and being 'taken for a born lady'. Rufus Lyon appears to be a quiet, supporting figure in *Felix Holt*, but his story is a startling and revolutionary one which paves the way for the revelation of Esther's true character and reveals a good deal about Eliot's religious philosophy. Like many of Eliot's generous and idealistic characters, Rufus Lyon is shortsighted. Along with Silas Marner and Dorothea Brooke, his limited physical vision suggests a deeper insight that allows him to perceive moral truths that are not visible within the narrow confines of society. Rufus Lyon was once the pastor of a large independent congregation, a leading public figure whose sermons were 'full of study and full of fire'. Then, to 'general astonishment', Rufus resigned from his position. It is revealed that walking home one evening, Rufus was waylaid by a woman with a baby who was weak with hunger. Across the span of her novels, Eliot creates several such women who stagger on a journey either heavily pregnant or with babies, desperate and at the end of their tether – Hetty Sorrel and Molly Cass are two. This time, the woman, Annette, is a French Catholic who is 'angelic-faced' and believes that her husband has died. Just as Silas Marner makes an instant commitment to baby Eppie, Rufus Lyon also instinctively takes and nurses this baby.

Despite it being fleetingly covered, Rufus's story is dramatic and passionate. He has stepped outside of the abstract confines of church teaching and taken action which affects people in the real world. His religion has clashed with his passion (in due course, he also recognises his sexual attraction for Annette) and caused him to sacrifice his successful career. Annette is a vagrant and while nominally a Catholic, essentially of no religion. Nevertheless, he adopts her baby, Esther. Later, it is Rufus who arranges for Esther to visit Felix in prison and by turning his back and pretending to write letters, he allows the two lovers to understand their love for each other. Rufus Lyon might be a minor character, but he embodies the difference between living a life within the realms of academic religious belief and making an impact in the real world.

In *Romola*, the extensive religious debate between Romola and Savonarola occupies a central plank of the story. After being pressurised by Savonarola to return to Florence, Romola continues to do her work, which she believes is 'God's will'. Romola lives her life with charity and kindness, in vivid contrast with the deceitful traitor Tito. As the political pressure mounts on Savonarola, Romola has a final debate with him about his religious philosophy in which she rebels against his strict interpretation of God's will, arguing for a more personal and compassionate approach to spirituality that transcends rigid dogma. This debate is the religious climax of the novel, and it is here that Romola dramatically and passionately turns the tables on Savonarola. It is a magnificent and well-organised argument in which Romola follows both her passion and her logic. She concludes: 'Father, I cannot hear the real voice of your judgement and conscience.'

Savonarola back-pedals and tries to take refuge in the male myth that these issues are all too complex for the female mind to grasp. This is the same labyrinth in which so many men try to hide and justify themselves throughout George Eliot's work. It is a sign of deceit and Romola will have none of it:

'She was so utterly in antagonism with him that what he called perplexity seemed to her sophistry and doubleness; and as he went on, his words only fed that flame of indignation.'

Romola goes on to speak 'almost with bitterness' and she concludes in a devastating blow to Savonarola: 'I do not believe it!' Her frame shakes with passionate repugnance. 'God's kingdom is something wider – else let me stand outside it with the beings that I love.'

It is easy to imagine the young Mary Ann Evans rehearsing some of these arguments with her father when she rejected the traditional Church of England beliefs. Perhaps she lost those arguments, but with George Eliot now writing the script for her, Romola wins her religious debate in resounding fashion. Savonarola is intellectually destroyed by Romola well before he is physically destroyed by the torture and fires which are lit for him.

By the time she started to write her final novel, *Daniel Deronda*, the Church had faded away for Eliot and was replaced by a new and more extensive investigation of faith. Daniel Deronda's journey of self-discovery is intimately bound up with understanding his Jewish heritage and involves a profound spiritual awakening. The narrative moves between the fractured relationship of Gwendolen and Grandcourt, defined by human selfishness and cruelty, and Daniel's efforts to live a meaningful life with Mirah. The novel concludes with the image of Mordecai's serene death and the idea that Mordecai's soul will fuse with Daniel's, implying a kind of spiritual unity.

Unlike Jane Austen, who confines herself to the social and financial aspects of life in the clergy as a country parish vicar, George Eliot extensively explores the meaning of faith through a wide array of different religious perspectives. Her novels range widely through different faiths, featuring Dissenters, Methodists, Dominican monks and Jewish mystics. Jane Austen would no more be able to accommodate the religious debates by idealistic believers like Dinah, Savonarola, Romola, Daniel Deronda or Mordecai among her clergymen than George Eliot would be able to find a place for vicars such as Mr Elton, who are angling to secure the necessary stipends (ideally two stipends) along with a wealthy wife in order to afford the capons for their lavish Sunday lunches.

* * *

CHAPTER 6

THE HEROINE'S JOURNEY

It is tempting to imagine that Jane Austen's and George Eliot's heroines each have a little of their authors in them. Take Jane any Austen heroine, whether extroverted and able to dazzle a room like Elizabeth and Emma or shy and reserved like Fanny and Anne, and we see that they all have something in common. Like Austen herself, they are perceptive and sharp, alert to every social cue, no matter how subtle. Quick to see and quick to judge, their antennae detect the slightest variation in manners, shades of differences in matters of taste and nuanced breaches of social etiquette. Within pairs of sisters it is inevitably the older sister, Elinor Dashwood and Jane Bennet, who is the more measured, patient and accepting of their fate and the younger sister, Marianne and Elizabeth, who is the more effervescent, quicker to judge and indignant. These characteristics echo the personalities of Jane and her older sister Cassandra.

George Eliot's heroines are often rather gauche and appear blind to social conventions. Bookish, aloof and comfortably solitary, they give little thought to their popularity. Several of them are described as 'short-sighted', and this often implies that they have some kind of inner sight instead. Dorothea pushes away Sir James's gift of a tiny white Maltese puppy partly because she has no interest in fashion accessories but also because she cannot really see it and is afraid that she will trip over it: 'The objectionable puppy, whose nose and eyes were equally black and expressive, was thus got rid of, since Miss Brooke decided that it had better not have been born.' Dorothea's mind is focused on greater, more philosophical endeavours. Her misjudgements, and those made by many of Eliot's heroines, often stem from this kind of blind or partially sighted idealism.

Nothing could be more alien to Jane Austen. Her characters are defined by seemingly insignificant actions that her heroines immediately detect – a stiffer than usual bow of the head, a mere touching of a hat (one such touch prompts Elizabeth to wonder: 'What could be the meaning of it? It was impossible to imagine; it was impossible not to long to know'), slipping past a locked gate into a park, pausing for a moment on the staircase – and that all have far-reaching consequences. As her characters interact and form relationships, they reveal their manners, their judgements and eventually their true nature. Along the way, Austen builds up the tension in the gap between what a character thinks they want and what the reader knows they need. As each relationship between the heroines and their prospective partners develops, there are key scenes which shift the ground, change the direction of the narrative and need forensic interpretation.

Inevitably, the first moment of introduction is vital. Social visiting and leaving calling-cards was a daily custom of the Regency era, so there are many opportunities for people to meet. Whether it is Darcy stepping into the Bennets' parlour as he accompanies Bingley on his reciprocal morning call to Mr Bennet or Catherine Morland lining up at the Bath Pump Room for the Master of Ceremonies to introduce her to the next available dancing partner, Austen often sets her plots going with the minimum of fuss. Generally, visitors simply walk into a room. Sometimes it is more dramatic, as when Anne catches William Elliot's eye as they pass by on the stairs in the coaching inn or when Marianne tumbles down a rainy hillside, sprains her ankle to be swept off her feet by Willoughby. However they meet and whether it is the exact angle of the bow of the head or the faintest pressure of the touch of their fingertips, the electric charge of attraction of a first encounter is unmistakable. As the relationships develop, these small details of behaviour or misbehaviour change and have to be minutely scrutinised. Austen's heroines are keenly aware that each tiny deviation from the accepted social pattern has important consequences for a relationship.

In Jane Austen's world, the first exploratory conversations can be so intricate that at first reading, they might seem abstract. Her characters make virtually no contemporary references and because they do not discuss aspects of life such as politics, social reform, religion or logistics including trade or household management (with the energetic exception of Mrs Norris), they must rely instead on rather ephemeral issues. For instance, the first dialogue between Elizabeth and Darcy is charged with the magnetic push-pull of attraction and resistance, yet it is so self-referential as to be virtually abstract in that it is a conversation about how such a conversation should be had:

> After a pause of some minutes she addressed him a second time, with:
> 'It is *your* turn to say something now, Mr Darcy. *I* talked about the dance, and *you* ought to make some kind of remark on the size of the room, or the number of couples.'

> He smiled and assured her that whatever she wished him to say should be said.
>
> 'Very well; that reply will do for the present. Perhaps, by-and-by, I may observe that private balls are much pleasanter than public ones; but *now* we may be silent.'
>
> 'Do you talk by rule, then, while you are dancing?'

The stirring of interest and attraction between them is clear. More significantly, Elizabeth is also starting to shape one of the central themes of their relationship: the process of her teaching manners to Darcy. As their conversations expand and test the boundaries, our sympathy and admiration for Darcy grow because we understand the rationale for his behaviour. As others are drawn into their circle, they too provide opinions and judgements that lead to considerable misunderstandings. At first, initiated and slyly manipulated by Wickham, these misunderstandings are comic, but eventually these rumours are so widely believed that as they are trumpeted by the deluded Mrs Bennet, Darcy and Elizabeth's relationship is in jeopardy.

Just when it appears impossible for Elizabeth and Darcy to trust each other, Jane Austen uses a device which recurs in all her novels and which later George Eliot uses extensively in her novels – she sends her heroine on a journey. This journey allows the heroine to reassess and reset their relationship, to learn more about their potential partner and more about themselves. Often this information is provided by a key witness from the past, a minor character who makes a crucial intervention at a crucial time. When Elizabeth joins her uncle and aunt on their holiday jaunt to the north, she has already rejected Darcy's self-obsessed and self-pitying marriage proposal. Though she no longer believes that Wickham has been wronged, she still feels confident in her assessment that Darcy is a proud, selfish, bad-tempered bully. When their holiday plans change, they find themselves in Derbyshire, close to Darcy's stately home, Pemberley. In his absence, they decide to visit the house. It proves to be the critical turning point. During her visit, the ground is completely cut from beneath her by Darcy's housekeeper Mrs Reynolds.

At first, the talk is of whether Mr Darcy will ever marry. Mrs Reynolds comes out with what Elizabeth thinks is a stock response: 'I do not know who is good enough for him.' Elizabeth smugly feels that she knows better and is about to put this down to Darcy's arrogance, but then Mrs Reynolds staunchly emphasises:

> 'I say no more than the truth, and what everybody will say that knows him,' replied the other. Elizabeth thought this was going pretty far, and she listened with increasing astonishment as the housekeeper added, 'I have never had a cross word from him in my life, and I have known him ever since he was four years old.'
>
> This was praise, of all others most extraordinary, most opposite to her ideas. That he was not a good-tempered man had been her firmest opinion. Her keenest attention was awakened; she longed to hear more.

Elizabeth has to reconsider as she hears more: 'He is the best landlord and the best master that ever lived. Not like the wild young men nowadays, who think of nothing but themselves. There is not one of his tenants or servants but what will give him a good name.'

This is the vital piece of evidence that transforms Elizabeth's opinion and marks the turning point of their relationship. Just like the thunderbolt that hits Emma Woodhouse ('Mr Knightley must marry no one but herself!'), in this instant Elizabeth realises the overwhelming imperative for her to question all her prejudices. Elizabeth turns all her attention to what will enable her to fulfil her destiny as the heroine who can match Darcy. When Elizabeth receives the appalling news of Lydia's flight with Wickham which plunges the Bennet family into scandal, she instinctively confides in Darcy. Taking responsibility for failing to reveal Wickham's treacherous nature, Darcy determines to pay Wickham off and force him to marry Lydia. This saves the Bennet family from social disgrace and financial ruin and paves the way for him to marry Elizabeth.

As soon as Darcy and Elizabeth trust each other, they begin to work together as a well-matched pair who can play to each other's strengths. We enjoy their shifting perspectives and the heightened drama created by Austen's pitch-perfect sense of timing. The reader finds out that Darcy is an exemplary gentleman just before Elizabeth does, and she herself realises this just before her family does. With delicious tension, Elizabeth realises that she loves Darcy at exactly the same moment she realises that any association with her disgraced family must be impossible for him. There is something intensely private about Elizabeth being sure of her love for Darcy before anyone else even suspects. The dawning sense that the plot might resolve itself makes Elizabeth's encounter with Lady Catherine exquisitely enjoyable. The journey to Derbyshire is the trigger that transforms Darcy into a hero; equally, it transforms Elizabeth into a heroine.

* * *

While *Pride and Prejudice* illustrates the most finely attuned example of a heroine's transformation, *Mansfield Park* provides the most

THE HEROINE'S JOURNEY

thorough. Fanny Price's journey to becoming a heroine is charted over an eight-year period. When Fanny leaves her parents' impoverished, shambolic home in Portsmouth and arrives at her aunt's grand house, Mansfield Park, she is just ten years old. At first, she is treated little better than a servant and her older cousin Edmund first discovers her sitting halfway up the attic stairs, too anxious to come down. This is an apt metaphor for her journey because Fanny is caught between two worlds. Bullied by her cousins and scorned by Mrs Norris, Fanny is a very long way from establishing herself as the heroine of the book.

At first, Edmund is Fanny's tutor, teaching her social etiquette and good judgement and helping her to feel secure at Mansfield Park. But as time passes, Fanny gradually displays more and more of her own judgement and begins to exert power. In parallel with Fanny's growing maturity, Edmund grows increasingly infatuated with the seductive Mary Crawford and stops being able to exercise correct judgement. While Edmund falters and is compromised, Fanny gathers strength and authority and starts rising up the ladder to justify her eventual status as heroine.

As with *Pride and Prejudice*, it is a journey that lays bare the true nature of hero and heroine and settles the destinies of each of the prime characters. Fanny's cousin Maria Bertram is engaged to Mr Rushworth, who with an annual income of £12,000 a year is Austen's richest man. However, Rushworth is rather dim-witted and Maria is attracted to Mary's suave brother Henry Crawford. A day's outing to admire Rushworth's estate at Sotherton takes place and as they set off to explore the grounds the party divides into two trios: Maria, Rushworth and Henry Crawford; and Edmund Bertram, Mary Crawford and Fanny. During this walk (a journey within a journey), each character is placed out of context and reveals critical truths, which sets the stage for the impending love affairs. As they walk around the gardens and into the woods, the balance of power shifts and reforms. Fanny is secretly in love with Edmund, but he is infatuated with Mary. When Edmund persuades Fanny to sit and rest on a bench leaving her 'to think with pleasure of her cousin's care, but with great regret that she was not stronger', he is in reality ditching the gooseberry Fanny so that he can be alone with Mary and they disappear together for what they promise will be just 'a few minutes'. When the other trio finds Fanny, they immediately understand Edmund's and Mary's plan:

'How ill you have been used by them!'

Then Maria opens up a new possibility:

'Miss Bertram, observing the iron gate, expressed a wish of passing through it into the park, that their views might be more comprehensive. It was the very thing of all others to be wished, it was the best, it was the only way of proceeding with any advantage.'

Henry Crawford picks this up: 'He directly saw a knoll not half a mile off, which would give them exactly the requisite command of the house. Go therefore they must to that knoll, and through that gate.'

But the gate is locked. While Rushworth dashes back to the house to find the key, Henry Crawford and Maria have a risky conversation in which they use blatant imagery to sound each other out on the possibility of an illicit relationship. Henry Crawford's opening gambit is:

'You have a very smiling scene before you.'

'Do you mean literally or figuratively? Literally, I conclude. Yes, certainly, the sun shines, and the park looks very cheerful. But unluckily that iron gate, that ha-ha, give me a feeling of restraint and hardship. "I cannot get out," as the starling said.'

> As she spoke, and it was with expression, she walked to the gate.

Henry Crawford then pushes Maria to be more explicit:

> 'And for the world you would not get out without the key and without Mr Rushworth's authority and protection, or I think you might with little difficulty pass round the edge of the gate, here, with my assistance; I think it might be done, if you really wished to be more at large, and could allow yourself to think it not prohibited.'

His seductive offer to embark on an affair is eagerly accepted:
> 'Prohibited! Nonsense! I certainly can get out that way, and I will.'

Fanny ineffectually tries to stop Maria:
> 'You will hurt yourself... you will be in danger ... You had better not go,'

but to her horror, Henry Crawford and Maria slip past the gate and outside the garden. Fanny is 'astonished at Miss Bertram, and angry with Mr Crawford'. Henry Crawford and Maria disappear into the wilderness and they banish themselves from Rushworth's garden. Their relationship has shifted to a new territory. From this moment, their physical affair and adultery is just a matter of timing.

Meanwhile, Edmund is flirting with danger with Mary Crawford. Fanny is looking for them when:

> The voice and the laugh of Miss Crawford once more caught her ear. The sound approached ... They were just returned into the wilderness from the park, to which a side gate, not fastened, had tempted them very soon after their leaving her, and they had been

across a portion of the park into the very avenue which Fanny had been hoping the whole morning to reach at last ... This was their history. It was evident that they had been spending their time pleasantly and were not aware of the length of their absence.

Despite their promise of leaving Fanny for only a few minutes, Edmund and Mary have been away for over an hour and Fanny is curious 'to know what they had been conversing about all that time'.

A closer look at Jane Austen's prose reveals the subtle metaphors she uses to describe various transgressions against social norms. While Maria and Henry stepped past a locked gate and were lost into the wilderness beyond, Edmund and Mary passed through only an unfastened side gate and have strayed into limited territory, 'a portion of the park'. However, they have briefly inhabited the 'very avenue which Fanny had been hoping to reach at last'. This is too guarded a metaphor to interpret clearly, but we might assume that during this hour, Edmund and Mary enjoyed a pretty passionate time. It was a steamy summer's day and they were out of sight. Whatever the interpretation of visiting 'the very avenue' means (although Sigmund Freud would have no qualms about interpreting it, possibly even to Austen's surprise), to answer Fanny's naive curiosity, they have probably not been 'conversing all that time'. Throughout this outing to Sotherton, crammed with its own series of vital mini-journeys, Fanny remains a disengaged observer. While her judgement of what she sees around her is perceptive, at this stage she is still too weak, passive and ineffectual to be considered a heroine. Her journey up the ladder continues.

After the episode in the Sotherton gardens, the tension and attraction between Edmund and Mary continues to be ratcheted up. Edmund and Maria's father Sir Thomas has written to announce a date for his return home that will precipitate both Maria's marriage to Mr Rushworth and Edmund's entry into the Church. After Mary mocks Edmund's decision to become a clergyman and turns away to play the piano, Fanny staunchly tries to stick up for him. For a brief moment Fanny seems to have triumphed and established a bond with Edmund. They stand alone together looking out of the window. They share a taste for the 'sublimity of Nature':

'*You* taught me to think and feel on the subject, cousin,' Fanny says.

'I had a very apt scholar.'

At this point, Edmund looks up at the stars:

'There's Arcturus looking very bright.'

When Fanny suggests going outside to look at the starlit sky together, her lifelong devotion to Edmund is reflected in the star that Austen has pinpointed. Close to the Great Bear star constellation, Arcturus was known as 'The Bear Follower' and often described as 'chasing the bear around the sky'. Just like Edmund's slavish devotion to Mary, Fanny also has slavish devotion to Edmund – they are both chasing bears. Edmund agrees that they should go out:

'We must go out on the lawn for that. Should you be afraid?'

'Not in the least. It is a great while since we have had any star-gazing.'

'Yes; I do not know how it has happened.'

But just as they might go outside together with Fanny's declaration that she would 'not in the least' be afraid beside Edmund, a clue to her love for him that he blanks, Mary starts playing a light tune, a 'glee', on the piano. Fanny watches with 'mortification' as Edmund leaves her and approaches Mary 'moving forward by gentle degrees towards the instrument'. Edmund is still on his journey inching towards Mary and he is 'among the most urgent in requesting to hear the glee again'. At this point, Mary starts to eclipse Fanny in Edmund's eyes. She will continue to be his heroine for now, while we share in the heartache of our own heroine Fanny: there will be no star-gazing for her that night.

Unlike the constant twists and turns of Darcy and Elizabeth's romance, Fanny's gradual climb up the ladder to claim her place as heroine and as Edmund's bride is a slow and laboured journey. The final page concludes with Fanny's triumph as heroine in securing her goal. The narrator appeals to us directly:

'I only entreat everybody to believe that exactly at the time when it was quite natural that it should be so, and not a week earlier, Edmund did cease to care about Miss Crawford and become as anxious to marry Fanny as Fanny herself could desire.'

This is the heroine's perfect ending, but it feels rather subdued. Fanny and Edmund's marriage lacks the sense of brio and heightened pleasure that rings out from Jane Austen's other endings. *Mansfield Park* is Austen's most conspicuously moral tale, and perhaps part of the problem with Fanny is that she is always right. For a heroine never to be wrong about anything means that she never makes mistakes or has to admit to herself that she has blundered. Fanny is never surprised by a sudden passion or struck by a revelation, and consequently neither are we. Fanny's journey is remorselessly straightforward. Other heroines such as Catherine Morland, Elizabeth Bennet and Emma Woodhouse are gloriously wrong in many of their judgements so along their paths to becoming consummate heroines they have to perform excruciating about-turns and frantically dig themselves out of gaping holes. Catherine is giddy, clumsy and her imagination runs riot; Elizabeth falls for Wickham's deceit; Emma is mistaken in every single judgement except the final crucial one that she herself must marry Mr Knightley. There are echoes of Fanny in Anne Elliot, who quietly and steadily gains stature and strength in her relationship with Captain Wentworth. Like Fanny, Anne is largely correct in her judgements and is unable to influence the unfolding dramas that she witnesses, but her vulnerability and self-doubt make her flawed and with this she is a natural heroine who catches our sympathy in a way that just eludes Fanny.

Immediately after *Mansfield Park*, Austen went to the opposite extreme. The character of Emma and the journey she takes as she creates chaos across Highbury society could not be more different to Fanny. Whereas Fanny was shy, circumspect and infallibly right, Emma is outspoken, headstrong and infallibly wrong. Unlike the meticulously documented incremental shifts in Fanny's journey to become the heroine of *Mansfield Park*, events in Highbury unfold at whiplash speed.

Emma is the most geographically concentrated of Jane Austen's novels, with most of the action taking place within the single village of Highbury. There are just two outings: one for a picnic at Box Hill and the other to Mr Knightley's house, Donwell Abbey, to pick strawberries. Once again it is these journeys which bring the plot to a crescendo. While most of Emma's schemes are merely absurd and comically misguided, when she is drawn into Frank Churchill's deceit, she begins to lose her moral bearings. As she follows this path, she begins to lose her lustre as the leading lady of Highbury and as the heroine of the story. Mr Knightley has not been privy to Emma's barbed treatment of Jane Fairfax when she has been hinting that Jane had had an affair with Mr Dixon, but he is at the Box Hill picnic when Emma starts publicly flirting with Frank Churchill. This causes an awkward silence. As part of the group's attempts to fill the silence, Miss Bates jokes that she says three dull things whenever she opens her mouth, at which point Emma turns the joke into a moment of cruelty by responding that it would be a wonder if she could limit herself just to three:

'Miss Bates, deceived by the mock ceremony of her manner, did not immediately catch her meaning; but when it burst on her, it could not anger, though a slight blush showed that it could pain her.'

After the picnic Mr Knightley takes Emma to task:

'I cannot see you acting wrong, without a remonstrance. How could you be so unfeeling to Miss Bates? How could you be so insolent in your wit to a woman of her character, age and situation? Emma, I had not thought it possible.'

This stinging criticism of Emma is the abrupt turning point in their relationship. Mr Knightley shows that he cares – he could almost be said to show passion for the first time. Emma is rightfully mortified. Until this point, she had been impulsively and without responsibility conjuring up ideas for matchmaking and indulging in vicarious romantic fantasies. When she starts hinting that Jane has had an affair and ridiculing Miss Bates, neither of whom can stand up to her due to their lower social rank, her breach of manners reveals her lack of judgement. Emma has crossed a line and is in danger of losing our sympathy and admiration as heroine. Mr Knightley pulls her back and effectively rescues her. Misunderstanding her silence as defiance when it is really the silence of remorse, he 'stiffly' hands her into the carriage. When she turns to look back at him, he had already turned away; 'It was just too late.' Mr Knightley's rebuke jolts Emma and redirects her to her path where she can become his heroine.

Later when Harriet confides to Emma that she loves Mr Knightley and she believes that he may well love her in return, Emma is forced to question herself and her behaviour. Her perceived position of power where she believed that she held the reins of social influence has been exposed as an absurd illusion. Emma has no power; indeed, all her attempts to guide and manipulate Harriet have been nothing but folly. With a sudden flash of insight, Emma realises she has been compromised and waylaid. When she asks herself what she is really doing, she has the revelation that she herself loves Mr Knightley. From that moment on, she must stop her farcical matchmaking and social meddling. She must just focus upon the single important thing in her life: her own marriage and her future, which are the true priorities for a heroine. Just in the nick of time, Emma takes the crucial final step in her journey and becomes a Jane Austen heroine.

* * *

If Jane Austen's heroines make their journeys along a path that eventually leads to their perfect marriages, George Eliot's heroines often find themselves married at a surprisingly early stage of the story. Their paths take the apparently happy state of marriage as their starting points from which they have to navigate their future. Their journeys then become increasingly fraught and uncertain.

In *Romola*, the story revolves around noblewoman Romola de' Bardi and Tito Melema, who has been shipwrecked with no apparent family. As with Austen, the moment of introduction between hero and heroine is crucial. By the time Tito meets Romola, Eliot has laid the foundation for Tito's deceit with care. He has been found asleep on the street by Bratti, a local Florentine market trader who brings him to the barber's shop to be spruced up. Clues about Tito's history, secrecy and duplicity are dropped at every turn. Before he is introduced by name, we hear the loaded opinion in the barber's shop: 'He would make a stepping-stone of his father's corpse.' The local painter Piero looks him up and down and immediately wants to paint a portrait of his face, as a traitor. Tito is reluctant to give his name. Only after several other introductions is it revealed:

'His name is... You said your name was?'
'Tito Melema,' said the stranger, slipping the ring from his finger.

The ring will prove to be significant.

Bratti hears that Bardo is looking for an assistant librarian and takes Tito along to be interviewed. Life moves fast for Tito – from waking up on the streets as a shipwreck survivor, he finds himself being interviewed by the elderly scholar Bardo. Bardo is blind and his beautiful daughter Romola looks after him.

In the opening exchanges, Bardo unfairly criticises Romola in front of Tito:

'I constantly marvel at the capriciousness of my daughter's memory, which grasps certain objects with tenacity, and lets fall all those minutiae whereon depends accuracy, the very soul of scholarship.'

Romola seems resigned to such criticism. Inaccurate and biased, this is classic male prejudice which will later be echoed by both Mr Brooke and Casaubon to Dorothea in *Middlemarch*. It might represent an autobiographical note for the self-educated scholar from Coventry. But in a surprise move which captivates Romola, Tito turns the tables on Bardo and allies with her:

'When Bardo made this reference to his daughter, Tito ventured to turn his eyes towards her, and at the accusation against her memory his face broke into its brightest smile, which was reflected as inevitably as sudden sunbeams in Romola's. Conceive the soothing delight of that smile to her!'

With this first smile that lights up the library, we hope that Tito will be redeemed. Tito has shone a light on Romola, and it feels as if it is the first time she has ever experienced joy:

> Romola had never dreamed that there was a scholar in the world who would smile at a deficiency for which she was constantly made to feel herself a culprit. It was like the dawn of a new sense to her – the sense of comradeship. They did not look away from each other immediately, as if the smile had been a stolen one; they looked and smiled with frank enjoyment.

This is a glorious pellucid moment. Their relationship seems spontaneous, mutually enhancing and full of the potential for happiness, as if it could light up the world. But this radiant moment is immediately punctured when Eliot dips into their respective minds:

> 'She is not really so cold and proud,' thought Tito.
> 'Does *he* forget too, I wonder?' thought Romola. 'Yet I hope not, else he will vex my father.'

On the one hand, Romola is innocently thinking of Tito as a scholar, taking him at face value; on the other hand Tito is appraising Romola and concludes that he can seduce her. Their relationship can be nothing but flawed.

We know that Tito is not a scholar; in fact, he is bogus. Their smile is compromised – in reality, Tito is an opportunist on the make. He will deceive and exploit Bardo as surely as he goes on to deceive and exploit Romola. The mystery about his past flickers again as the conversation turns to the value of his ring:

> 'Five hundred ducats!' exclaims Bardo when he hears of the estimated value. 'Ah, more than a man's ransom!'

Tito gave a slight, almost imperceptible start, and opened his long dark eyes with questioning surprise at Bardo's blind face, as if his words – a mere phrase of common parlance, at a time when men were often being ransomed from slavery or imprisonment – had had some special meaning for him. But the next moment he looked towards Romola…

We immediately register the reference of an 'almost imperceptible start' and realise that there is an unpaid debt in Tito's past. We are unsure what it is, but it is ominous. Soon we will read the note from Baldassarre, who is Tito's adoptive father and has been captured and held in slavery. Baldassarre begs Tito to sell the jewels that he gave him to release him from slavery, but Tito ignores this plea. In the meantime, Tito pushes ahead with his parallel seductions of the *contadina* (peasant woman) Tessa and the scholar's daughter Romola. Both women will fall in love with him, both with touching innocence:

'I do love you,' murmured Romola. She looked at him with the same simple majesty as ever, but her voice had never in her life before sunk to that murmur. It seemed to them both that they were looking at each other a long while before her lips moved again; yet it was but a moment till she said, 'I know now what it is to be happy.' The faces just met and the dark curls mingled for an instant with the rippling gold. Quick as lightning after that, Tito set his foot on a projecting ledge of the bookshelves and reached down the needful volumes.

In this instant, we see both Romola's blindness to Tito and his manipulation. Tito invariably moves 'quick as lightning'. Cunning and slippery, he will stay one step ahead of every situation – whether it is Florentine politics, his two lovers or his demented adoptive father who decides to murder him – right up until he dives into the River Arno to escape a violent mob. Even then he would have backed himself to survive, but he is washed ashore on a mud bank where the vengeful Baldassarre is waiting to see what the river might bring to him.

Tito is certainly one step ahead when he decides to deceive the obvious heroine Romola and seduce Tessa, the simple *contadina*. In a revealing insight into a male mind, Eliot sets out Tessa's attraction for Tito: 'Tito felt an irresistible desire to go up to her and get her pretty trusting looks and prattle: this creature who was without moral judgements that could condemn him, whose little, loving ignorant soul made a world apart.'

Tito is aware of his own treachery and he acknowledges that he wants something other than the ethereal pre-Raphaelite heroine Romola: he wants a woman to be wholly subservient, trusting, unconditional and virtually enslaved to him. Most important of all, he wants to avoid 'moral judgements'. This profound immorality defines Tito, who would indeed make 'a stepping-stone of his father's corpse,' and collides with Romola's compassionate and heightened morality.

There is a vein of erotica as Tessa is regularly beaten by her step-father and Tito pointedly asks how often and how painful these beatings are. This is an aspect of the physical relationship that he cannot entertain with the idealised, noble Romola. Eliot understands that her heroine Romola, who is beautiful, intelligent and occupies the moral high ground, cannot compete with a sexy, unjudgemental peasant girl. Both women have an innocence to them, yet Tessa is so docile and compliant that she appears almost mentally impaired. Believing that she and Tito are married by the conjurer, Tessa is readily persuaded by Tito not to tell anyone and responds to his physical threats with abject obedience.

Like Victorian wives, Renaissance wives had to cede all authority and possessions to their husbands, and for Romola this includes her beloved library, which she inherited from her father. Tito decides to sell the library behind her back and although 'his freedom from scruples did not release him from the dread of what was disagreeable', he is determined to take the money. Romola can barely believe this betrayal and asks: 'Are faithfulness, and love, and sweet grateful memories, no good?' It is a horrible awakening for her. For the first time in her life, Romola experiences scorn and anger and finally accuses him of what he is: 'You are a treacherous man!'

Her passionate, articulate argument forms the crescendo at the conclusion of Book 1. As heroine, Romola simply has no power and no answer to the brutal assertion of power by the husband: 'The event is irrevocable. The library is sold. And you are my wife.'

These three curt sentences, each a hammer blow, send Romola falling to her knees in front of the painting of her blind father and 'bursting into sobs'.

The relationship that started with a spontaneous radiant smile that ignited feelings which Romola had never felt before has collapsed. Like Dorothea in *Middlemarch* and Gwendolen in *Daniel Deronda*, Romola is caught in a vicious and unyielding trap. If she is to emerge as the heroine she wants to be, a figure who can steer a course between the extreme religious factions of Florence, look after the poor and help transform society, Romola needs to break off her relationship with Tito. She plans to escape from Florence.

Just like Austen's heroines before her, Romola will embark upon a pivotal journey. But unlike Austen, who gives her heroines little psychological space to prepare, Eliot builds a detailed psychological picture while Romola contemplates her journey ahead. Trying to escape from her marriage, which has broken, and her husband, who has deceived her, Romola hurriedly starts packing her bags:

'When she had fastened the door, she took her taper to the carved and painted chest which contained her wedding clothes. A great sob arose as she looked at them: they seemed the shroud of her dead happiness.'

It is a devastating image of the lost happiness that a heroine should have expected to have enjoyed. Romola has to accept that the happiness of falling in love with Tito in the library has vanished. Romola considers whether to remove her wedding ring and in a moment of startling honesty weighs up the impact: 'It brought a vague but arresting sense that she was somehow violently rending her life in two.'

Romola almost compromises, but then: 'There was a passionate voice speaking within her that presently nullified all such muffled murmurs. "It cannot be! I cannot be subject to him. He is false. I shrink from him. I despise him!" She snatched the ring from her finger and laid it on the table.' As Romola moves into more complex emotional territory and her relationship approaches breaking point, the ornate language of her early scenes gives way to direct, powerfully charged sentences.

Trying to assert herself and follow her own path as heroine, Romola attempts to escape from Florence. She almost succeeds in her journey, but at the moment of her escape she is recognised and ensnared by Savonarola, who persuades her to return and to become his disciple. Outside the gates of Florence, Romola is forced to capitulate. At first she resists: 'I will not return. I acknowledge no right of priests and monks to interfere with my actions. You have no power over me.'

But during their extended discussion about religious philosophy and duty, Romola loses ground to him: 'As the anger melted from Romola's mind, it had given place to a new presentiment of the strength there might be in submission.'

Her arguments and her sense of self are pushed increasingly backwards and the balance of power between them changes. Like Austen, Eliot picks out the incremental shifts with each line of dialogue:

"'I should never have quitted Florence," said Romola, tremulously.'

Moments later she tries to refute his arguments, but she is weakening:

'Speaking in a tone of anguish, as if she were being dragged to some torture: "Father, you may be wrong."'

Finally, Romola capitulates: "'Father, I will be guided. Teach me! I will go back."

'Almost unconsciously, she sank on her knees. Savonarola stretched out his hands over her.'

This intense discussion of religious philosophy results in her complete and physical capitulation to Savonarola. In what is couched almost as an erotic scene, certainly a scene of domination, Savonarola forces Romola to kneel in front of him and lays his hands over her. Romola starts their relationship as his wholly subservient disciple. The religious fervour which Eliot channels through Savonarola is high voltage – a long way from Austen's vicar Dr Grant ordering too many capons for his Sunday lunch in *Mansfield Park*.

As with Janet Dempster and Gwendolen, Romola has to endure physical violence from her husband. The plight of women was a pressing social issue in the Victorian era, and Eliot tackled it fearlessly and with a deep understanding of human psychology. For Romola, whose early years were spent quietly working with her father in the library, the way in which Tito dominates her comes as a total shock. When Tito and Romola are outside one evening and Tito is approached by another menacing political faction, Romola understands that Savonarola is in danger. When she tries to extract the truth from Tito, he is evasive. At length she tells him:

'Tito, it is of no use. I have no belief in you.'

Given how opaque much of the syntax is throughout *Romola*, this direct, heartfelt sentence is all the starker. It should be that these words are enough: the relationship should end there. But words are insufficient in the face of physical violence and Romola's intellect offers no defence:

'You shall not!' said Tito in a bitter whisper, seizing her wrists with all his masculine force. 'I am master of you. You shall not set yourself in opposition to me.'

For Romola, a kind and gentle heroine, this violence is an agonising fall from grace. Nothing in her life has prepared her to manage in such a situation. The life journey that she assumed that she would take towards fulfilment and happiness has instead brought her to a place of desolation. Romola warns Bernardo, her godfather: 'Trust nobody. If you trust, you will be betrayed.' These words could almost be the strapline for a modern-day spy thriller, but they mark the low point of Romola's life. Her father is dead, his work destroyed, Bernardo is executed, she is dominated by Tito and Savonarola and she has lost all her trust in the possibility of any positive human interaction.

Romola tries one last time to escape from Florence. Once again she disguises herself, and this time she successfully leaves the fast-deteriorating world of the city behind. In a moment of sudden and arresting calm, Romola finds herself on the shores of the Mediterranean. Her journey now takes on a surreal quality of allegory.

Romola watches a fisherman and buys his small fishing boat. She sets sail towards the horizon, lies down with her cowl over her face and passes out. Romola does not care where she is taken – she is seeking death: 'Presently she felt that she was in the grave.' She has lost all hope of being the heroine of her earlier ideals.

When Romola wakes up, she finds herself in a new life. She walks ashore into an apparently empty village that she realises has been decimated by plague. Peering into abandoned houses, she finds the villagers are either dead or dying. She comes across a dead family where only a baby is still alive and with the bringing of milk and the burying of the dead, the landscape is an allegory for a Christian rebirth. Romola has emerged purified from her suffering in Florence. Unafraid of death and not scared to handle people with the plague, she nurses the sick and rebuilds the community. It is a surreal world where time does not seem to apply and where the village seems to exist in isolation. Romola emerges to take control of the village and as she does, she metamorphoses into an almost mythical heroine, a Madonna. When she returns to Florence, Tito and Savonarola are dead and this provides her with the freedom to reinvent herself and rebuild a new uncompromised life.

At the conclusion of her journey, Romola is reborn as a very different heroine from her introduction in her father's library.

In Eliot's final novel, *Daniel Deronda*, Gwendolen Harleth is entangled in a web of complex relationships with the enigmatic Daniel Deronda and the imperious Grandcourt. The story opens in the casino in Leubronn with the compelling question: 'Was she beautiful or not beautiful?' While this conundrum might be posed by the narrator, it also might belong to Daniel Deronda, who is watching from a distance. Radiant and poised, Gwendolen commands the spotlight and is clearly destined to be the heroine. The question about her beauty seems rhetorical – she is clearly beautiful and she is also winning handsomely at roulette. But when she sees that Daniel is watching her, her luck changes. Even before they have been introduced their relationship is charged, because from across the casino floor, Daniel has changed her fate. It is Daniel who watches her go to the pawn shop and writes the message: 'A stranger who has found Miss Harleth's necklace returns it to her with the hope that she will not again risk the loss of it.' Gwendolen is mortified that Daniel has helped her and indignant about the high moral tone of his advice. The third chapter rewinds the story, taking us back to a year before Gwendolen arrived at the casino. Gwendolen's father has just died and as they settle into their new home at Offendene, the housekeeper tells the lady's maid to take the key 'to her Royal Highness'.

'I don't know who you mean, Mrs Startin,' said Bugle.
'I mean the young lady that's to command us all – and well worthy for looks and figure,' replied Mrs Startin.

Wherever she goes, Gwendolen is admired and rather feared. Imperious and calculating, she confidently assumes that all relationships will be struck on her terms. Compliments range from 'certainly, a fine woman never looks better than on horseback, and Gwendolen has the figure for it' to 'by George! Who is that girl with the awfully well-set head and jolly figure?' As she kisses her own reflection in the mirror, Gwendolen certainly has vanity but correctly feels that she has much to feel vain about. As she sets out to conquer society, we are prepared to forgive this because we see how Gwendolen is the only one in her family who can secure their future.

When Gwendolen first meets the wealthy aristocrat Grandcourt, it is to her – and to us – a meeting of equals. In her mind she is destined to be the heroine of the narrative and as his name suggests Grandcourt will be her romantic hero. Their first conversation uses a brilliantly original narrative technique to set out Gwendolen's thoughts alongside the dialogue. It is very funny and brings us particularly close to Gwendolen:

'I suppose you are a first-rate shot with a rifle.' (*Pause, during which Gwendolen, having taken a rapid observation of Grandcourt, made a brief graphic description of him to an indefinite hearer.*)
'I have left off shooting.'
'Oh, then you are a formidable person. People who have done things once and left them off make one feel very contemptible … I hope you have not left off all follies, because I practise a great many.' (*Pause, during which Gwendolen made several interpretations of her own speech.*)
'What do you call follies?'
'Well, in general, I think, whatever is agreeable is called a folly.' (*Pause, wherein Gwendolen recalled what she had heard about Grandcourt's position and decided that he was the most aristocratic-looking man she had ever seen.*)

And so the dialogue continues with the reader eavesdropping on both the spoken words and Gwendolen's thoughts:

(*Pause, during which Gwendolen thought that a man of extremely calm, cold manners might be less disagreeable as a husband than other men, and not likely to interfere with his wife's preferences.*)
(*Pause, wherein Gwendolen speculated on the probability that*

the men of coldest manners were the most adventurous, and felt the strength of her own insight, supposing the question had to be decided.)

This startling and intimate device has since been widely copied, even in modern films such as *Annie Hall* and *Love Actually*.

Planted in this comic scene are the seeds of Gwendolen's impending tragedy. Gwendolen is proved completely wrong. While she has self-confidence, our access to her thoughts reveals a tragic list of misunderstandings:

'(*Pause, wherein Gwendolen was thinking that men had been known to choose someone else than the woman they most admired, and recalled several experiences of this kind in novels.*)'

We see Gwendolen unmasked – her innermost thoughts are founded on scant experience. Despite putting on such a confident display to Grandcourt as the sophisticated heroine of the moment who can converse with wit and charm, Gwendolen is touchingly revealed as an ingenue whose experience of the world is based on novels, and who has not yet realised that she is out of her depth. The relationship which Gwendolen thinks lies in her favour and which she considers to be her rightful due as heroine is actually a sprung trap.

The second time Gwendolen is given jewellery, which mirrors the return of her necklace by Daniel Deronda, is on her wedding night. It is also accompanied by a revealing letter. Gwendolen has been entranced by the prospect of Grandcourt's diamonds, preparing herself to exult over them in the same fashion as she did over the sight of their magnificent horses being brought to the front of the house for them to ride. The Grandcourt diamonds, which she will inherit upon their wedding day, will signify the wealth, status and independence she has craved for her and for her family. Feeling confident that her role as heroine is secure, Gwendolen composes herself to open the package on her wedding night and to gloat over the diamonds. To her horror, the letter she reads is devastating:

'Perhaps you think of being happy, as she once was, and of having beautiful children such as hers, who will thrust hers aside. God is too just for that. The man you have married has a withered heart.'

Mrs Glasher, Grandcourt's former mistress, writes from experience:

'Will he think you have any right to complain when he has made you miserable? You took him with your eyes open. The willing wrong you have done me will be your curse.'

Her curse irrevocably shifts Gwendolen's relationship with Grandcourt, and the chapter ends with Gwendolen screaming with 'hysterical violence' in front of Grandcourt: 'In some form or other the Furies had crossed his threshold.'

Gwendolen's relationship with Grandcourt has cartwheeled. From fancying herself his equal, the heroine to his hero, she now enters a ghastly vortex. From this moment until his death, she loses control of her destiny and will become his captive.

As the story moves away from their relationship and returns to Daniel, the complex web entangling him with Gwendolen and Grandcourt tightens briefly when they visit the house of Sir Hugo Mallinger, Daniel's guardian. By this time Gwendolen is no longer 'saucy', which was the adjective most often used to describe her before her marriage. Grandcourt's dominance is now palpable and Gwendolen's resistance has collapsed:

The belief in her own power of dominating was utterly gone. She had found a will like that of a crab or a boa-constrictor which goes on pinching or crushing without alarm at thunder. Not that Grandcourt was without calculation of the intangible effects which were the chief means of mastery; indeed, he had a surprising acuteness in detecting that situation of feeling in Gwendolen which made her proud and rebellious spirit dumb and helpless before him.

Gwendolen tries repeatedly to turn to Daniel for support, but each time Grandcourt thwarts her. Eventually, Gwendolen realises she is trapped in a dead marriage from which she sees no escape. She will only be released from captivity by Grandcourt's death.

After Grandcourt dies, Gwendolen assumes that she will be able to form a relationship with Daniel. To her mind, this would have been an obvious and justified assumption, and as the leading heroine of the story, she feels that this would be her due. However, once again Gwendolen is wrong footed and disappointed by Daniel, who announces that he will be married to Mirah. Just as he did in the casino, Daniel kills her luck and changes her destiny. Rather than being Daniel's heroine, Gwendolen is forced back into another form of isolation: life as a solitary widow.

On the face of it, Gwendolen gives her blessing to Daniel and Mirah in a letter which, in an echo of Mrs Glasher's curse to her, arrives on their wedding day:

'Do not think of me sorrowfully on your wedding-day...'

It is revealing that Gwendolen assumes they will think of her on their wedding day at all. Gwendolen has promised her mother that she shall live and she now assures Daniel: 'It shall be better with me because I have known you.'

When we close the book and consider who causes Gwendolen the most suffering, the answer is not as obvious as we might assume.

On the face of it, Grandcourt is clearly sadistic and suffocating while Daniel is as 'angelic' as Mirah emphatically believes. Yet a more nuanced reading suggests that Daniel causes Gwendolen the most suffering by providing her with a scintilla of hope that he might one day be her partner. She herself has to extinguish this hope. The shift in their relationship which she longed for never happens and because of him Gwendolen faces a very different ending from the one she expected. Her life will not be alongside Daniel's and their relationship will remain unconsummated.

In the very last ending that she would ever write, George Eliot shows that not all heroines' plans succeed. Their life journeys can take unexpected turns and sometimes they arrive at a very different place from their expected destination. Gwendolen will have to redefine what her role as heroine will be. All that she can conclude is that her future will be solitary, but she will survive.

While Jane Austen's heroines learn a great deal about themselves and their partners, they end their stories fulfilled and happily married. The sense of satisfaction comes from a journey that has almost come full circle, in that the next generation of the social order has been established and the social order itself has been perpetuated. The heroines have finally arrived to take up the new role of wife in the top ranks of society where they were always destined, even if they were diverted along the way. Ultimately, George Eliot's most ambitious and extensively drawn characters are her three heroines Romola, Dorothea and Gwendolen. Their journeys do not come full circle but break the pattern. Each of these women eventually emerges as a very different sort of heroine from the role that she had expected to play at the beginning of her journey.

Examining how Jane Austen and George Eliot explore and

develop the characters of their respective heroines, whether romantic or realist, brings us very close to the centre of their storytelling.

* * *

CHAPTER 7

VILLAINS AND VICTIMS

In the novels of Jane Austen and George Eliot, villains and victims don't just cause the twists and turns of the plot; they force us to explore questions of character, context and consequence. Inevitably, the choices the authors make for their characters offer a window into their distinctive worldview and we see that while Austen's villains often face social censure without catastrophic fallout, Eliot's undergo profound reckonings and face spiritual damnation.

While there are villains across all Austen's novels, there are scarcely any victims. Both the villains and their victims, with the single exception of Eliza in *Sense and Sensibility*, are shielded from any fate worse than temporary ignominy and an exclusion from the final curtain calls. Generally, the villains have made an attempt to ensnare the heroines and once the heroines have seen through them and rejected them, these villains are effectively redeemed by their own failure.

Notable villains such as Willoughby, Wickham, Henry Crawford and William Elliot are all let off lightly. But the list of their crimes is not trivial. Willoughby seduces the young Eliza and abandons her with their baby. After failing to seduce Darcy's sister Georgiana,

Wickham successfully seduces Lydia and holds the Bennet family to ransom. With his demand for a settlement of £10,000, he is callously prepared to ruin the Bennets. Henry Crawford is cynically intent upon 'making Fanny love him' without any intention of loving or marrying her himself. Such a seduction would see Fanny expelled from Mansfield Park, abandoned by her family and unable to marry. No doubt she would be flogged by her father, who comments ominously upon Maria's and Henry's adulterous affair: 'By God, if she belonged to *me*, I'd give her the rope's end as long as I could stand over her. A little flogging for man and woman too would be the best way of preventing such things.' Instead, Crawford seduces Maria Bertram and causes her marriage with Rushworth to collapse, which so precipitates her banishment. William Elliot's refusal to repay his debts to Mr Smith ruins him and leaves Mrs Smith living in poverty. She warns Anne: 'His heart is black and hollow.'

Yet none of these villains suffers for his crimes. The closest a villain comes to physical harm is the duel reported between Colonel Brandon and Willoughby in *Sense and Sensibility*, but both their pistol shots miss – a disappointing result, given Colonel Brandon's military training – and Willoughby emerges unscathed. His only punishment is to be married to a wealthy heiress while whimsically regretting that he had been unable to marry Marianne. Wickham is given his £10,000 and posted to a regiment based in the north. Perhaps the worst punishment is meted out to Maria Bertram, who left her husband Rushworth to move in with Henry Crawford. At the conclusion of *Mansfield Park*, we hear what happened:

> She hoped to marry him, and they continued together till she was obliged to be convinced that such hope was vain, and till

the disappointment and wretchedness arising from the conviction rendered her temper so bad, and her feelings for him so like hatred, as to make them for a while each other's punishment, and then induce a voluntary separation.

Austen then devises a specific punishment for Maria:

It ended in Mrs Norris's resolving to quit Mansfield Park and devote herself to her unfortunate Maria, and in an establishment being formed for them in another country, remote and private, where, shut up together with little society, on one side no affection, on the other no judgement, it may be reasonably supposed that their tempers became their mutual punishment.

To be thrown out of Jane Austen's 'cultivated garden', as Charlotte Brontë called it, to somewhere remote and private, another country even, is the worst punishment we hear of and Austen is clear that 'punishment' is the right word – she uses it twice in that paragraph. The other punishments given to those who have broken the rules and threatened the happiness of the married partners are little more than gentle condemnations. Incidentally this is why the title of P. D. James's follow-up to *Pride and Prejudice* is such a brilliant and arresting choice: *Death Comes to Pemberley*. With Austen, the worst fate that might befall Pemberley is that its 'shades might be polluted' by the arrival of Elizabeth and her mother's tradesmen family relations, but death is not allowed on stage in any of her books. No death comes to Pemberley, nor to any other Jane Austen location.

The only two people who die during the narratives and whose deaths therefore have an impact upon the plots are Dr Grant, whose death frees up his vicar's living for Edmund and Fanny to take over in *Mansfield Park*, and Mrs Churchill, who is Frank Churchill's aunt in *Emma*. Both these deaths take place off stage and are reported with a richly comic touch:

'Mrs Churchill, after being disliked at least twenty-five years, was now spoken of with compassionate allowances. In one point she was fully justified. She had never been admitted before to be seriously ill. The event quitted her of all the fancifulness and all the selfishness of imaginary complaints.'

This convenient death is a pivotal moment in *Emma*. It halts Frank's deceitful manoeuvres in Highbury and prevents them from having serious consequences, primarily for Jane Fairfax but also for Emma. Frank, whose name ironically belies his duplicity, has been sending out deceitful messages while he waits for his inheritance. After Mrs Churchill's death, he returns to Highbury to show himself in what he wants society to accept as his true colours. Armed with his inheritance from Mrs Churchill, Frank is able to announce his engagement with Jane Fairfax and save her from accepting the post as a governess. He cheerfully endeavours to clear up all misunderstandings. Now endowed with his own capital, Frank Churchill can ostensibly join the ranks of monied gentlemen. As far as Highbury society takes it, Frank Churchill is redeemed by his aunt's death and all is understood and forgiven – except by Mr Knightley, who still warily views him as the scheming 'trifling fellow' of his first appearance. In the nick of time, Mrs Churchill's death prevents Frank, who is an accomplished liar and manipulator, from developing into a worse villain. At the same time, Jane Fairfax is transformed from being cast off into obscurity as a governess and suffering as one of Frank Churchill's victims to becoming his bride.

Jane Fairfax is Austen's most sustained study of a woman who is trapped and subject to extended emotional stress. She is one of the

VILLAINS AND VICTIMS

few characters who is closest to becoming a genuine victim. Invariably described as 'cold', 'pale' and without an 'open temper', there is never any hint of comedy around Jane Fairfax or anything she says. In fact, Jane is in turmoil because she is hiding a secret – she and Frank Churchill are secretly engaged. In order to provide a smokescreen to conceal their engagement, when Frank arrives in Highbury he publicly flirts with Emma and also fools her into believing that Jane is in love with her friend's husband, Mr Dixon. Frank and Emma flirt to such an extent that Highbury society assumes that they have an attachment. During the outing to pick strawberries at Donwell Abbey, unable to bear the strain any longer and believing that Frank is attracted to Emma, Jane Fairfax leaves the party in a distraught state:

> I am fatigued; but it is not the sort of fatigue – quick walking will refresh me. Miss Woodhouse, we all know at times what it is to be wearied in spirits. Mine, I confess, are exhausted. The greatest kindness you can show me, will be to let me have my own way and only say that I am gone when it is necessary.

The following day, Frank and Emma flirt again during the Box Hill picnic and Emma also insults Jane's aunt, Miss Bates. In an excruciating scene, Frank Churchill oversteps the lines of decency: 'You order me, whether you speak or not. And you can be always with me. You are always with me.' He then announces to the assembled party: 'I am ordered by Miss Woodhouse (who, wherever she is, presides) to say that she desires to know what you are all thinking of.'

Unable to interfere, both because of her social status and also in order to preserve the secret of their engagement, Jane has to watch

Frank's excessive flirting with Emma. At Box Hill, it becomes too much for her, and that evening she breaks off her engagement with Frank Churchill and accepts the post as a governess. This is a life-changing moment for her and she collapses. When Emma tries to offer comfort to Jane, she is refused entry to her room. When Emma sends some arrowroot for her to use as an infusion, it is returned to her in a quiet but powerful rejection:

> Some arrowroot of very superior quality was speedily dispatched to Miss Bates with a most friendly note. In half an hour the arrowroot was returned, with a thousand thanks from Miss Bates, but 'dear Jane would not be satisfied without its being sent back; it was a thing she could not take – and, moreover, she insisted on her saying that she was not at all in want of anything.'

Jane Fairfax sees Emma as responsible for the collapse of her engagement to Frank Churchill. Her likely future as a governess, with an income set at less than a servant's pay and little access to society, would set her on a similar path to her aunt Miss Bates. This is a telling portrait of a young woman with limited options, a precarious position on the edge of society whose future hangs by a thread. It is understandable that Jane Fairfax repudiates Emma. Blinded by her collusion with Frank Churchill and with her arrowroot pointedly rejected, Emma has become the villain of the piece.

As soon as his aunt dies and his inheritance is released, Frank Churchill renounces his earlier treachery and takes his place with Jane as the third couple in the novel set to be happily married. Without his aunt's death, Frank Churchill was set to become one of Jane Austen's most pernicious villains. Jane Fairfax would have suffered most, but even Emma with her wealth and social position may have forfeited her marriage to Mr Knightley and risked a future as 'an old maid like Miss Bates'. We should make no mistake that Frank Churchill is – as Mr Knightley is aware – every bit as dangerous to women as a villain like Willoughby or Wickham.

The only death reported by Jane Austen in any detail is in *Sense and Sensibility*, where Colonel Brandon describes the death of his first love, Eliza. Both she and her daughter (also called Eliza) are crucial to our understanding of Willoughby's villainy, but Austen struggles to accommodate this death within the narrative and instead keeps Eliza's seduction and collapse into poverty at arm's length. Effectively, Eliza's death is twice removed from the narrative: firstly, it is a back story which takes place before the action of *Sense and Sensibility* starts, and secondly, as told by Colonel Brandon it is a story within a story, rather than part of the main plot. The emotional depths are further clouded by his deliberately obtuse storytelling and euphemisms:

'To be brief, when I quitted Barton last October – but this will give you no idea – I must go farther back. You will find me a very awkward narrator, Miss Dashwood; I hardly know where to begin.'

As Colonel Brandon begins to describe Eliza's tragic life, his language grows evasive: 'My brother had no regard for her; his pleasures were not what they ought to have been, and from the first he treated her unkindly.'

Colonel Brandon uses such stilted, strangled and remote language that it is virtually impossible to decipher his emotion beyond stock images of despair, such as: 'he could say no more, and rising hastily walked for a few minutes about the room … a few minutes more of silent exertion enabled him to proceed with composure.'

Colonel Brandon explains how he found Eliza:

'Regard for a former servant of my own, who had since fallen into misfortune, carried me to visit him in a spunging-house [a debtors' prison], where he was confined for debt; and there, in the same house, under similar confinement was my unfortunate sister.'

But having mentioned this extraordinary visit – a 'spunging-house' is an unprecedented location in Jane Austen – there are no further details. We are given no idea what the inside of a spunging-house looks like. Austen backs away from exploring this territory in further detail:

'What I endured in so beholding her – but I have no right to wound your feelings by attempting to describe it – I have pained you too much already.'

Just when we wanted to follow Colonel Brandon into the spunging-house and really understand what it was like for poor Eliza to be living there, the language remains steadfastly vague and generic: 'I was with her in her last moments.'

It feels as if the deadpan phrasing has been deliberately employed by Austen to dampen the emotional impact of the account and so avoid offending the reader. When Colonel Brandon turns to Eliza's daughter, Austen continues warily to circle the tragedy from a distance. Finally, when Colonel Brandon's story reaches its climax with the revelation that Eliza's daughter has recently been seduced and abandoned and there is a baby, the story is abruptly stopped.

The subject matter is highly emotionally charged, but Austen determinedly avoids this loss of control, and Colonel Brandon, who had warned Elinor she would find him 'a very awkward narrator', continues the evasive language: 'In short, I could learn nothing but that she was gone; all the rest, for eight long months, was left to conjecture. What I thought, what I feared, may be imagined; and what I suffered too.'

Only the mention of 'eight months' alerts us to the young Eliza's seduction and ensuing pregnancy. But what he 'thought', what he 'feared', what he 'suffered' is left unspoken and remains impossible to imagine because he covers it with a veil of euphemism and cliche. Aware that the purpose of the Colonel's story was to throw some light on Willoughby so that Elinor could assess his suitability to marry her sister Marianne, Elinor finally joins the dots and is jolted into a response:

'Good heavens! Could it be? Could Willoughby...?'

And Willoughby's treachery is revealed.

Yet Elinor does not then censure Willoughby or sympathise with Eliza. She does not even ask Colonel Brandon for further details. Elinor only has one question about the poor woman who has been seduced, abandoned and left with a baby:

'Is she still in town?'

Colonel Brandon confirms: 'I removed her and her child into the country, and there she remains.'

The matter is closed. Thereafter Elinor asks no questions about Eliza, who now slips off the radar of the novel. We have no idea what happened to her or to her baby (a third-generation Eliza?) and she does not reappear until she is slightingly referred to by Willoughby when he recounts his own version of events to Elinor. Once again, rather astonishingly, Elinor does not take Willoughby to task or question him further.

Of all the crimes committed by Jane Austen's villains, Willoughby's is the worst. Of all the victims, Eliza the mother and Eliza the daughter suffer the most. Yet despite her mother's wretched death in a spunging-house and then her own seduction by Willoughby and the unwanted illegitimate baby, Eliza remains off stage, shrouded in silence. In contrast, Willoughby is partially forgiven and ends up enjoying his country estate and London house with a rich heiress and his dogs and horses. It is difficult to know how to interpret this treatment of a villain and his victim. Perhaps Austen is simply acknowledging the pragmatic, unsentimental truth that a man who can gain a fortune will always fall on his feet and that lovers like Eliza will just be abandoned. Eliza and her baby are placed on the other side of Austen's highly cultivated garden wall; they are emphatically 'not in town'. Perhaps it is not a question of social class, but simply that as her caustic black humour reveals in this letter to Cassandra, Austen was always unsentimental about death and even poked fun at it: 'Mrs Hall, of Sherborne, was brought to bed yesterday of a dead child, some weeks before she expected, owing to a fright. I suppose she happened unawares to look at her husband.' Without missing a beat, the next sentence goes on unperturbed: 'There has been a great deal of rain here for this last fortnight.'

Jane Austen admits that she does not wish to explore difficult subjects or any depraved aspects of human nature in her work. As the loose ends of *Mansfield Park* are tied up and she sorts out the final division between villains and victims, Austen cheerfully addresses the reader: 'Let other pens dwell on guilt and misery. I quit such odious subjects as soon as I can, impatient to restore everybody not greatly at fault themselves to tolerable comfort, and to have done with all the rest.'

Perhaps Eliza is simply collateral damage, thrown under the turning wheels of the plot. Her suffering will not be addressed and she and her baby will be abandoned by the narrative just as they have been abandoned by Willoughby. We can at least hope that Colonel Brandon and Marianne as his new wife might find a cottage for them on their estate.

Rather than seeing any villain die, Austen prefers a softer version of death, which is just to kill their reputation. At the endings of her stories, she effectively judges her characters and hands out rewards and punishments. We have seen the rewards given to the leading men and women – a happy marriage and a comfortable income. As for the villains, they are typically left out of these happy endings. We do not know what happens to John Thorpe or Frederick Tilney at the end of *Northanger Abbey*; in *Sense and Sensibility*, we hear that Willoughby is not in an ideal marriage, although Sophia Grey with her capital of £50,000 cannot be too bad; and at the end of *Mansfield Park*, contact with Mary Crawford is severed as she stays with Mrs Grant, and the flawed characters of Maria and Julia are quite literally removed from the park. Fanny is left as the sole focus of Sir Thomas Bertram's affections – 'Fanny was indeed the daughter that he wanted' – and with adroit succession planning, Fanny's younger sister Susan even inherits Fanny's less enviable role as Lady Bertram's constant companion: 'Delighted to be so!' *Persuasion* concludes with Anne Elliot's conceited sister and father fading away while Anne has all the pleasure of her marriage to Captain Wentworth. The prime villains of the plot are her cousin William Elliot and Mrs Clay. They may not get a happy curtain call, but they will get by because after all he has the inheritance of a baronetcy to look forward to. There is a hint that they may even marry each other.

Jane Austen is generous to her villains. As a self-defined comic writer, her priority is to celebrate the happiness of her heroines. In this context, she is content to show that the villains have been removed from the heroine's path and cannot cause any more mischief. Taking Charlotte Brontë's image of the cultivated garden, whether they have been tidied up and planted in a chilly northern corner of the garden like Wickham or tipped over the garden wall and left to their own devices like Henry Crawford, these initially dangerous men who threatened to ruin the lives of a sequence of women have been defused or negated. The heroines' happiness is unassailable, and the villains are effectively emasculated.

* * *

If Jane Austen's approach to avoiding death in her fiction stems from her decision to 'let other pens dwell on guilt and misery' and to 'quit such odious subjects' as soon as she could, then George Eliot's writing answers that challenge – she certainly wields one of those 'other pens'. Deaths of all kinds occur throughout her work. For Eliot, there are essentially two kinds of death. There are the physical deaths of her villains, which are often tortuous, violent and described in graphic detail. There are also metaphorical deaths, in which the victims suffer from the sort of guilt and misery that Austen anticipates and pushes away. In these metaphorical deaths, characters enter a state of paralysis where they lose control of their lives and become trapped in a form of purgatory. Eliot describes Silas: 'Marner's thoughts ... were baffled by a blank like that which meets a plodding ant when the earth has broken away on its homeward path.' As with Silas Marner, Romola, Mrs Transome and Gwendolen are frozen into barely animate existence; their paralysis can only be broken by a powerful shock.

For George Eliot, an exploration of death, whether it is the long planned deranged murder of a villain or the desperate drowning of a sister and brother, is the natural extension of the premise of her writing. Just as surely as Austen tells us what she will not write about, Eliot tells us what she will write about. She sets out her approach in those opening lines of *Adam Bede*: 'With a single drop of ink for a mirror.' With this image, George Eliot brings us intensely close to her creative process. We (the 'chance comer') are invited to focus upon the drop of ink as it is poised at the tip of her pen, about to touch the paper. From this microscopic perspective, we look into this drop of ink at the end of her pen that is bulging with infinite possibilities and prepare to experience the world that she creates with it. We are invited to feel as close to her writing as we possibly can. If we follow her process of creation, George Eliot is making a commitment to us as readers, a promise, to reveal 'far-reaching visions'. We need to follow the ink.

As narrator, George Eliot proceeds to conjure up the reality of her locations. The first scene she creates in *Adam Bede* is the roomy workshop of Mr Jonathan Burge, but once we follow the ink we are led from this carpenter's workshop all the way through the novel to the powerful vision of Hetty Sorrel's disoriented and fractured mind as she tries to find a dark enough pond in which to drown herself.

George Eliot's explicit commitment to take us into the heart of her scenes extends to those which confront death. Invariably, these deaths are tangled with the emotions of the surviving characters, the victims, who sometimes have so fervently wished for the death of these villains that they have been tempted to commit murder themselves. These deaths provoke compassion, but this is complicated because it is also laced with grief, guilt and relief. When a surviving victim such as Romola or Dorothea is freed from an abusive relationship by the deaths of their husbands, they experience a powerful rebirth.

Adam Bede is framed by two deaths. The first is Adam's father. At the outset of the novel, we hear of 'a green valley with a brook running through it, full almost to overflowing with the late rains, overhung by low stooping willows'. We hear of Adam's father and his drunkenness and then as Adam and his brother Seth are walking by the river, Seth remarks:

'Why, what's that sticking against the willow?'

It is such a matter-of-fact question, so simply put. With no melodrama, Adam runs forward and drags the body out. They look at the 'glazed eyes' of their dead father. They carry him home and Adam makes the coffin. The death of Adam's father is a simple accident with no villains. The slight complexity in emotions in the family is that he had become a heavy drinker and an increasingly disruptive figure. The Bede family are better off without him. Without his father, Adam can take over the management of the family workshop and his path is clear to becoming the land agent for the Donnithorne estate. This early death in her first novel is the simplest death across all her books. From then on, the deaths involve villains and victims and are analysed in extensive psychological detail, perhaps none more so than the second death in *Adam Bede*: the murder of Hetty Sorrel's newborn baby.

Immediately after delivering the final manuscript of *Adam Bede*, Eliot wrote in her journal about the inspiration which prompted her to attempt this first full-length novel:

The germ of *Adam Bede* was an anecdote told me by my Methodist Aunt Samuel (the wife of my father's younger brother): an anecdote from her own experience. We were sitting together one afternoon during her visit to me at Griff, probably in 1839 or '40, when it occurred to her to tell me how she had visited a condemned criminal – a very ignorant girl who had murdered her child and refused to confess; how she had stayed with her praying through the night, and how the poor creature at last broke out into tears and confessed her crime. My aunt afterwards went with her in the cart to the place of execution.

Touchingly, Eliot concludes her diary entry about *Adam Bede*:

'I love it very much and am deeply thankful to have written it, whatever the public may say to it – a result which is still in darkness, for I have at present had only four sheets of the proof.'

The death of Hetty's baby at the heart of *Adam Bede* is disturbing and heart-wrenching. As Eliot explains in the same diary piece, by building the novel around the death of Hetty's baby she had to work hard to make Hetty a strong enough character to sustain the narrative:

> The problem of construction that remained was to make the unhappy girl one of the chief *dramatis personae* and connect her with the hero ... When I began to write it, the only elements I had determined on, besides the character of Dinah, were the character of Adam, his relation to Arthur Donnithorne and their mutual relation to Hetty, i.e. to the girl who commits child-murder – the scene in the prison being, of course, the climax towards which I worked. Everything else grew out of the characters and their mutual relations.

Seduced by the feckless Arthur Donnithorne, loved unswervingly by the stoic and wholesome Adam Bede, Hetty is caught between these two men. Compared with George Eliot's later villains, such as Tito and Grandcourt, Arthur is rather lightweight. While written in 1858, *Adam Bede* was set in 1799. There are clear traces of eighteenth-century and Regency figures in Arthur Donnithorne. Looking at Arthur through the lens of Jane Austen, it is possible to identify traces of Bingley in that he is the squire and he is anxious to please. There are also darker traces of Wickham in that Arthur is a seducer. He understands that he should stop the flirtation and budding relationship with Hetty, but he justifies his actions because after all she is so very pretty and he cannot help himself. The flirtation in the woods escalates into seduction in the isolated Hermitage with appalling consequences that eventually destroy Hetty and her baby.

The death of Hetty's baby is vividly recounted from two perspectives. Firstly, we watch Hetty as she moves across the landscape in agonising slow motion and breaks down in suicidal desperation. We have 'followed the ink' and Eliot has taken us to a very desolate place. After her arrest, Hetty refuses to speak. Only when Dinah arrives to comfort her in the prison cell does she eventually break her silence to tell her version of the story. Hetty's retelling of the story from her own perspective in her broken vocabulary is harrowing. We relive this from within Hetty's tortured mind:

> 'Dinah,' Hetty sobbed out, throwing her arms round Dinah's neck, 'I will speak ... I will tell ... I won't hide it any more.'
>
> At last, Hetty whispered –
>
> 'I did do it, Dinah ... I buried it in the wood ... the little baby ... and it cried ... I heard it cry ... ever such a way off ... all night ... and I went back because it cried.'

By using Hetty's voice with her simple country English, George Eliot captures her confused, passionate feelings and brings us intensely close to the trauma of her suffering:

> 'I thought there'd perhaps be a ditch or a pond there...'

Hetty's mind is in turmoil as she wrestles with her exhaustion, suicide and her baby:

'It was like a heavy weight hanging round my neck; and yet its crying went through me, and I daren't look at its little hands and face ... I walked about but there was no water.'

It is a profoundly moving account of what might now be diagnosed as the effects of serious post-natal post-traumatic stress disorder.

This is a very different narrative treatment from Jane Austen's depiction of Eliza's death in the spunging-house. It is as if in their first full-length novels each author is setting out the parameters of what they intend to write about – and what will be left out. Austen clearly signals that she will not engage with her victims. She will not examine Eliza too closely or explore any moral questions about Willoughby's responsibility for her daughter's seduction and abandonment. The prime role for Eliza and her daughter is to illustrate Colonel Brandon's loyalty and Willoughby's treachery, but then she is ruthlessly dropped from the narrative. Eliot takes the opposite approach. By building the whole construction of the novel around Hetty's confession in the prison cell as she sits through the night waiting for her execution, Eliot brings us ever closer to the victim.

The last words spoken by Hetty about her baby are searing and unanswerable. We know Hetty buried her baby under a tree and we have been told that its hand was sticking out of the mud. Hetty has given us her experience and repeatedly described the baby's incessant crying inside her head. She concludes her story with a last question to Dinah:

'Dinah, do you think God will take away that crying and the place in the wood, now I've told everything?'

While *Adam Bede* is framed by the first death of Adam's father and the second death of Hetty's baby, there is a third death. It is referred to fleetingly in the epilogue and she is not named, but it is of Hetty herself. Rather than being executed for the murder of her baby, Hetty was transported to Australia. Dinah comments: 'And the death of the poor wanderer when she was coming back to us has been sorrow upon sorrow.'

Hetty's death concludes the tragedy that Adam and Dinah will absorb and take with them as they look to their own future.

* * *

George Eliot uses the same narrative technique where a death is recounted by a surviving participant to great effect across her fiction, most poignantly in her final novel, *Daniel Deronda*.

Just as with Hetty's story of her baby's death, when Gwendolen recounts how Grandcourt died on their sailing trip it is the complexity of the relationships around the death and the questions of responsibility which is the psychological territory Eliot explores.

Grandcourt's death is surrounded by ambiguity. We have followed his increasingly vicious control of Gwendolen with rising concern. There appears to be no way for her to escape him. His all-encompassing, suffocating control culminates in their yachting trip around the Mediterranean. The sense of Gwendolen's captivity in the hands of a predator is overwhelming: 'Quarrelling with Grandcourt was impossible: she might as well have made angry remarks to a dangerous serpent ornamentally coiled in her cabin without invitation.'

Grandcourt clearly takes sadistic pleasure in this domination:

VILLAINS AND VICTIMS

Grandcourt had an intense satisfaction in leading his wife captive after this fashion: it gave their life on a small scale a royal representation and publicity in which everything familiar was got rid of, and everybody must do what was expected of them whatever might be their private protest – the protest (kept strictly private) adding to the piquancy of despotism.

Grandcourt has squeezed the self-confidence and the life out of Gwendolen. When Daniel arrives in Genoa, Grandcourt forces Gwendolen, his trophy wife, to come out with him on a small sailing boat for the day so that she does not catch sight of the man he perceives as his rival. Gwendolen has no choice but to agree:

'Oh, let us go,' said Gwendolen. The walls had begun to be an imprisonment, and while there was breath in this man he would have mastery over her. His words had the power of thumbscrews and the cold touch of the rack. To resist was to act like a stupid animal unable to measure results.

Gwendolen is a victim trapped in the role of the living dead. She has lost all hope of release or of regaining her own self-confidence. As they are in the boat together, Gwendolen's final capitulation is simply: 'God help me.' She is, however, forced by Grandcourt into the admission that 'I shall like nothing better than this', to which Grandcourt replies: 'Very well; we'll do the same tomorrow. But we must be turning in soon. I shall put about.'

Leaving Grandcourt and Gwendolen poised at this point, Eliot opens a new chapter that shifts to Daniel Deronda's perspective. He becomes aware of a sailing boat being rowed ashore. At first, the rumours are of a lady who has drowned, but then he sees Gwendolen, who tells him: 'It is come, it is come! He is dead!'

We realise it is Grandcourt who has drowned. His death, coming against all our expectations, is breathtaking and abrupt.

The confession which Gwendolen then makes to Daniel tells the episode from her point of view. Given that so much of the narrative perspective has been Gwendolen's, we are surprised by how many secrets have been kept from us along the way: the thin knife she keeps in a box, her fantasy that she would hide it under her pillow and how she would use it, dropping the key overboard yet wondering whether she can find a locksmith to open the box. How did we not know these things? The one thing we did already know was her mounting despair and rage against her torture and the sense that she had virtually died inside:

> I want to tell you what it was that came over me in that boat. I was full of rage at being obliged to go – full of rage – and I could do nothing but sit there like a galley-slave ... We never looked at each other, only he spoke to order me. The very light about me seemed to hold me a prisoner and force me to sit as I did.

She continues with her confession:

> I knew no way of killing him there, but I did, I did kill him in my thoughts ... All the while I felt that I was getting more wicked ... The evil longings, the evil prayers came again and blotted everything else dim, till, the midst of them, I don't know how it was, he was turning the sail, there was a gust, he was struck, I know nothing, I only know that I saw my wish outside me.

Gwendolen recounts Grandcourt's last words as he was swept overboard. It is his final order to her: 'The rope!'

But Gwendolen holds the rope in her hand and she does not throw it. She concludes: 'And I held my hand, and my heart said, "Die!" – and he sank.'

It was in Gwendolen's gift to throw the rope and to save Grandcourt. She chose not to. Holding the rope, she saw Grandcourt's face above the water, then below the water: 'There was the dead face – dead, dead. It can never be altered. That was what happened. That was what I did. You know it all. It can never be altered.'

With this shattering sequence of four and five word sentences, Eliot takes us to the heart of Gwendolen and shows us her passion, her entrapment and her faltering grip on her own identity. As with the confession told by Hetty to Dinah, this account brings us inside the mind of a traumatised woman. During his life, she was full of murderous thoughts and now in his death, she is racked by terrible guilt. She is a victim in both his life and his death.

Grandcourt is the most brutal of villains and his is a brutal death. As Eliot so often does, she mirrors one death with another, and Grandcourt's violent and unpitied death is followed by the peaceful death of Mordecai, who is a sort of serene prophet in *Daniel Deronda*.

While Grandcourt dies struggling and fighting in full view of Gwendolen withholding the rope, Mordecai gently slips to another existence with Daniel's and Mirah's arms around him, thereby releasing Daniel and Mirah to their united future. Mordecai has been a visionary for Daniel and Mirah, rising above day-to-day life. His death is so lyrically depicted that it is presented to us as not so much a death as more of a rebirth into his preferred state of existence: 'He chose to be dressed and sit up in his easy chair as usual, Deronda and Mirah on each side of him ... with eyes full of some restful meaning, as if to assure them that while this remnant of breathing-time was difficult, he felt an ocean of peace beneath him.'

Mordecai's last words to them are:

Death is coming to me as the divine kiss which is both parting and reunion – which takes me from your bodily eyes and gives me full presence in your soul. Where thou goest, Daniel, I shall go. Is it not begun? Have I not breathed my soul into you? We shall live together.

It is a wonderfully calm, uplifting ending. Mordecai is transported into a spiritual future. In his death, Mordecai becomes a new life force.

* * *

While it is tempting to categorise villains and victims, there are many instances in George Eliot's fiction where the lines are blurred. In *Silas Marner*, another solitary woman with a baby is struggling across a desolate landscape. Molly is secretly married to Godfrey Cass, but Godfrey has cast Molly off and is under pressure from his domineering father to marry Nancy, the daughter of the neighbouring landowner. Only Godfrey's brother Dunstan knows his secret. Impoverished and now an opium addict, Molly is walking through the snow on New Year's Eve to give Godfrey their daughter and try to force him to take responsibility for her. Waylaid by the snow, Molly is lost, exhausted and drugged with opium. Like

Hetty Sorrel, she wants to use her baby almost as proof of the relationship. Also like Hetty, she has been wholly abandoned. Eliot draws a fine line between feeling actively suicidal as Hetty feels and feeling just beyond the ability to care and look after herself and her baby as Molly feels. Molly sinks first into despair and then into an opium-induced state of mind and the soft, apparently comforting snowdrift. Molly is clearly a victim. When Molly dies, her baby Eppie is released and toddles across the snow towards the golden light streaming out of Silas Marner's open door.

This is both a rebirth for Eppie and for Silas, who has suffered a metaphorical death by being banished from the religious sect based at Lantern Yard. Falsely accused of theft and arriving at Raveloe as a refugee, Silas starts the story as a solitary myopic figure working in isolation and excluded from the community. Silas too is a victim, especially when his life savings of gold coins are stolen by Dunstan. The story of Silas's rebirth is all the more powerful because there appeared to be no way back to life for him. He is a 'poor mushed creature' whose 'head was all of a muddle'. It is impossible to conceive that a baby would enter his life and that he would adopt it.

The second virtual 'death' is that of Godfrey Cass and his marriage. This is a quiet and poignant affair. All along Godfrey has been effectively the villain of the story. Godfrey had married Molly then dismissed her, he had refused to identify her dead body and he had refused to admit that the baby which had crawled into Silas Marner's cottage was in fact his. He suggests to Silas that he take the baby to the workhouse and gives him a shilling. Assuming that he has managed to cover everything up, Godfrey marries Nancy. But after their first baby girl dies in infancy, their marriage is childless. When Dunstan's skeleton is found in the well sixteen years later, along with Silas's gold coins, Godfrey decides to confess the truth about his past to Nancy. The lines between villain and victim begin to blur:

> There was no indignation in her voice – only deep regret. 'Godfrey, if you had but told me this six years ago, we could have done some of our duty by the child. Do you think I'd have refused to take her in, if I'd known she was yours?' At that moment Godfrey felt all the bitterness of an error that was not simply futile, but had defeated its own end.

Nancy goes on:

> 'And – oh, Godfrey – if we'd had her from the first, if you'd taken to her as you ought, she'd have loved me for her mother – and you'd have been happier with me: I could better have bore my little baby dying and our life might have been more like what we used to think it 'ud be.'
> The tears fell, and Nancy ceased to speak.

Partly hoping to provide Eppie with a better life and partly seeking their own redemption, Godfrey and Nancy set off to reclaim Eppie as their daughter. They entertain the expectation that she will gratefully accept their offer; after all, Silas is a lowly weaver living in a tiny cottage with an earth floor and Godfrey is the squire of the village living in the grand hall. To their surprise, their offer is passionately rejected by Silas, who then turns to give Eppie the choice. In the second critical turning point of the novel, Eppie also 'passionately' and 'impetuously' rejects Godfrey and Nancy. Mortified, they leave the cottage and return home. There is a sense of quiet death. They let themselves into the house: 'Nancy laid down her bonnet and shawl.'

'That's ended!' says Godfrey.

The conversation is simple and has the gentle cadence of a forlorn couple. It is a scene of quiet domestic disappointment; something inside them has been extinguished. It is harsh for Nancy – and harsher still given that her own baby girl died, and she keeps the baby's little white dress folded up in her chest of drawers.

In contrast to this virtual death and the barren future which Godfrey and Nancy face, Silas and Eppie are looking ahead to an enlarged family as she marries Aaron: 'You won't be giving me away, father,' she had said before they went to church. 'You'll only be taking Aaron to be a son to you.'

In a glorious scene of rebirth, the wedding party of Silas, Dolly, Eppie and Aaron walk towards the Stone-Pits cottage with its fertile garden. They have combined as a new and bigger family. Their new life has been earned the hard way and has only been made possible by the life-changing moment when Silas stood up and made the far-reaching emotional commitment to the baby, the very same commitment that Godfrey failed to make. Silas is no longer a victim; he is now surrounded by a loving family and they walk together towards their future bright and brim-full of hope and life. Equally at this point, it no longer seems appropriate to define Godfrey as the villain; he has now become a victim of his own past life and his failure to take in and love his own baby.

* * *

Whether for her villains or her victims, Jane Austen prefers to sidestep death. If death cannot be avoided, she arranges for it to take place remotely, where she can mockingly present it in parenthesis to the main action. She uses a death as a key to unlock the plot and to provide the necessary inheritance or living to a beneficiary's advantage.

Within George Eliot's work, death is graphically presented within the main action and occurs in many different ways. Violent death can strike down the villains either as a long-sought revenge against which no chainmail vest can provide protection, or it can merely represent their just deserts as they trip into a deep well after robbing a solitary weaver of his life savings or slump head down on a garden bench. For the victims who die, their death is presented as an all-encompassing embrace that overwhelms them, such as the torrential flood water or a deep snowdrift. For those victims who witness the death of their tormentors close up and survive, it can provide both a form of closure from their abusive relationships and an opening to a future life – a new and hard-earned freedom alive with possibility.

* * *

CHAPTER 8

ENDINGS AND ECHOES

As 1816 progressed, Jane Austen managed to complete the manuscript that she was calling *The Elliots*, but towards the end of the year she was suffering from poor health. It is now commonly suspected that she suffered from Hodgkin's lymphoma, meaning that she would have been susceptible to unusually severe infective illnesses as well as chronic conjunctivitis that probably impeded her ability to write. It is difficult to be certain of a diagnosis, though, because medical records are scant and Cassandra destroyed many letters in which she detailed her symptoms. Writing to her old friend Alethea Bigg (whose brother was Harris) on 24 January 1817, Austen comments:

> I think I understand my own case now so much better than I did as to be able by care to keep off any serious return of illness. I am more and more convinced that bile is at the bottom of all I have suffered, which makes it easy to know how to treat myself.

By emphasising bile with her underlining, she believed that she was suffering from the same illness which Henry had suffered from two years previously. At the time, the prescribed cure was calomel, a mercury-based mixture. Unfortunately, if she was treating herself with calomel, she would only have been poisoning herself further. One of the side effects of swallowing mercury is vomiting, bloody diarrhoea and acute cramps, which unfortunately were then all taken as signs that the calomel was working and purging the system to flush out the disease.

Despite her illness, Jane Austen rises to the occasion with humour, as she invariably does in all her letters. She had an instinctive wish to rise above any pain, cast off anything 'odious' and delight any audience. Her letter to Alethea goes on to note that the rain has been so bad they cannot go out in the cart meaning 'our donkeys are necessarily having so long a run of luxurious idleness that I suppose we shall find that they have forgotten much of their education when we use them again'. This is the letter where she also touches upon Henry's first sermon: 'It will be a nervous hour for our pew.'

Although she makes light of her illness, laughs about their lazy donkeys and makes no direct mention of Henry's catastrophic bankruptcy, it is possible to detect how far Jane Austen and her brother have fallen. She is treating herself with toxic mercury, her household clearly cannot afford a horse and carriage but just two donkeys and a cart, the village roads are flooded and Henry has crashed from being a high-flying London banker to a lowly parish curate.

Four months later, her family moved Jane closer to medical care in Winchester, but by then it was too late. Jane Austen died on 18 July 1817. While she could solve all the problems that beset her heroines and provide them with happy endings that involved good husbands, good health and plenty of money, in the end she could not solve these problems for herself.

ENDINGS AND ECHOES

* * *

From the time of her death, a new reality was created around the life of Jane Austen that would echo through the ages. As we have seen, in the final twist of her life story Jane Austen left a surprise for her brother Henry to find: two unpublished manuscripts in her desk. Henry took responsibility for renaming the typescripts and arranging their posthumous publication with John Murray as *Northanger Abbey* and *Persuasion*. As he did so, he took this as his chance to start reinventing his sister's story.

In Henry's ponderous foreword, we begin to see the new myth of Jane Austen being created. Right from the opening sentence, it is clear that the Austen literary genes have bypassed him:

> When the public, which has not been insensible to the merits of *Sense and Sensibility*, *Pride and Prejudice*, *Mansfield Park*, and *Emma*, shall be informed that the hand which guided that pen is now mouldering in the grave, perhaps a brief account of Jane Austen will be read with a kindlier sentiment than simple curiosity.

The expression 'mouldering in the grave' would have had Austen scoffing in her grave, and for a man who earlier delighted in writing exuberant letters to John Murray (unless of course that letter was actually dictated by Jane and just signed by Henry), the tone is oddly both pompous and muted. Henry seemed eager to frame his sister's life as a virtuous existence devoid of any drama. A new image is born, one that she has never shaken off: the image of Jane Austen as the prim spinster aunt:

'Short and easy will be the task of the mere biographer. A life of usefulness, literature and religion was not by any means a life of event.'

Given that Henry, along with his sister Jane, had an expansive charm, loved company and enjoyed playing to an audience, it is strange that he seemed to want to squeeze the wit and vibrancy out of her life. Perhaps his self-confidence was affected by his bankruptcy, or perhaps his lugubrious tone comes from his new role as a pious clergyman. In any event, Henry's sombre and low-key approach was echoed by the next generation of family biographers. In the 1867 account *My Aunt Jane Austen: A Memoir*, Caroline Austen opens with an introduction to 'a very private and rather uneventful life'. If this was not enough to put off her readers, she continues: 'My Aunt's life at Chawton, as far as I ever knew, was an easy and pleasant one – it had little variety in it, and I am not aware of any particular trials, till her own health began to fail.'

In the first expanded biography published in 1869, *A Memoir of Jane Austen*, Edward Austen-Leigh continues the myth of the spotless spinster aunt, intoning:

> Of events, her life was singularly barren: few changes and no great crisis ever broke the smooth current of its course … Her talents did not introduce her to the notice of other writers, or connect her with the literary world, or in any degree pierce through the obscurity of her domestic retirement.

He went on to dismiss her letters as domestic and trivial:

'A wish has sometimes been expressed that some of Jane Austen's letters should be published. Some entire letters, and many extracts, will be given in this memoir; but the reader must be warned not to expect too much from them.' He goes on to patronise them: 'The style is always clear, and generally animated, while a vein of humour continually gleams through the whole; but the materials may be thought inferior to the execution, for they treat only of the details of domestic life.'

With excruciating condescension, he remarks:

'They may be said to resemble the nest which some little bird builds of the materials nearest at hand, of the twigs and mosses supplied by the tree in which it is placed, curiously constructed out of the simplest matters.'

On the death of Fanny Knight (Austen's niece) in 1882, a real treasure trove of Jane Austen's life was discovered. Fanny's son Edward Knatchbull-Hugessen found a box in his mother's attic containing a collection of ninety-six letters, which Cassandra had tied up with ribbons and left to Fanny. This more than doubled the number of letters that have been preserved. In 1884, Knatchbull-Hugessen published the collection of these letters with a preface that also entirely missed the point of their joyful gossip, vivid domestic detail and irrepressible wit:

'In truth the real beauty of Jane Austen's life really consisted in its being uneventful: it was emphatically a home life and she the light and blessing of a home circle.'

Reviewing the publication of this second collection of letters, *The Times* agreed with the general Austen family line and concluded that they were of rather trifling importance, describing them as 'nothing'.

As well as finding echoes of Jane Austen's zest for life in her fiction, we can pick them up most readily in her surviving collected letters. It is necessarily an incomplete history and many of the echoes that we find are unanswered. Just as her fiction requires careful analysis to 'catch her in the act of greatness', as Virginia Woolf put it, so her letters provide many disguised hints that need forensic analysis. Throughout her correspondence, there are comments which stand out and make her presence feel so immediate. Her tart observations on the lives of those around her can be enjoyed as much as any of the social commentary of her novels.

Here she is recounting a family trip to the dentist in 1813. We have all been to the dentist and we feel as if we are right beside her:

> The poor girls and their teeth! We were a whole hour at Spence's, and Lizzy's were filed and lamented over again and poor Marianne had two taken out after all, the two just beyond the eye teeth, to make room for those in front. Fanny, Lizzy and I walked into the next room, where we heard each of the two sharp hasty screams. Fanny's teeth were cleaned and, pretty as they are, Spence found something to do to them, putting in gold and talking gravely and making a considerable point of seeing her again before winter.

She concludes: 'I would not have him look at mine for a shilling a tooth and double it – it was a disagreeable hour.'

It is difficult not to feel close to Jane Austen, and to wince on the recipient's behalf, when reading such astringent comments as her correction of her nephew's manners in this letter to Edward James Austen on 9 July 1816:

'You never thanked me for my last letter which went by the delivery of the cheese. I cannot bear not to be thanked.'

The waspish tone echoes Mrs Norris, and so does the mention of the cheese. By combining deliveries, Jane Austen was economising just like Mrs Norris and so ensuring that she saved the cost of posting the letter.

In September 1796, there had been an earlier trace of Mrs Norris in this acerbic remark:

'Louisa's figure is very much improved; she is as stout again as she was. Caroline is not grown at all coarser than she was, nor Harriet at all more delicate.'

And here she is chivvying people for lost clothing:

'I do not believe that any of the party were aware of the valuables they had left behind; nor can I hear anything of Anna's gloves.'

She is not above congratulating herself:

'We are very busy making Edward's shirts and I am proud to say that I am the neatest worker of the party.'

And she signs off: 'I know nothing of my mother's handkerchief, but I dare say I shall find it soon.'

Like Mrs Norris, we can see her setting off along the corridors on a mission to track down the missing gloves and handkerchief. These are echoes of a domestic life which we instantly recognise. A more unusual and thought-provoking echo of her imagination is her advice to Anna, one of her nieces who has just asked for help with the plotting of a novel. Anna is struggling to bring a curate to life on the page and her Aunt Jane provides this startling advice which is a beguiling echo of a literary path that she might herself have taken:

> What can you do with Egerton to increase the interest for him? I wish you could contrive something, some family occurrence to draw out his good qualities more, some distress among brothers or sisters to relieve by the sale of his Curacy – something to take him mysteriously away and then heard of at York or Edinburgh – in an old great coat.

Sadly, Anna did not publish her novel and this stunning advice was never taken up. It shows Austen's imagination effortlessly creating situations and mystery from a detail as seemingly insignificant as a coat. The addition of an old greatcoat injects pace and suspense and feels much more modern than her own writing. Of course, she never lived to see the craze for old greatcoats worn by so many twentieth-century icons such as Sherlock Holmes, Charlie Chaplin and the tramps in *Waiting for Godot*.

By insisting that their aunt lived the dull, worthy blameless life of an old maid, Jane Austen's family and their five assorted biographies all missed the point. They missed the real clues that are scattered across her letters and illuminate her personality – that their Aunt Jane could be acidic, acerbic, sharp, gossipy and flirtatious. She could attract and repulse men; she was petulant, greedy, generous and loving. Their Aunt Jane was neither a remote icon of literary perfection nor an unblemished spinster aunt but endearingly human. Put another way, if Jane Austen had embodied only the saintly and spinster aunty qualities which her family tried to insist on, she simply could not have written the novels she did.

Perhaps her family were trying to shoehorn their Aunt Jane into a neatly defined box in just the same way that her novels packaged everyone into neat boxes. The collection of letters provides many unfinished endings and mysteries which are left unanswered. In her real life, Jane Austen had many frustrating gaps in which aspects of her private life fade away without explanation. Perhaps her family wanted to have a sense of control, but unless she chose to write and explain herself she was unanswerable to anybody. After her death, the Austen family read her letters and tried to piece the jigsaw puzzle of her life together, but they were just as much in the dark as we are today.

Like us, they would have wondered at the long list of unfinished stories and episodes of Aunt Jane's life that had no clear-cut endings. There is the dancing partner who had to be teased to dance and was the 'flirt and genius' of the evening but who then vanished; Tom Lefroy, the good-looking young Irishman with whom she was 'most profligate and shocking in the way of dancing and sitting down together' but who then failed to propose to her; the succession of dancing partners who kept her on the dance floor all evening but who then faded away; Harris Bigg-Withers, the stammering younger brother of a neighbourhood friend who did propose to her and who was joyfully accepted for one evening – what did they do that night? – but who was then rejected the next morning; Charles Haden, the ardent London apothecary who provocatively declared that he preferred *Mansfield Park* to *Pride and Prejudice* – but who then might have never said goodbye; and James Clarke, the Prince Regent's predatory librarian who tried to seduce her by inviting her to stay in his secret hidden rooms in Golden Square. These loose, unconnected endings are not neatly tied up in the manner of a Jane Austen novel with the dots seamlessly joined by an invisible author's imagination. Instead, whether from her life in Hampshire or her more unaccounted-for time in London, they are the thread of the real life that Austen lived, necessarily incomplete with all its pauses, gaps and unanswered questions. It was much easier for the Austen family to ignore all this and pretend that their Aunt Jane was just everyone's favourite spinster aunt.

Unlike this personal life of half-finished stories, Jane Austen made her inward imaginative life perfectly ordered. The world of her fiction was her chance to exert her omniscient authorial control. The obvious and compelling quest for marriage drives the endings of each of Jane Austen's novels and she ties off all the narrative threads into neat marriage bows. The satisfaction created by these neatly tied-up endings makes Austen one of our most celebrated authors who is invariably cited as the key inspiration by every subsequent writer of romantic comedy.

Right up until the last year of her life, when she wrote *Persuasion*, Jane Austen's stories all pivot irresistibly towards comedy as they reach their endings. Comedy needs a punchline and Austen understood how to deliver the punchline of a happy ending.

Marianne Dashwood could have been written in a very different way. After seeing her exulting in Willoughby's company, Colonel Brandon takes her sister Elinor to one side. He starts to say how much Marianne reminds him of another young woman he once knew, but then he stops. Later we hear that this woman is the tragic figure of Eliza. Colonel Brandon has tried to warn Elinor, but to no effect. When Willoughby abandons Marianne and refuses to acknowledge her, cutting her in public at the London ball, Marianne collapses. Unlike Eliza, she has not been seduced, but her story could have been just as tragic. However, at heart Jane Austen is a comic writer and *Sense and Sensibility* will be a romantic comedy. From the moment of Marianne's collapse Austen shifts gear and introduces a comic twist to Marianne's suffering. As she staggers off to her bedroom, Mrs Jennings moves forward:

'Poor soul!' cried Mrs Jennings. 'How it grieves me to see her! And I declare if she is not gone away without finishing her wine! And the dried cherries too!'

Later, Mrs Jennings offers further help:

I have just recollected that I have some of the finest old Constantia wine in the house that ever was tasted, so I have brought a glass of it for your sister. My poor husband! How fond he was of it! Whenever he had a touch of his old cholicky gout, he said it did him more good than anything else in the world. Do take it to your sister.

The gout-curing wine never makes it to Marianne, because since Elinor is suffering from Edward's protracted absence, she sees no harm in swigging the glass herself.

News of Willoughby's treachery spreads, but the reactions all undermine any sense of sincere passion or tragedy and heighten the comedy:

> Sir John could not have thought it possible. 'Such a good-natured fellow! He did not believe there was a bolder rider in England! He wished him at the devil with all his heart ... Such a deceitful dog! It was only the last time they met that he had offered him one of Folly's puppies! And this was the end of it!'

At the beginning of the novel, Marianne is first introduced as a young woman who might break the limits of convention and possibly live a life of risk. Standing for sensibility, she is presented as Romantic with a capital R, an impetuous idealist in the vein of Percy Shelley or Lord Byron. As they approach the end of the novel, Marianne and Elinor are swept up in the all-encompassing comic plot and become diminished. Through the eyes of Mrs Jennings, the Dashwood sisters are reduced to the same status as her own daughter, Charlotte: they are just two young girls trying to secure husbands like everyone else, who most likely will be 'married by Michaelmas'. On the final page of the book, Marianne falls into the arms of Colonel Brandon, the man whom she had previously considered much too old to marry. She betrays all her idealistic principles by adopting the role of a conventional landed gentleman's wife:

> Marianne Dashwood was born to an extraordinary fate. She was born to discover the falsehood of her own opinions, and to counteract, by her conduct, her most favourite maxims. She was born to overcome an affection formed so late in life as at seventeen, and with no sentiment superior to strong esteem and lively friendship, voluntarily to give her hand to another! ... a man ... whom two years before she had considered too old to be married – and who still sought the constitutional safeguard of a flannel waistcoat! But so it was.

The punchline is superbly polished and witty – the final reintroduction of Colonel Brandon's flannel waistcoat steals the show.

The supreme wit with which Jane Austen writes and the tightness of her endings puts charm at a greater premium than any exploration of more ragged and complex issues. But of course such polish also means it is superficial, and writing to her sister Cassandra, Austen admitted of *Pride and Prejudice*: 'The work is rather too light and bright and sparkling; it wants shade.' She then laughingly suggests a solution:

> It wants to be stretched out here and there with a long chapter – of sense, if it could be had, if not, of solemn specious nonsense, about something unconnected with the story; an Essay on Writing, a critique on Walter Scott, or the history of Buonaparte – or anything that would form a contrast and bring the reader with increased delight to the playfulness and Epigrammatism of the general style.

Anyone falling for that suggestion would be falling into a trap, but it is these endings that no doubt made Brontë exclaim of Austen with exasperation that 'the passions are perfectly unknown to her; she rejects even a speaking acquaintance with that stormy sisterhood'.

The only novel in which Austen allows a thin strand of uncertainty to slide into the ending is *Persuasion*. Against all odds and obstacles, Anne Elliot and Captain Wentworth have triumphed and we reach the last page. The last paragraph of the last page opens with what appears to be one of Austen's usual statements of complete happiness to frame a happy ending:

'Anne was tenderness itself, and she had the full worth of it in Captain Wentworth's affection.'

However, uniquely for Austen she then takes a different line. The final sentences of the book cast an unexpected possibility and with it some unexpected doubt. Perhaps this is the 'shade' that she told Cassandra that romantic comedies such as *Pride and Prejudice* were lacking:

> His profession was all that could ever make her friends wish that tenderness less; the dread of a future war all that could dim her sunshine. She gloried in being a sailor's wife, but she must pay the tax of quick alarm for belonging to that profession which is, if possible, more distinguished in its domestic virtues than in its national importance.

For the first time in the endings of her novels, Austen introduces the sense that the concluding marriage is not a self-contained bubble but will be impacted by the outside world. This new and unexpected element of realism introduces a more optimistic note. Anne Elliot has come further than any other Jane Austen heroine.

Initially described as 'faded and thin', 'haggard' and with a 'bloom that had vanished early', by the end of the book Anne has been recreated as a dazzling vibrant bride who 'glories in being a sailor's wife'. Together with Captain Wentworth, she is ready to respond to any kind of crisis – just as she did in Lyme Regis, where she saved Louisa's life. Jane Austen has opened up a new dimension for her.

The ending is different because, most unusually, Austen has allowed the reader into Captain Wentworth's perspective. Before these final lines, in a piece of theatrical brilliance she manages to stage a scene within a crowded room, where it seems impossible for there to be any kind of revelation. Five people are in a room at the White Hart inn: Anne is stuck talking to Captain Harville about the nature of female commitment, Mrs Musgrove and Mrs Croft are unhelpfully discussing the drawback of a long engagement and Captain Wentworth is writing a letter.

As Mrs Musgrove's and Mrs Croft's conversation grows increasingly personal, Anne feels its pointed relevance to her and checks across the room:

'Her eyes instinctively glanced towards the distant table. Captain Wentworth's pen ceased to move, his head was raised, pausing, listening, and he turned round the next instant to give a look – one quick, conscious look at her.'

The pen ceasing to move is a minute but monumental stage direction.

From this moment, Anne grows confused and from her perspective the conversation turns into 'only a buzz of words'. In the crowded room, Anne's interpretation of what she sees starts to falter. Looking at Captain Benwick's miniature portrait, Anne and Captain Harville discuss the cliched topic of whether men or women are most 'constant'. As Anne injects passion into her defence of women, Captain Wentworth's pen, which previously 'ceased to move', now falls to the ground. Anne is 'startled at finding him nearer than she had supposed'.

The staging of the room seems to keep moving around and closing in on Anne. The tension and confusion within the room rises when Mrs Croft takes her leave and asks her brother a question, but 'Captain Wentworth was folding up a letter in great haste and either could not or would not answer fully'. The confusion has spread to Captain Wentworth. When the gentlemen leave, Wentworth 'hurried' and 'agitated', Anne is left alone with Mrs Musgrove. For the first time in the novel, Anne is bewildered and cannot see or think clearly:

'Anne knew not how to understand it.'

Then at a stroke, all confusion is lifted. Ostensibly returning to retrieve his gloves, Captain Wentworth pulls out a second letter from beneath the piles of scattered paper on the desk and places it in front of Anne. Austen has managed to pull off a dramatic theatrical coup. Within the most constricted scene, where there is no place to hide and where even a whispered conversation is overheard, Captain Wentworth has written a second letter right under everyone's nose. It is an astounding conjuring trick.

Anne immediately realises the life-changing significance of what she is about to open:

'On the contents of that letter depended all which this world could do for her.'

Captain Wentworth's letter is just as powerful and passionate as she might hope: 'I can listen no longer in silence … you pierce my soul. I am half agony, half hope … A word, a look, will be enough to decide whether I enter your father's house this evening or never.'

The image of a writer at a desk desperately trying to carve out some privacy while people teem around the room could be an image of Jane Austen herself. Her father had given her a small folding writing-desk for her 19th birthday, which is now in the British Library. With a large family of six brothers, one sister and over thirty nephews and nieces and frequent social visitors, she would likely have written many of her novels while other people were coming in and out of the room.

In a letter to one of her nephews, who asked for her advice about his writing, Austen laughingly refers to her own writing process:

'What should I do with your strong, manly, vigorous sketches, full of variety and glow? How could I possibly join them on to the little bit (two inches wide) of ivory on which I work with so fine a brush, as produces little effect after much labour?'

The image of Captain Wentworth writing at the small desk and surreptitiously hiding a letter among the scattered papers is far from a scene of 'little effect'. The letter which Captain Wentworth writes is a bombshell. At last, he has sufficient self-knowledge to make this renewed declaration of love for Anne. The letter is life-changing for both of them and precipitates the conclusion of the novel. Leaving Anne speechless, Austen steps in as narrator and wryly observes:

'Such a letter was not to be soon recovered from.'

The sublime power of an author – especially an author as sublime as Jane Austen – is that in Anne Elliot she can create a heroine for whom she can rewrite history, recast reality and achieve an ending where anything is possible. The 'tax of quick alarm' distracts from the usual romantic comic punchline and reads like a door that is opening for Anne into a different world.

Like manipulating a Rubik's Cube, Jane Austen arranges her plots so that at various points in the narrative all appears to be in utter and irretrievable confusion. With progressive plot twists, the heroines seem ever more remote from their desired partners until the very last twist when suddenly – often within the turn of the final page – all is abruptly reconfigured. In the final few breathless pages, the plots accelerate towards their conclusions and all becomes possible, all is redeemed, money is found, the right partners are aligned, marriages are made and all loose ends are tied up.

With the final turn of her author's wrist, all sides of the Rubik's Cube are made perfect.

* * *

George Eliot approached her endings in an entirely different way. After she finished *Adam Bede*, she reflected in a letter to John Blackwood in May 1857: 'Conclusions are the weak points of most authors, but some of the fault lies in the very nature of the conclusion, which is at best a negation.'

In order to avoid this sense of negation, George Eliot takes the conclusion of her novels as an opportunity to reassess the cast of characters, bring together the survivors and provide them with different responsibilities. They then set out on a new path, where they often face an unclear future. This multi-directional approach is perfectly encapsulated by this striking image which appears in *Middlemarch*, written as a direct address from the author to the reader:

> An eminent philosopher among my friends ... has shown me this pregnant little fact. Your pier-glass [mirror] or extensive surface of polished steel made to be rubbed by a housemaid, will be minutely and multitudinously scratched in all directions; but place now against it a lighted candle as a centre of illumination and lo! the scratches will seem to arrange themselves in a fine series

of concentric circles round that little sun. It is demonstrable that the scratches are going everywhere impartially, and it is only your candle which produces the flattering illusion of a concentric arrangement, its light falling with an exclusive optical selection. These things are a parable.

This 'parable' is exactly how George Eliot draws her characters and plots. They are scratched lines which do not neatly fit into patterns, do not have a regular or controlled shape and they remain unfinished. As her characters pass through the light of her attention, they are illuminated and the meaning of their actions is made clear. At the end of her novels, Eliot withdraws the light with which she has examined them and their futures are left unclear.

These open endings reflect Eliot's philosophy that life is always in flux. Across her fiction, Eliot leaves a number of relationships unresolved and often leaves their moral position hanging in the balance. In *Middlemarch*, Bulstrode's downfall is a mixture of truth and rumour. He did not commit murder, yet he wanted Raffles to die, and his placing of the alcohol beside Raffles might have triggered his death – or Raffles might have died anyway. Equally, while Bulstrode's loan to Lydgate is not an outright bribe, it taints and compromises Lydgate and perhaps stops him from accusing Bulstrode of any wrongdoing. Despite the incomplete evidence, Middlemarch society joins the dots and expels Bulstrode from the civic society of gentlemen. Yet while his public disgrace is certain, within the privacy of his marriage Eliot allows much to be unspoken and open-ended. At first, Bulstrode's wife, Harriet, cannot understand why the town is avoiding her until she visits her brother who blurts out 'with his impulsive rashness':

'God help you, Harriet! You know all.'

When she understands the full extent of the allegations, Harriet returns home. She locks herself in her bedroom, takes off all her ornaments and puts on a 'plain bonnet-cap, which made her look suddenly like an early Methodist'. She then approaches her husband's bedside. The only spoken words in the scene are: 'Look up, Nicholas.'

Eliot then illustrates how within a relationship silence can be as revealing as speech:

> He raised his eyes with a little start and looked at her half amazed for a moment: her pale face, her changed, mourning dress, the trembling about her mouth, all said, 'I know', and her hands and eyes rested gently on him ... They could not yet speak to each other of the shame which she was bearing with him, or of the acts which had brought it down on them. His confession was silent, and her promise of faithfulness was silent ... She could not say, 'How much is only slander and false suspicion?' and he did not say, 'I am innocent.'

It is a profoundly ambiguous ending to the portrait of this relationship. No more is said between them and this is the last we see or hear of Bulstrode. As with so many other marriages in George Eliot's novels, in the face of his unspoken guilt and her unspoken forgiveness the Bulstrode marriage will have to find a way to endure beyond the end of the book. Their life in Middlemarch has ended and their marriage is compromised by mutual silence, but even as they face this bleak future, Eliot manages to introduce an element of uncertain sympathy for them.

Reflecting the complexities of the random scratching on the 'glass or polished steel surface', the endings of her novels each articulate that there is unfinished business – human damage which cannot be resolved and must simply be incorporated into future daily life. In *Adam Bede* the damage that will be done to Hetty Sorrel was foretold at the moment of her secret triumph when she tried on a pair of illicit earrings in her bedroom:

> It is too painful to think that she is a woman, with a woman's destiny before her – a woman spinning in young ignorance a light web of folly and vain hopes which may one day close round her and press upon her, a rancorous poisoned garment, changing all at once her fluttering, trivial butterfly sensations into a life of deep human anguish.

Nine years later, when the epilogue brings the novel to a close, the tragedy of Hetty is still at the heart of the story. Eliot opens by rooting the reader in a realistic scene of everyday life: 'It is near the end of June, in 1807. The workshops have been shut up half an hour or more in Adam Bede's timber-yard…'

Adam has gone out to meet Arthur Donnithorne, and Dinah and their children Addy and Lisbeth are waiting for him to return. Adam tells Dinah how it still affects him:

'"It's cut me a good deal, Dinah," Adam said at last, when they were walking on.'

He recounts their meeting and explains that both men acknowledged the tragedy in their lives. They find it impossible to tie up any neat ends and their conclusion is raw:

'There's a sort of wrong that can never be made up for.'

It would have been easier to leave Arthur offstage at the ending, but instead he is brought back so that Arthur and Adam, two men who have grown up together, worked together and fought each other can confront what happened and accept that they cannot come to terms over Hetty's tragedy.

Then, with a quiet sense of realism with which George Eliot so often manages to move seamlessly from tragedy to everyday life, the ending comes lightly. These last two lines conclude the novel:

'Why, there's Mr and Mrs Poyser coming in at the yard gate,' said Seth.

'So there is,' said Dinah. 'Run, Lisbeth, run to meet Aunt Poyser. Come in, Adam, and rest; it has been a hard day for thee.'

We are left with an open ending that feels natural and true to life. As with *Middlemarch*, much is left unsaid. There is no neat conclusion for the characters and their relationships with each other. The tragedy of Hetty and her baby together with the ensuing destruction of Arthur's life will cast a permanent shadow.

The exception to these open endings is that of *The Mill on the Floss*. Painfully autobiographical, it tells the story of Maggie Tulliver, whose intellectual curiosity and longing for independence divides her from her coldly puritanical brother – just as happened with the young Mary Ann and her brother Isaac. In the novel, the brother and sister are reconciled just before they drown together in the flood. As she wrote these last chapters, Eliot was reported to have been constantly sobbing. In real life, the tragedy was that she was never reconciled to her brother Isaac. In February 1860, Eliot wrote to John Blackwood to confess that although she knew Blackwood preferred happy endings, she had other plans for *The Mill on the Floss*:

'I am preparing myself for your lasting enmity on the ground of the tragedy in my third volume. But an unfortunate duck can only lay blue eggs, however much white ones may be in demand.'

When *The Mill on the Floss* was published, the American novelist Henry James praised Eliot's creation of Maggie and Tom as exceptionally truthful and touching:

> English novels abound in pictures of childhood; but I know of none more truthful and touching than the early pages of this work. Poor erratic Maggie is worth a hundred of her positive brother, and yet on the very threshold of life she is compelled to accept him as her master.

The one thing Henry James found fault with was the ending:

> The chief defect – indeed, the only serious one – in *The Mill on the Floss* is its conclusion ... The story is told as if it were destined to have, if not a strictly happy termination, at least one within ordinary probabilities. As it stands, the dénouement shocks the reader most painfully. Nothing has prepared him for it; the story does not move towards it; it casts no shadow before it.

My own view is that the critical flaw in the novel's tragic ending is not the drowning itself but that Maggie's tragedy is belittled by Stephen Guest's wholly uninspiring and vapid character. Everything is undermined by Stephen Guest and his 'attar of roses' – he never recovers from his introduction:

'The fine young man ... is no other than Mr Stephen Guest, whose diamond ring, attar of roses, and air of nonchalant leisure at twelve o'clock in the day are the graceful and odoriferous result of the largest oil-mill and the most extensive wharf in St Ogg's.'

'Nonchalant' might not be too damning, but 'odoriferous' certainly is. After this it is difficult to take Stephen Guest seriously as a lover or as a character of substance. Stephen Guest never recovers either from his early ridicule as he is introduced lying at Lucy's feet:

'The foolish scissors have slipped too far over the knuckles, it seems, and Hercules holds out his entrapped fingers hopelessly … the scissors are drawn off with gentle touches from tiny tips, which naturally dispose Mr Stephen for a repetition *da capo*.'

If George Eliot aimed for her novels to follow the illuminated truth of those scratched lines, then *The Mill on the Floss* is perhaps her only failure, for here the lines are drawn in a contrived circle towards the tragic ending, despite the fact that it is not plausible to have a passionate and ultimately tragic love affair based upon Stephen Guest. Eliot seems to embed the plans for the tragedy and the accompanying flood in the core of the narrative and then she shoehorns the characters to fit the story. Accordingly, *The Mill on the Floss* is her one novel in which there is a tightness and an artificiality to the unfolding of events, which creates a discrepancy between what we think Maggie might do, based on her character as portrayed in the novel, and the actions she ultimately takes. And if, with her final scene of reconciliation between brother and sister, George Eliot was sending a message to Isaac, it went unanswered.

More often, though, the conclusions of Eliot's novels are open-ended. The epilogues of *Romola*, *Middlemarch* and *Daniel Deronda* mirror each other. Their endings each set out that the surviving women shall take a new and open path. As Romola leaves the allegorical village, she has become a Madonna. Back in Florence, Eliot grounds the reader in real life, meticulous about the time and the date:

'On the evening of the 22nd May 1509, five persons, of whose history we have known something…'

Like so many of George Eliot's epilogues, the scene is touchingly domestic and intimate – Romola is not exactly the Madonna for 'her people' on a large scale. But the epilogue also contains within it the seeds of the future: Romola is teaching Lillo (the illegitimate son of Tito and Tessa) and there is a hint that with her schooling, he will not repeat Tito's callous behaviour. In her closing words of the novel, Romola is candid in her assessment of Tito, and these words will act as a warning to Lillo:

'He came at last to commit some of the basest deeds – such as make men infamous ... Calamity overtook him.'

She is more forgiving of Savonarola:

'Perhaps I should never have learned to love him if he had not helped me when I was in great need.'

These are the last words of the novel. The slight touch of uncertainty introduced by the use of 'perhaps' adds to the sense of reality – with no easy answers, Romola is feeling her way forwards. Nevertheless, given the trauma which Romola has suffered this is a rather benign and thoughtful reflection. As with all Eliot's novels, the final scene encompasses a tight-knit domestic group of the core survivors. These are the characters who have emerged strengthened by their ordeals and armed with self-knowledge, they have found a viable basis from which to build a new life.

The conclusion of *Daniel Deronda* is as open-ended as *Romola*. Daniel and Mirah are preparing to embark on a journey to the East. Mordecai had been planning to travel with them, but as the novel draws to a close he dies in their arms in a moment of union and rebirth. As Daniel and Mirah look ahead to the future and to their vague destination in 'the East', they prepare to carry with them their shared experiences and losses, just as Adam and Dinah must carry Hetty's death and Romola bears the deaths she has witnessed in her family. Perhaps the most touching gift which Daniel will carry forward is the letter of blessing from Gwendolen. She accepts that her path will be a solitary one once Daniel has left, but she offers a blessing and a release to him:

'You must not grieve any more for me. It is better – it shall be better with me because I have known you.'

Gwendolen's letter to Daniel is a mirror image of the curse she received in a letter from Mrs Glasher on her wedding day. While her blessing frees Daniel, it also reminds us of the bond between them – a bond of attraction which is never quite destroyed and becomes another unresolved part of the ending of the novel.

With such complex stories and with characters following such intricate lines on the scratched surface of the polished glass, they will not easily fall into the satisfactory shape of a neat ending.

* * *

When her novels reach their endings, George Eliot often provides a sense that the leading characters fade back into the wider society. In cinematic terms, it is as if the camera pulls away from a close up. As *Middlemarch* draws to a close, we see a number of compromised lives that illustrate why the novel is subtitled *A Study of Provincial Life*. In the final chapter, Dorothea, who started the book as an impatient idealist with an ardent wish to reform, is now married to Will Ladislaw with a baby. She has moved from occupying the radical foreground to taking a place in the conventional background. Eliot tells us:

'Her full nature, like that river of which Cyrus broke the strength, spent itself in channels which had no great name on the earth. But the effect of her being on those around her was incalculably diffusive.'

As the protagonists fade into the background of society and take their place among the wider cast, Eliot shows how minor characters can shape the destiny of the major ones, no matter how slight their role. The smallest exchange captures these characters. When Hetty finally arrives in Windsor, where she hopes to find Arthur, she clambers down from the coach. She is heavily pregnant, exhausted and destitute. Nudging her to give him a tip, the coachman asks her to 'Remember him'. But Hetty is down to her last shilling.

> As she held out the shilling, she lifted up her dark tear-filled eyes to the coachman's face and said, 'Can you give me back sixpence?'
>
> 'No, no,' he said, gruffly, 'never mind – put the shilling up again.'

It is just a single line, but with these words 'put the shilling up again' the coachman makes a choice. He has recognised how desperate Hetty is and decides not to take her money. The coachman takes pity on Hetty and in this moment, gruff and terse as he is, he emerges as a kinder man. We will indeed 'remember him' for it.

Hetty's last conversation before she gives birth to her baby is with an age-old farm labourer. This man does not refuse her payment because he is being kind but because he wants nothing to do with her. He scolds Hetty for wandering across the landscape like a mad woman:

> 'I want none o' your money. You'd better take care on't, else you'll get it stool from yer, if you go trapesin' about the fields like a mad woman a-thatway.'

ENDINGS AND ECHOES

Now abandoned by every person across the landscape, Hetty is alone. Intent upon drowning herself, she enters a very desolate place by herself.

> Life now, by the morning light, with the impression of that man's hard wondering look at her, was as full of dread as death – it was worse; it was a dread to which she felt chained, from which she shrank and shrank as she did from the black pool and yet could find no refuge from it.

All the minor characters across the landscape make choices which combine to shape the path of Hetty's tragedy towards her ending.

The concluding words of *Middlemarch* speak for all choices made by Eliot's characters:

'The growing good of the world is partly dependent on unhistoric acts; and that things are not so ill with you and me as they might have been is half owing to the number who lived faithfully a hidden life, and rest in unvisited tombs.'

With the address to 'you and me', George Eliot directly invites her readers to be involved in this observation. She draws us into a complex multi-layered world where the main characters' futures are open and uncertain, interwoven as they are with those myriad minor characters who 'lived faithfully a hidden life, and rest in unvisited tombs'. We – the 'chance comers' – understand it to be a highly realistic world made from those myriad random scratchings on the polished glass which Eliot briefly illuminates with the light of truth.

As we leave *Middlemarch* with these words, we remember all those minor characters who provide the backdrop to her literary world. To take just one example, there is a poignant scene in *Adam Bede* where Bartle Massey, the retired schoolteacher, is trying to teach three grown men to read. These men, a stonemason, a brickmaker and a dyer, are craftsmen who are trying to educate themselves, and Eliot shows immense compassion in her description of their evening class:

'It was touching to see these three big men, with the marks of their hard labour about them, anxiously bending over the worn books and painfully making out, "The grass is green"; "The sticks are dry"; "The corn is ripe."'

Their labour skills are rooted in the eighteenth century, but the year is 1799 and the century is turning. Their world is changing fast, and to use a modern expression Bartle Massey is encouraging these craftsmen to 'upskill'. When these three craftsmen learn to read, they will change their businesses and help drive the industrialisation of the nineteenth century forward. They too will be partly responsible for making 'things not so ill with you and me as they might have been'; they too will live hidden lives (apart from the moment when the author's lamp is shone on them in their evening classes) and eventually at the conclusion of their lives – just as at the conclusion of the lives of the leading characters – they too will occupy unvisited graves.

* * *

When George Eliot died in 1880, the Church of England did its best to ensure that her grave would be unvisited. Refusing permission for her to be buried in Westminster Abbey by citing her 'adulterous relationship with George Lewes', the Church insisted that she should be buried in unconsecrated ground. Her grave is in Highgate Cemetery in an area reserved for dissenters and agnostics. She would have been content to have known that John Cross arranged for her to be buried alongside the real love and partner of her life, George Lewes. One of the people who did visit her grave was her long-estranged brother Isaac, now able to offer his condolences to his official brother-in-law, John Cross. In 1980, on the centenary of her death, a memorial plaque to her was placed in Poet's Corner in Westminster Abbey.

Just as a myth around Jane Austen was created after her death, so a myth was created around George Eliot.

In 1884, Eliot's publisher William Blackwood and Sons published an 'autobiography'. Compiled by John Cross, who had married her in the last year of her life, it was entitled *George Eliot's Life as Related in her Journals and Letters* and was drawn solely from Eliot's own writing of letters and journals. Like Austen, Eliot was a prolific correspondent, and although many of her letters were destroyed after her death, some 1,000 letters have been preserved together with her journals. John Cross included excerpts of nearly 900 of these letters, but of course, as the editor he controlled the narrative.

Just as Austen's family biographers had done twenty years earlier, John Cross left out details that he thought might taint Eliot's respectability. When Henry James reviewed it, he noted that Cross failed to admit the reader 'behind the scenes, as it were, of her life'. Instead, 'the curtain is lowered whenever it suits the biographer'. Henry James concluded:

> What is remarkable, extraordinary – and the process remains inscrutable and mysterious – is that this quiet, anxious, sedentary, serious, invalidical English lady, without animal spirits, without adventures or sensations, should have made us believe that nothing in the world was alien to her; should have produced such rich, deep, masterly pictures of the multiform life of man.

Again, just as Jane Austen would have scorned her classification as a prim spinster aunt, George Eliot would have scorned the description of her as 'sedentary' or 'without adventures'.

Despite John Cross's loyal editing, the letters and journals of Eliot are still full of echoes of the life she lived. Just as we feel close to Jane Austen when we read of her scolding her naughty donkeys or boasting about her new black bonnet, we feel intensely close to George Eliot when we read of the personal details of her life, such as her packing her carpet-bag to head to London or her exhaustion when writing her faltering poem, *The Spanish Gipsy*: 'Ill and very miserable. George has taken my drama away from me.'

Moments that linger in my mind are of her as the young radical woman who has just left her home to live in John Chapman's boarding house in London; meeting George Lewes in William Jeff's bookshop in the Burlington Arcade with the brothels upstairs; their passionate affair and scandalous flight across the Channel into the dawn breaking over Antwerp; and perhaps most endearingly, the image of her in her long black crinoline skirts, scrambling over the rock pools at Ilfracombe, clutching her shrimping nets and buckets of seawater while dreaming of writing a novel.

Henry James had first met George Eliot some twenty years earlier. In describing her as 'without animal spirits', perhaps he had forgotten that first thrill. He provided an account of his first meeting and it echoes down the ages as true and vivid. Writing to his father, Henry James brilliantly conveys the strange and compelling power of George Eliot's attraction:

'The one marvel as yet of my stay is having finally seen Mrs Lewes ... I was immensely impressed, interested and pleased. To begin with she is magnificently ugly – deliciously hideous ... Now in this vast ugliness resides a most powerful beauty which, in a very few minutes steals forth and charms the mind, so that you end as I ended, in falling in love with her. Yes, behold me literally in love with this great horse-faced bluestocking. I don't know in what the charm lies, but it is thoroughly potent.'

* * *

EPILOGUE: A MEETING OF MINDS

It is another wet day in January. In a house on a hill near the Welsh border, I am sitting at my desk. Outside, my view is of a damp lawn littered with brown leaves. On the desk, two piles of books are stacked on either side of my computer: on the left, a pile of seven weighty novels, and on the right, a smaller pile of six slimmer ones. These are Penguin paperbacks, their black spines rounded and cracked with marbled streaks where they have been repeatedly bent open.

As I look at these two piles of books, the combined novels of Jane Austen and of George Eliot, I feel immensely privileged to have been able to spend so long in such extraordinary company. Like the Egyptian sorcerer conjured up by Eliot, both authors 'reveal far-reaching visions of the past' and like all these authors' readers, I have travelled far and wide across the magnificent worlds that they created.

These two authors, each possessed of a dazzling intellect and charm, never met. Having learned so much about each of them when looked at together, I wonder what they would have made of each other. What would George Eliot, who lived with such a fierce and determined streak of idealism, have made of Jane Austen's equally fierce and determined pragmatism? What would Jane Austen with her neatly resolved plotlines have thought of George Eliot's exploration of the complex layers of life and the realism that sends her characters off into such uncertain futures?

Were Eliot to cast Austen as a heroine in her fiction, she would write much more slowly and methodically about her than Austen wrote about herself. She would be unlikely to lead with her appearance, as Austen often did in her entertaining letters to Cassandra – 'my black cap was openly admired by Mrs Lefroy and secretly I imagine by everybody else in the room' – although she might pick up the aside that Austen made about corsets:

> I learnt from Mrs Tickar's young Lady, to my high amusement, that the stays now are not made to force the Bosom up at all – that was a very unbecoming, unnatural fashion. I was really glad to hear that they are not to be so much off the shoulders as they were

and reframe it into an amusing metaphor about the suffocating restrictions placed on lady novelists.

No, surely Eliot would seek to introduce much more measured introspection than Austen ever allowed herself. She would discuss and unpick the shadowy men who appear on the edges of Austen's life – she would explore why Tom Lefroy, in his highly visible and impractical white coat, so abruptly left Steventon and abandoned the 21-year-old Jane; she would dwell on Harris Bigg-Withers's blurted marriage proposal in more detail, articulating Jane's fleeting acceptance and then try to provide some explanation of what changed during the night which led to the next morning's awkward rejection. She would recognise this decision as the critical turning point in Austen's life – if she had woken up and smiled at Harris Bigg-Withers, in that moment her life would have changed direction. With marriage and children, her writing career would have been brought to a dead end.

Jane Austen laughingly mentions to her sister Cassandra that *Pride and Prejudice* 'wants shade'; George Eliot would have provided that shade. She would have explored the many difficult areas of life which Austen gaily refuted as 'odious'. Perhaps we would learn more about her disabled brother George living all his life in a private nursing home and apparently never visited or discussed by the Austen family. We would have a greater understanding of the death of her father and how the three single women cooped up in their small roadside house in muddy Chawton managed their daily lives. Eliot would have probed into the morality of Henry Austen's banking operations and explored how much his closest sibling Jane Austen knew about it and his dramatic financial ruin: 'Austen & Maunde have failed for a million and we are totally ruined.' Eliot would have examined Jane and Henry's life in London and articulated the sudden whiplash for them when it was all over.

Given how Eliot liked to arrange an early, disastrous relationship for her heroines, perhaps she would conjure up some key and damaging relationship from which Austen would have had to make a great effort to recover. She would not have been content with the throwaway line in her letters that people were laughing at Tom Lefroy and so he ran away when Austen visited his house. After the collapse of such a relationship and her rejection of the suitor, Austen would emerge stronger, and this, together with the death of her father, would have formed a framework for her ambition to become independent.

Eliot would have recognised and applauded her successful earnings from the book sales but perhaps made her more idealistic and less concerned with money. As with so many of her own books, Eliot might have approached the ending in two different ways: one way would be to pace Jane's writing of *Persuasion* against the growing knowledge that she was suffering from an incurable illness; the other choice would be to relish and trumpet her final unmarried status – like Romola, Jane Austen has earned the right to face her own future on her own terms. I think that for George Eliot, this would have been the most powerful ending.

And what of Jane Austen? How would she have cast Mary Ann Evans and her alter ego George Eliot as a heroine in her fiction? I like to think she would have been thrilled – if a little scandalised – to examine the sequence of unsuccessful love affairs with married men that Mary Ann had before she met Lewes. Quite how Austen would have described their intellectual connection, their sexual chemistry and the freedom of their open relationship is harder to gauge because it would be completely unchartered territory for her. Looking at Lewes's flair for organising house parties and theatrical events and his rather chameleon-like ability to become an expert on any subject, Austen would probably draw on Henry Crawford as a model for Lewes. She would likely have been amazed at Mary Ann's blatant physical enjoyment of her affair with him and would struggle to couch their flight across the Channel to Antwerp as a successful bid for freedom rather than an ignominious elopement like Lydia's and Wickham's. She might have to ask her naval brothers to help describe the boats, the travel, the sense of adventure and exploration that Mary Ann felt in the face of the sea, the breaking dawn and the open horizon of their future.

Surely, too, Austen would have delighted in the creative freedom provided by the adopted identity of George Eliot, and above all she would have been thrilled at her earning so much money from her books. Writing as George Eliot, she really earned a ton of *pewter* and Austen would have described the mounting royalties with admiration and glee – and then she would have had a great deal of fun in spending large chunks of money. Being so pragmatic, she may have cut out the mental anguish that Eliot suffered as she wrote, considering it 'odious' and something to be ignored. She would have undoubtedly included a great deal of sparkling dialogue between the Lewes couple about the books they loved, the money they made and how they spent it. Overall, Austen would have made Eliot sound rather feistier and less academic – in terms of the Bennet sisters, she would have cast her more like the saucy Elizabeth than the owlish Mary.

With her interest in fashion, Austen would have dressed her better, nudging her a little closer to the high society around her on the Continent. Austen would have had no patience for the sort of wry self-deprecation that Mary Ann suffered when she wrote from Geneva:

> The people dress, and think about dressing, here more even than in England. You would not know me if you saw me. The Marquise took on her the office of *femme de chambre* and dressed my hair one day. She has abolished all my curls and made two things stick out each side of my head like those on the head of the Sphinx. All the world says I look infinitely better; so I comply, though to myself I seem uglier than ever – if possible.

She would have given Mary Ann a thorough makeover and kept her in the eye of fashion.

Above all, somewhere in her storyline Jane Austen would surely have married her to George Lewes, just to tie up that nagging loose end. And while she was about it, she might have been tempted to photoshop his famously simian appearance, tidy up his shaggy whiskers and make him a little taller – perhaps as tall as Mr Darcy. No longer attracted to 'the most amusing little fellow in the whole world', as with all her other heroines Jane Austen would have ensured that Mary Ann Evans from Coventry put her trade roots behind her and a married a gentleman.

* * *

In 1799, when Jane Austen was putting the finishing touches to her manuscript that eventually became *Northanger Abbey*, Adam Bede was working late in his workshop putting the finishing touches to his father's coffin. Perhaps then, as Eliot did so seamlessly in *Romola*, we can blend fact and fiction to create a shared world for Jane Austen and George Eliot.

If we fast-forward five years, those three craftsmen who we met earlier in Bartle Massey's evening class – the stonemason, the brickmaker and the dyer – have been enjoying the swelling economic boom of the early 1800s. They have successfully built up their trades into commercial businesses, borrowing from banks like Henry Austen's in Alton, Hampshire. A year later, in 1805, these three craftsmen, now self-made businessmen with several hired hands working in their workshops and beginning to think of expanding their companies, might meet for a drink in The Green Dragon. Grateful to old Bartle Massey for teaching them to read, they discuss the newspaper reports of the Battle of Trafalgar. Jane Austen herself would have read these reports and anxiously wondered whether her brother Charles had been involved. She was not to know until afterwards that at the last minute his ship *Endymion* was dispatched back to Gibraltar to pick up supplies and therefore missed the battle.

Ten years later, in 1815, these three men would be owners of what were then called manufactories, later simply known just as factories, employing hundreds of workmen. As Bartle Massey predicted, the dyer has built up his textiles business so successfully that in 1815, he is elected as Town Councillor, just in time to help arrange the municipal celebrations for the Battle of Waterloo.

By 1816, these tradesmen have worked their way up in the world and we imagine them living in substantial town houses in Middlemarch. Within the town civic society, they now no longer think of themselves as craftsmen, but more as 'gentlemen among gentlemen'. Thanks to their newly acquired wealth, they have social ambitions for their children to marry up in society. Aware of the current recession and the string of banking failures (they might not have understood the implications of the newspaper reports about the appointment of Lord Moira as Governor General of India, but they would have read about the collapse of another London bank, Austen & Maunde), they are thinking about the prospects of their businesses and how to safeguard the money they have made.

One fine day, when there is finally a break in that summer's incessant rain, the dyer might take his daughter out for a walk. Fancying herself in love with a local country squire in possession of a good fortune, she might lead her father across the street to the circulating library and pick up a novel for herself, something by a lady novelist – perhaps *Emma*, recently published by John Murray of 50 Albemarle Street, written by 'the Author of *Pride and Prejudice*', and look! It's dedicated to the Prince Regent himself. Perhaps there will be another hero like that dashing Mr Darcy. It's clearly a romantic book and will turn her head, but her father is happy to indulge her.

Jane Austen and George Eliot, two authors who were writing fifty years apart but drawing from the same well of human experience, can spark an imagined conversation in the mind of any reader who chooses to open their books.

Both authors might have found satisfaction in such a connection with each other – a touch of their fingertips across the bookshelves of their fictional world.

* * *

INDEX

Adam Bede 18, 61, 77, 90, 124–5, 149, 214–20, 248–9, 255–6
American Civil War 16
Annie Hall 197
Antwerp 27, 258, 264
Austen, Caroline (niece) 232
Austen, Cassandra (sister) 5, 12, 65–9, 72–3, 83, 100, 101, 110, 137, 171, 212, 229, 233, 240–41, 262–3
Austen, Charles (brother) 15, 16, 118
Austen, Edward (brother) 3–5, 72, 103, 113, 116, 144
Austen, Francis (brother) 4, 15, 16, 111, 118, 267
Austen, George (brother) 263
Austen, Henry (brother) 1, 3–7, 9, 11, 13, 58, 67, 72, 110–20, 122, 132–3, 229–32, 263, 266
Austen, James (brother) 118, 162
Austen, Jane
  clergy 162–6
  death 230
  death in novels 205–12, 219, 227–8
  Elinor & Marianne 1, 3
  Elliots, The 9, 11, 12, 13, 14, 121, 229
  Emma 5–10, 62, 70, 78–81, 86–7, 101, 113, 117, 141–8, 164–5, 182–5, 206–9
  endings 237–45
  heroines 172–84, 200, 201
  illness 229, 230
  Lefroy, Tom 67, 68, 70, 72–4, 237, 262, 263
  letters 233, 234, 235, 236
  letters to her sister 65, 66, 68, 72, 73, 101, 212, 240
  Mansfield Park 4, 15, 58, 73, 84, 87, 89, 103, 105, 115, 117, 132, 163–6, 176–83, 204–6, 212–13
  on marriage 81–90
  marriage proposal 69, 70
  on money 99–112, 119, 120
  Mrs Ashton Dennis 2, 116
  myth 231, 232
  naval officers 161
  Northanger Abbey 1, 14, 55, 119–20, 132, 213, 231, 266
  Persuasion 14, 62, 70, 79, 82–4, 87, 89, 120–22, 161, 213, 231, 241–4, 264
  Pride and Prejudice 3, 5–10, 42, 44, 62, 68–70, 81, 84–7, 108, 110, 116, 138–40, 173–6
  Sense and Sensibility 3, 10, 70, 83–7, 102, 106, 110, 162, 203–4, 209–13, 219, 238
  Susan 1, 2, 9, 12, 13, 116, 119, 120, 133
  Tom Lefroy 67, 68, 70, 72–4, 237, 262, 263
Austen, Reverend George (father) 1, 9, 19, 69, 244, 263

Austen-Leigh, Edward (nephew) 136, 137, 232, 233

Bath 69
Bigg-Withers, Harris 67, 69, 70, 74, 83, 118, 237, 262, 263
Bismarck, Count Otto von 16
Blackwood, John 58, 61, 123–8, 245, 249
Blackwoods Magazine 41
Bonaparte, Napoleon 10, 17, 113
Bray, Cara 21, 22, 28, 75, 76
Bray, Charles 21, 22, 28, 29, 30, 76
Brontë, Anne 36, 44, 49
Brontë, Charlotte 35–40, 42–55, 57, 59–63, 97, 126, 241
   death 55, 59
   Jane Eyre 36, 38–40, 42, 43, 44, 49, 50, 51, 62, 63, 127
   letters to George Lewes 36–46, 49, 50, 52, 53
   letters to William Smith Williams 36, 37, 47, 48, 49, 52
   Professor, The 36, 37
   Shirley 48, 49, 51
Brontë, Emily 36, 44, 49, 54, 63
Byron, Lord 5, 239

Chapman, John 22, 24–7, 31, 34, 100, 258
Clarke, Reverend James 6–8, 70, 71, 74, 100, 133, 237
Combe, George 29, 30
Copenhagen, Battle of 15
Coventry 19–21, 25, 26, 28, 186, 266
Crosby, Richard 1, 2, 9, 10, 13, 116, 119, 120, 133
Cross, John 26, 30, 132, 256–7

Daniel Deronda 18, 90, 92, 97, 129, 151, 159–61, 194–200, 220–24, 251–3
Darwin, Charles 33
Das Leben Jesu (The Life of Jesus) 22, 167
Dickens, Charles 61, 127

Egerton, Thomas 3, 4, 235
Egremont, Lord 71

Elinor & Marianne 1, 3
Eliot, George
   Adam Bede 18, 61, 77, 90, 124–5, 149, 214–20, 248–9, 255–6
   burial 256, 257
   clergy 167–9, 204–5
   Daniel Deronda 18, 90, 92, 97, 129, 151, 159–61, 194–200, 220–24, 251–3
   death 256
   death in novels 214–24, 228
   endings 245–55
   Felix Holt 18, 77, 127, 150–51, 160, 167
   Fortunes of Amos Barton, The 58, 59, 123, 124
   heroines 171–2, 184–201
   Janet's Repentance 60, 80
   letters 257, 258
   on marriage 90–97
   Middlemarch 18, 19, 63, 90–96, 125, 129–30, 152–60, 245–7, 253–5
   Mill on the Floss, The 23, 91, 92, 249–52
   on money 123–131
   Mr Gilfils Love Story
   myth 257–7
   relationship with Lewes 74–7, 80, 95, 131, 132, 256
   Romola 18, 20, 90, 92, 97, 127, 130, 135, 167, 168, 185–94, 251–3, 266
   Silas Marner 77, 129, 150, 167, 168, 214, 224–7
   Spanish Gypsy, The 258
Elliots, The 9, 11, 12, 13, 14, 121, 229
Emma 5–10, 62, 70, 78–81, 86–7, 101, 113, 117, 141–8, 164–5, 182–5, 206–9
Evans, Chrissey (sister) 19, 30
Evans, Isaac (brother) 19, 20, 30, 31, 100, 249, 251, 257
Evans, Mary Ann (*see* Eliot, George)
   birth 14
   faith 21, 22
   journalism 55–6, 123
   Silly Novels by Lady Novelists 55, 56, 57
Evans, Robert (father) 19, 20, 21, 22, 23, 95, 100

INDEX

Felix Holt 18, 77, 127, 150–51, 160, 167
First Impressions 1, 3, 9
Fortunes of Amos Barton, The 58, 59, 123, 124
Franco-Prussian War 16
Fraser's Magazine for Town and Country 38

Gaskell, Elizabeth 40, 41, 52
George III, King 14
George IV, King 14

Haden, Charles 72–4, 113, 116, 122, 237
Hennell, Sara 24, 40, 61, 27
HMS *Cleopatra* 15
HMS *Elephant* 15, 16
HMS *Endymion* 15, 16, 267

Ilfracombe 33, 55, 258

James, Henry 250, 257, 258
Jane Eyre 36, 38–40, 42, 43, 44, 49, 50, 51, 62, 63, 127

Knatchbull-Hugessen, Edward 233
Knight, Fanny 4, 136, 233

Lefroy, Tom 67, 68, 70, 72–4, 237, 262, 263
Lewes, George 26–55, 57–63, 74–7, 123–8, 131, 256–8
Life of Jesus, The (*Das Leben Jesu*) 22, 167
Love Actually 197

Mansfield Park 4, 15, 58, 73, 84, 87, 89, 103, 105, 115, 117, 132, 163–6, 176–83, 204–6, 212–13
Memoir of Jane Austen, A 232
Merchant of Venice, The 72
Middlemarch 18, 19, 63, 90–96, 125, 129–30, 152–60, 245–7, 253–5
Midsummer Night's Dream, A 87
Mill on the Floss, The 23, 91, 92, 249–52
Moira, Lord 114–15, 121, 267
Murray, John 4, 5, 6, 9, 12, 13, 117, 127, 231, 267
My Aunt Jane Austen: A Memoir 232

Northanger Abbey 1, 14, 55, 119–20, 132, 213, 231, 266
Norton, Charles Eliot 32

On the Origin of Species 33

Parkes, Joseph 22, 30
Persuasion 14, 62, 70, 79, 82–4, 87, 89, 120–22, 161, 213, 231, 241–4, 264
Pride and Prejudice 3, 5–10, 42, 44, 62, 68–70, 81, 84–7, 108, 110, 116, 138–40, 173–6
Professor, The 36, 37

Ranthorpe 38, 43
Reform Act of 1832 18, 30, 96, 153, 160
Regency, the 6, 10, 14, 108, 135, 166, 172
Romola 18, 20, 90, 92, 97, 127, 130, 135, 167, 168, 185–94, 251–3, 266
'Rosehill circle' 21
Royal Navy 4, 14, 15, 103, 115, 118, 161

Sand, George 12, 40, 41, 45, 46
Scenes of Clerical Life 20, 60, 124
Scott, Sir Walter 117
Seaside Studies 33, 34, 123, 124
Sense and Sensibility 3, 10, 70, 83–7, 102, 106, 110, 162, 203–4, 209–13, 219, 238
Shelley, Percy 239
Shirley 48, 49, 51
Silas Marner 77, 129, 150, 167, 168, 214, 224–7
Silly Novels by Lady Novelists 34, 55, 56, 57
Strauss, David Friedrich 22
Susan 1, 2, 9, 12, 13, 116, 119, 120, 133

Tenant of Wildfell Hall, The 44
Times, The 233
Tom Jones 67, 72
trade 148, 149–52
Trafalgar, Battle of 15, 166, 266

Victoria, Queen 14, 131

Waterloo, Battle of 10, 166, 267
Wellington, Duke of 10, 53

271

Westminster Review 25, 26, 27, 40, 55, 74
William IV, King 14
William Jeff's bookshop 36, 63, 74, 258
Williams, William Smith 36, 42, 47, 48, 49, 52, 53
Winchester 12, 13, 230
Wuthering Heights 44, 63